The Mayor of Aihara

The Mayor of Aihara

A Japanese Villager and His Community,
1865–1925

Simon Partner

UNIVERSITY OF CALIFORNIA PRESS
Berkeley · Los Angeles · London

University of California Press, one of the most
distinguished university presses in the United
States, enriches lives around the world by advancing
scholarship in the humanities, social sciences, and
natural sciences. Its activities are supported by
the UC Press Foundation and by philanthropic
contributions from individuals and institutions.
For more information, visit www.ucpress.edu.

University of California Press
Berkeley and Los Angeles, California

University of California Press, Ltd.
London, England

Library of Congress Cataloging-in-Publication Data

Partner, Simon.
    The mayor of Aihara : a Japanese villager and his
community, 1865–1925 / Simon Partner.
        p.   cm.
    Includes bibliographical references and index.
    ISBN 978-0-520-25858-7 (cloth : alk. paper)
    ISBN 978-0-520-25859-4 (pbk. : alk. paper)
    1. Aizawa, Kikutaro, 1866–1962.   2. Aihara-
mura (Kanagawa-ken, Japan)—History—
Biography.   3. Mayors—Japan—Aihara-mura
(Kanagawa-ken)—Biography.   I. Title.

DS894.49.K349A34   2009
952'.136—dc22   2008043138

Manufactured in the United States of America

18   17   16   15   14   13   12   11   10   09
10   9   8   7   6   5   4   3   2   1

This book is printed on Natures Book, which contains
30% post-consumer waste and meets the minimum
requirements of ANSI/NISO Z39.48–1992 (R 1997)
(*Permanence of Paper*).

This book is dedicated to my teachers,
Carol Gluck and Henry Smith,
with deepest gratitude.

Contents

Illustrations

Figures 1 and 2. The mayor of Aihara, ca. 1910
(left), and Aizawa in 1918 (right) (Both courtesy
Aizawa Family)

Introduction

An hour's ride outside Tokyo on the suburban Keiō railway line is a station called Hashimoto. It is located in the northern part of the city of Sagamihara, but there is little to distinguish it from the surrounding districts that merge into one another in a massive and often depressing suburban sprawl stretching the length and breadth of the Kantō Plain. Hashimoto as a place has no legal status, and little meaningful identity.

On a recent visit to Hashimoto, I stopped in at the Northern Citizens Counseling Office, on the sixth floor of a brand-new glass-walled building next to the station. The office was supposed to be an information center for the northern districts of Sagamihara.

I asked the uniformed woman behind the counter if she knew the location of the former Aihara village office—I knew it was somewhere in Hashimoto. She disappeared into a back room, out of which emerged a succession of increasingly responsible but equally nonplussed individuals, until I was finally ushered to the desk of the chief of the Northern Citizens Counseling Office. He was a suited, middle-aged man who was probably close to retirement. Yes, he was aware that there had formerly been a village office in Hashimoto. But the village had merged into Sagamihara years ago, and no, he had no idea what might have happened to the village records. No, he did not know where the village office had been. Nor did he know whom I could ask. Might he ask why I wanted this information?

Figure 3. Hashimoto in 2006

I explained that I was writing a biography of Aizawa Kikutarō, the former mayor of Aihara and the head of one of its most prominent families. Yes, said the chief, he had vaguely heard of Aizawa. He had lived in Hashimoto, hadn't he? Hadn't he kept a diary? No, he had no idea what had become of him or his family. Unfortunately, the chief himself was not from Hashimoto, nor was anyone else in the office. Oh, the Aizawa still lived in Hashimoto, did they? Well, perhaps I should go and talk to them—no doubt they would know more than he did.

. . .

A hundred years ago, Aizawa Kikutarō *was* Hashimoto. At the time of his birth in 1866, the Aizawa family was by far the wealthiest in a village of one hundred families. Hashimoto was a relatively isolated wheat- and silk-producing village on the northern edge of the Kantō Plain. It benefited from its location on a "highway" (a dirt and gravel track some six meters wide) leading to the coast, but it was still a long day's hike from the coastal towns of Kanagawa and Yokohama. The livelihood of its inhabitants depended almost exclusively upon agriculture. An American visitor to Hashimoto and the surrounding villages shortly before Aizawa's birth wrote of "small shops, old houses, temples and miyas [shrines] looking very like one another . . . scattered among a growth of bamboos and firs, surrounded with living fences of trees and flowering shrubs," ornamented with persimmon trees and "many beautiful varieties of azaleas, white, red, and purple." On a summer evening,

> The passer-by will see the steaming family wash tub by the road side and one or two or more members of the family in various stages of the bath having entered the tub by turns. . . . When the sun has gone down I see the lamp lit at the household altar, the smudge is kindled to keep off the swarm of mosquitoes, and the household gathers in the apartments, open on one side to the street, take their evening meal leisurely, and thereafter smoke and chat squatted in a circle men and women together. Then, as evening draws on, the mosquito tent is hung up within doors under which the children go to sleep, or the family gathers to while away the evening hours.[1]

When Aizawa Kikutarō turned sixty in 1926—the year in which I bring this story to a close—Hashimoto had already taken on many of the characteristics of the faceless suburb that it is today. It had lost its legal identity, swallowed by the administrative village of Aihara. The railway station was there, already surrounded by commercial buildings as it is today. Although agriculture was still the community's mainstay, more and more residents commuted to work in the metropolitan centers of Tokyo and Yokohama. Increasingly, the fields that had not yet been developed for residential property were lying fallow or being returned to woodland, as residents of Hashimoto found the rewards of factory and office work more alluring than the sweat and toil of farming. Aizawa himself was working as a bank manager.

How did this transformation come about? The question is an important one, because during the sixty years covered in this book, between 60 and 80 percent of the Japanese population lived in village communities. Studies of economic and social change in Japan during the period of rapid modernization starting in the 1860s have tended to focus on the cities. This, after all, is where most of the factories were. It is where modernity was most visible. But if we are to understand the process of social transformation in Japan's modern era, we *must* look in the villages. It is, quite simply, where most Japanese were.

The story of Hashimoto is not in any way typical of all Japanese villages. No village could fill that role; there was just too much diversity. But in spite of its many unique features, the residents of Hashimoto from the 1860s to the 1920s shared a variety of experiences with their fellow villagers throughout Japan. These experiences included government-mandated universal education; military conscription; participation in national projects of war and empire; increasing consumption of goods produced and sold in the national and even the international market; increasing communication outside the village through railways, telegraph services, and wheeled transportation; and increasing integration—for better and worse—into the cash-based national and international commercial and industrial economy. My goal in this book is to explore these experiences—both unique and common—through the lens of one man's life.

I chose my subject, Aizawa Kikutarō, because he was a prolific diarist. Aizawa began keeping his diary in 1885, when he was nineteen. He made an entry—sometimes brief, sometimes lengthy—without fail every day for the next seventy-eight years. The only days he missed were during one week in 1901, when he was hospitalized; and during the last week of his life in 1963, when he was ninety-seven years old. This extraordinary document, which chronicles many of the dramatic transformations of the Japanese village during the modern era, still sits in a storage house in the Aizawa family compound in Hashimoto. The family has thus far restricted full access to the diary, out of concern for the other families in the community who might be named in it. But Aizawa's son, the late Aizawa Yoshihisa, transcribed and privately published the section of the diary from 1885 to 1926, and it is primarily on this document that I have drawn my research.[2]

Aizawa is in many ways a less than ideal subject. As a relatively wealthy landlord, he represented only a very small fraction of Japanese village society. As a man in a patriarchal age, he was unfortunately oblivious to many of the concerns and activities of village women—whose lives are in some ways more interesting than those of the men because of the insights they give into the basic institution of village life, the farm family. However, one cannot easily reach back a hundred years into the past and talk to whomever one wishes. Villagers—particularly the less-influential members of village society such as women and poor tenant farmers—left relatively few traces of their life stories. The Aizawa diary, by contrast, is a wonderfully engaging and informative document that goes far beyond the laconic, businesslike entries of the typical specimen of this genre in Japan.

Moreover, although Aizawa's privileged status is problematic in some ways, it does permit us some unique insights into Japanese village life

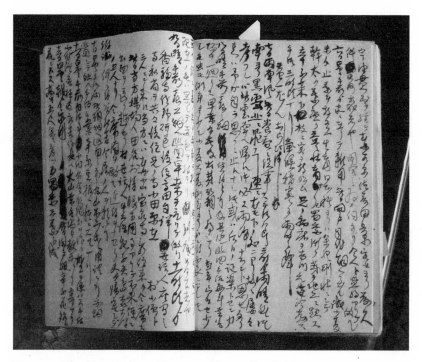

Figure 4. The Aizawa diary (Courtesy Aizawa Family)

in the Meiji (1868–1912) and Taishō (1912–26) periods. Aizawa's circle
of acquaintance was wide, and a huge variety of interesting characters
from all walks of life march through the pages of his diary. Aizawa had
a detailed knowledge not only of his own financial situation, but also
of those of his many debtors and tenants. Thus, it is possible to read
between the lines of the diary to get quite a full picture of the varying fortunes of many of the villagers of Hashimoto. Most importantly,
Aizawa served as deputy mayor and then mayor of Hashimoto's successor village, Aihara, for a period of twenty years. His experiences as
a village official, as documented in the diary, give us valuable insight
into the concerns of the village and villagers during this period. Perhaps
there are other sources that might have given me greater insight into
the transformation of the Japanese village. I have used those I could
find, and in many places I have delved beyond the diary for additional
sources on Hashimoto, its surrounding area, and on Japanese villages
in general. But for better or worse, it is on Aizawa and his diary that I
hang my story of village life in nineteenth- and early twentieth-century
Japan.

. . .

I am indebted to many people and institutions for support in the research and writing of this book. I carried out my fieldwork in Japan under the auspices of a Japan Society Research Fellowship. The staff of the Japan Society and my fellow Research Fellows were helpful and stimulating company, and I am grateful to them for their support. I especially thank Marcia Yonemoto for her valuable insight into early modern Japanese society. During this period, I was a visiting scholar at the School of International Liberal Studies at Waseda University. This was a wonderfully cozy institutional home, and I benefited from its generous facilities and excellent library services. My thanks go in particular to Kōichi Okamoto for once again sponsoring me at Waseda. I am grateful to the members of the Modern Japanese History Workshop at Waseda for valuable feedback after a presentation of my work in progress. Also in Tokyo, Kate Nakai was a precious source of advice and interpretation on a variety of arcane questions that baffled a relative newcomer to the Meiji period like myself. And John Mertz, my colleague from North Carolina who like me was on sabbatical in Japan, kindly helped me with some tricky linguistic questions.

In Hashimoto and Sagamihara, I am grateful to Mr. Kōki Aizawa, the great-grandson of Aizawa Kikutarō, and his wife. Mrs. Aizawa kindly opened her house to me and showed me the Aizawa diary and some mementos of its author. Mr. Aizawa found time amid his enormously busy schedule as an executive of the Pioneer Corporation to answer my questions and provide me with supporting materials. The archivists and librarians of Sagamihara were unfailingly helpful in my forays for subsidiary materials on Aizawa, Hashimoto, and Aihara village.

I am most grateful to two readers, Ann Waswo and Steve Ericson, for their thoughtful and very helpful comments on the manuscript. Dani Botsman and Dominic Sachsenmaier also read and commented on the conclusion, though I'm afraid that my analysis does little justice to their sophisticated input. Sheila Levine, Reed Malcolm, and the very professional team at the University of California Press have once again been ideal supporters and partners in the editing and publication process.

Reading and interpreting materials of the Meiji era is, for a naïve modernist like me, an enormously challenging endeavor. Researching and writing this book has been a thoroughly rewarding excursion into new territory—but I take full responsibility for any mistakes, egregious or otherwise, that I have made.

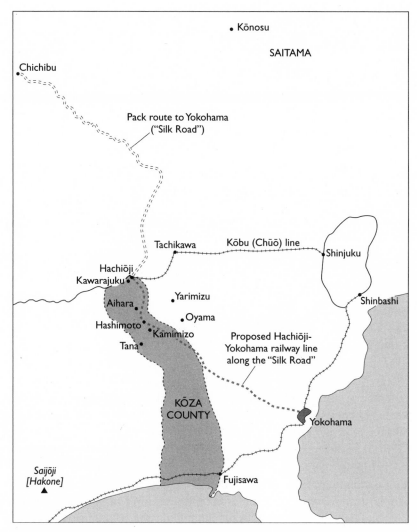

Figure 5. Kōza county and surroundings, ca. 1900 (Courtesy *Monumenta Nipponica*)

CHAPTER I

The Village Enters the Modern Era

1866–1885

BORN IN TROUBLED TIMES

February 20, 1866.

The village of Hashimoto lies nestled on the northwest edge of the Kantō Plain, tranquil and compact. Its one hundred or so houses are clustered on either side of a dirt-packed highway that, at the end of the village, crosses a stream over an arched wooden bridge, and begins its slow ascent up into the hills. A handful of travelers are on the road: a villager carrying a heavy load of brushwood down from a wooded hillside; a farmer returning from the Kamimizo market with a load of fishmeal fertilizer; a wholesaler looking to buy silk thread to take down to the foreign merchants in Yokohama; a merchant with a pair of pack mules, stopping at one of the village's roadside teahouses; and a pair of pilgrims, returning from a visit to Kamakura's famous Hachiman Shrine. The sound of their straw sandals on the packed earth barely stirs the somnolent village. A cow lows in a stable. A few chickens squawk from their cramped coop. The pale winter sun casts long shafts, hazy with the dust of the Kantō soil, between the ramshackle wooden houses of the villagers.

Spread out around the houses clustered near the road is a neat patchwork of fields, stretching off into the distance. Many of the fields are fallow, recently plowed and waiting for the spring wheat crop to be planted. Where they have been plowed, the soil is a deep black color.

This is the Kantō loam: a rich, crumbly volcanic mixture that lies three or more meters deep across the plain. Other fields are planted with mulberry trees two to three meters high, spread out in even rows, leafless as they await the warmth of spring. Patched in among the irregularly shaped fields are small groves of woods—a clump of ancient oaks, beeches, and cedars around the Zuikōji Temple bordering the village, and several groves of regularly spaced chestnut trees.

Immediately to the north of the village the road climbs into the first of the hills leading up to the Goten Pass. The hillsides are heavily forested with pine, beech, and chestnut trees. These are the foothills of the Kantō mountain range. On the other side of the Goten Pass, the road descends to the market town of Hachiōji, before climbing again into mountains that rise in craggy ranks of forest and rock, stretching off blue and green into the far distance. To the southwest, the setting is even more dramatic. A couple of kilometers away, the fields come to an end at the banks of the Sagami River, which has just descended from the mountains and still flows fast, strong, and icy cold. On the other side of the river, the mountain peaks are tipped with snow. In the summer months hundreds of pilgrims will pass through Hashimoto on the route to these high mountains. Rising behind them all, floating in the limpid air, is an unreal sight: Mount Fuji, its smooth sides dipped in snow, reflecting the sunlight in a blue-white sheen against the pale blue of the winter sky.

The houses of Hashimoto are for the most part small and plain. Built of wooden frames, with walls made of a stucco paste of mud and straw, and thatched roofs on low-hanging eaves, they sit close to the road surrounded by a few fruit trees, a bare work area, and perhaps a shed for storage. The houses offer solid shelter, but they reflect lives of simplicity and bare sustenance. Some of the owners are squatting in their dusty yards, doing winter chores—the fields are fallow after the winter wheat harvest, and now the farmers are making sandals and rope out of the straw. Their faces are dark from a lifetime out of doors, spare and angled with the simplicity of their food and the life of constant manual labor. Bareheaded in the chill winter afternoon, the men wear their hair pulled back from the forehead and closely knotted at the top of their heads. Their women work by their sides, the little children playing in the dirt.

Near the top of the village are a few simple teahouses and an inn, catering to the needs of passing travelers. Above them, close to the stream that marks the boundary, are a handful of grander dwellings.

Their compounds are enclosed by high fences of bamboo and wood, and gated to keep out intruders. The main houses are large imposing structures, and the compounds contain a variety of subsidiary buildings—storehouses of brick and plaster, lodges for retired family heads, stables for horses and cattle, well houses, and work sheds.

The last house in the village, nestled against the flowing stream and protected from prying eyes by a high wall, is the compound of the Aizawa family. Its main house is an imposing building, plastered white, with black wooden bars on the ground floor windows. Its distinctive high gables allow light and air into the upper floor, which is used for silkworm cultivation. It is roofed with fresh straw thatch and surrounded by a beautifully cultivated garden of ornamental trees and carefully trimmed bushes.

In this house, a familiar drama is taking place. Riu, thirty-one years old, is giving birth. She is attended by the local midwife, a woman from the village's lower class who is trained in the lore of childbirth. Also present is her mother-in-law, the matriarch of the Aizawa family, who is directing the maid to bring whatever is needed to make Riu as comfortable as possible. Riu's four-year-old son, Kenjirō, and her two daughters are being cared for by the *komori*, a young village girl hired to live with the family as a child-minder and maid. Riu's mother, from the Suzuki family in Asakawa village, two hours walk away over the Goten Pass, has been sent for. A farm hand will accompany her back to Hashimoto, where she will share with her daughter the first hours of this new life. Riu's husband, thirty-six-year-old Yasujirō, is busy with his village and farming duties. His job is to stay out of the way of the women's activities.

The new baby is a son. His birth is a cause for celebration, of course, but not on the same scale as the birth of Kenjirō, four years earlier. Throughout the first part of his life, the younger brother will live in the shadow of his elder brother's position as heir to the headship of the Aizawa family. A week after the birth, the family celebrates with rice and red beans, and Yasujirō registers the birth of the child with the family temple. His name is to be Kikutarō—"Chrysanthemum Boy."

The Aizawa family is the wealthiest in Hashimoto. Yasujirō possesses more than fifty hectares of farmland in the fields surrounding Hashimoto, as well as extensive holdings of forest land. He is also the hereditary *nanushi*, or headman responsible to the feudal lord, of part of Hashimoto village. Although Hashimoto is a village of only one hundred families, it is divided between four different feudal lords, part of an immensely complicated patchwork of ownership and fief that characterize the land of the Kantō Plain.[1] Because this land is readily accessible from the capital, the government of the shogun has allocated much of it to its immediate retainers—the *hatamoto* or bannermen—as a tax base for their income needs. Other pieces of land in the area are direct possessions of the shogun, and pay taxes to his official representative, the *daikan,* based in Shinagawa on the outskirts of Edo (the shogunal capital—later renamed Tokyo). Still others belong to one or other of the small independent domains that dot the area.

Yasujirō owes his allegiance, and service, to the Fujisawa family. The Fujisawa are the most powerful of the local *hatamoto* lords, with land valued at a total of fifteen hundred *koku* (the standard unit of income, one *koku* being equivalent to roughly 112 kilograms of rice). The greatest obligation of the villagers of Hashimoto is to pay taxes. As *nanushi,* it is Yasujirō's job to apportion these taxes among the villagers, supervise their collection, and deliver them to the Fujisawa family in Edo.

This relationship is both close and personal. The Fujisawa are the masters of their portion of Hashimoto in a very real sense. The villagers of Hashimoto provide not only tax money, but also personal services to the Fujisawa family: maids and servants to Fujisawa family members; loans or special payments to individual members of the Fujisawa family; and the delivery of local produce. The villagers are forced to observe a protocol of abject humility in all communications with their feudal lords, even while occasionally protesting at excessive exactions. In the feudal conception of the time, the farmers are lowly commoners whose function is to feed their warrior lords. In spite of the rulers' acknowledgment of the importance of farmers to the economy and sustenance of the realm, the truth is that farmers are powerless and despised by their samurai rulers. And yet, the samurai are also deeply dependent on the farmers, for the land is the source of the lords' livelihood.

The Aizawa family occupies an ambiguous status within the oppressively hierarchical world created by the Tokugawa shoguns. As landlord farmers, they enjoy a larger income than many of the ruling samurai class. The Aizawa's registered annual income is equivalent to seventy *koku* of rice—roughly equivalent to the stipend of a lower middle-ranking samurai in shogunal employ. In reality, the Aizawa are probably closer in wealth to an upper-middle-class samurai family, as villagers typically seek ways to understate their wealth, while the notional salaries of samurai retainers are usually subject to various deductions to help the government out with its perennial financial difficulties. But the protocol of the day requires farmers like the Aizawa to submit humbly to the often arrogant behavior of their samurai "masters." Farmers, including headmen unless specially exempted, are not permitted to use family names (this rule is generally ignored by wealthier families, except in official documents). And their clothing and housing are strictly controlled, with silk and other luxury items banned (again, many wealthier farmers ignore these edicts).

Four years earlier, an American journalist wrote after passing through Hashimoto and its surrounding villages: "To the stranger who wanders among their quiet hamlets, seeing so much of worldly peace and apparent content, and certainly so little of poverty or distress, there seems to be nothing wanting to their rustic happiness."[2] The villagers of Hashimoto are, indeed, in many ways privileged. Their land is blessed with a mild climate, although it lacks the irrigation resources to plant wet paddy rice, Japan's most valued food crop. Hashimoto is well located on a major road, with direct access both to the capital and to the international port of Yokohama. These are the conditions that have given rise to Hashimoto's major economic activities, the production of wheat and silk. Between them, these products provide the villagers with the cash income they need to pay their taxes and buy essential commodities, including fertilizer and rice, which they prefer as a staple over the locally grown grains.

The relatively warm climate of the Kantō region—protected from northerly winds by the mountains that surround it on three sides—allows the villagers to plant two crops a year, one in the winter and one in the spring. They plant a variety of grains, including barley, rye, dry-field rice, and millet as well as wheat. The farmers raise their crops with little help from animals or machinery: Hashimoto has only seven horses, all in the hands of the wealthiest families. All of the farming families, though, are heavily dependent on fertilizers to nurture the depleted soil. In addition to grass and leaves from the hillsides, wheat bran from their crops, and human manure collected under the commode in the outhouse, they also purchase rice bran or fishmeal on the open market, the latter coming from as far away as Hokkaido. Fertilizer is their greatest expense, costing as much as 70 percent of the total income from the crop according to one village estimate.[3]

Once they have harvested their crop, the village farmers sell it to local merchants, who in turn transport the grain to the city. With the cash income they receive, the villagers pay their rents or taxes, and buy rice and other essentials. The money economy is already highly developed in the Kantō area. Demand from the increasingly commercialized capital has spread cash through the region, and for many years now the villagers' taxes have been payable not in rice or equivalent crops—as is the case in most of Japan—but in *kan,* the copper currency in use among the local tradesmen. The tax system and the need for fertilizer, in particular, have prompted the farmers to do whatever they can to raise extra cash. Villagers sell firewood (sometimes buying the wood themselves, and hauling it down to Edo for resale) and work as carriers or packhorse-minders on the region's highways. Since the mid-Tokugawa era, they have turned increasingly to silk as an additional source of cash income.

The farmers of the non-rice-growing uplands around Hashimoto have been producing silkworms, silk thread, and silk and cotton cloth since at least the eighteenth century.[4] In recent decades Hachiōji, some six kilometers to the north of Hashimoto, has become a major regional market for silk and cotton fabrics, with merchants buying the products from local producers (either at the local markets or by traveling round the villages) and selling them to Edo tradesmen. Now, Hachiōji textiles are being sold not only in Edo, but also Osaka, Echigo, and other provinces throughout Japan. Although Japan's main centers for silk production are the Shindatsu district of Fukushima prefecture, the Kōzuke district of Gunma prefecture, and the mountainous areas of Nagano prefecture, Hachiōji is a well-established player in the national, and now international, silk market.

The opening of Japan to foreign trade through the commercial treaties (1858) with the United States and several European nations has brought a rapid increase in demand for silk. Western markets for luxury textiles are expanding in concert with the growth in industrial and trade wealth. In the early 1860s France, traditionally the major European supplier of silk thread, fell victim to silkworm blight. The French producers' misfortune represented a major opportunity for a new market entrant like Japan. Farmers in Japan's mountain villages who struggled for centuries against inhospitable terrain, harsh winters, and oppressive exactions are now responding eagerly to the new economic opportunity. "Families that formerly cultivated rice and dry fields are now becoming full-time silk producers," observed one commentator in the early 1860s. "The mountain regions are becoming prosperous, and fields and woods are now giving way to mulberry groves and tea plantations."[5]

Figure 6. A *zaguri* spindle (Courtesy Hachiōjishi Kyōiku Iinkai)

Given its ready access to Japan's major foreign port of Yokohama, Hashimoto is well positioned to benefit from foreign trade. The village is situated on the ancient Kōshū Kaidō highway, a route that connects it directly to the Tōkaidō highway just outside Yokohama. The road is one of the major arteries feeding the Edo metropolitan area, and it is a conduit for silk products descending on the foreign enclave from mountainous regions north of the capital—a role that is to earn it the label "Japan's silk road." Local merchants have responded to the demands of foreign buyers for greater consistency by introducing an inspection and certification system for locally reeled silk. This in turn has prompted reelers in the area to adopt the *zaguri* spindle, a relatively sophisticated machine that was developed in Japan near the turn of the nineteenth century, and introduced into the Kantō region only in the past two decades. The *zaguri* is superior to earlier reeling machines, because its wooden cog mechanism makes it extremely fast and consistent. *Zaguri* means "sitting and turning." The operator sits at the large machine and turns a handle attached to a set of wooden cogs, turning a drum on which the silk is reeled. The operator then

Figure 7. Silkworm cards (Courtesy Yokohama Shiruku Hakubutsukan)

picks a half dozen boiled cocoons from a cauldron and fixes the end of each cocoon thread to the drum. The *zaguri* then unreels the cocoons, twisting the threads together to make a strong strand of raw silk. As one cocoon unravels, the operator can attach another to its end, making extra long thread.[6]

"Silk is everywhere," wrote a foreign visitor to Japan's rural hinterland. "Silk occupies the best rooms of all the houses; silk is the topic of everybody's talk; the region seems to live by silk. One has to walk warily in many villages lest one should crush the cocoons which are exposed upon mats, and look so temptingly like almond comfits."[7] Families in Hashimoto take in silkworms according to the space they have available and their ability to provide mulberry leaves—either by purchasing or growing them. The silkworm eggs arrive on silkworm "cards" *(sanranshi)* made of thick Japanese paper. Specialized breeders mount egg-laying worms on squares within one of these cards, which contains the eggs of twenty-five to thirty silkworms. The eggs lie dormant until hatched by the silk rearing family. In their dormant state, they can be transported for long distances—indeed, since the silkworm blight in Europe, a significant part of Japan's silk exports have been in the form of these egg cards.

Hashimoto families buy the silkworm cards from merchants, who travel from the card-producing districts of Nagano prefecture. There follows a six-week-long process of painstaking nurturing, involving the labor of the whole family, but particularly its female members, to rear the silkworms until they spin cocoons using the silk thread produced in their bodies. Here is the process as described by an English visitor:

> The silk season here begins in early April by the [egg-]cards being hung up. In about twenty-two days the worms appear. The women watch them most carefully, placing the cards on paper in basket trays, and brushing them each morning with a feather for three days, till all the worms are hatched. The mulberry leaves with which they are fed are minced very fine and sifted, so as to get rid of leaf fibre, and are then mixed with millet bran. The worms on being removed from the paper are placed on clean basket trays over a layer of matting. They pass through four sleeps, the first occurring ten days after hatching. The interval between the three remaining sleeps is from six to seven days. For these sleeps the most careful preparations are made by the attendants. Food is usually given five times a day, but in hot weather as many as eight times, and as the worms grow bigger their food grows coarser, till after the fourth sleep the leaves are given whole. The quantity is measured with great nicety, as the worms must neither be starved nor gorged. Great cleanliness is necessary, and an equable temperature, or disease arises; and the watching by day and night is so incessant, that, during the season, the women can do little else. After the fourth sleep the worms soon cease to feed, and when they are observed to be looking for a place to reel in, the best are picked out and placed on a straw contrivance, on which they reel their cocoons in three days. When the cocoons are intended for silk they are laid out in the sun on trays for three days, and this kills the chrysalis.[8]

Once the cocoons are ready, most families in Hashimoto reel their own silk, using the *zaguri* or simpler homemade implements. Silk thread is the single most economically important product of Hashimoto (as in all the surrounding villages), exceeding wheat and other grains in value.[9] The villagers of Hashimoto sell their silk thread to visiting merchants, or they take it themselves to the markets of Kamimizo or Hachiōji. These markets are themselves an important feature of the cash economy. Established in the seventeenth century, they are held six times a month. The Kamimizo market caters to the full range of local agricultural products, as well as farm supplies imported into the region. Hachiōji, on the other hand, has a specialized silk market, where farmers and merchants sell both spun silk and silk and cotton cloth.

Figure 8. *Mabushi* cocoon frame (Courtesy Yokohama Shiruku
Hakubutsukan)

Some Hashimoto families own wooden looms, on which they weave
the silk thread into cloth. For the most part, they weave plain, undyed
cloth (gauze, crepe, twill, or chiffon) for kimono makers to work on. In
some cases, the cloth is even sent for export. In the neighboring village,
Aihara, silk weaving is a major enterprise, substantially exceeding silk
thread in annual revenues. Yarimizu, to the north, also has half a dozen
cloth-making families, each employing two or three female workers.

. . .

In spite of the peaceful and prosperous façade that Hashimoto presents,
the world into which Kikutarō is born is by no means a stable or secure
one. Indeed, Japan is on the brink of momentous change, and many of
the strains that are shaking its political system to the very foundations
are already apparent in the smaller universe of Hashimoto's village
community.

For the past decade or more, the political system that brought more
than two hundred years of peace to Japan has been reeling from a series
of blows, starting in 1853 with Commodore Matthew Perry's appear-

ance on Japanese shores at the head of a squadron of steam-powered gunboats, charged with bringing to an end Japan's long-standing policy of political and economic seclusion. The ensuing exposure to Western markets and technology has been deeply destabilizing, creating ruinous inflation and offering the opportunity for hostile domains with long-standing grudges against the Tokugawa shogunal family to arm themselves with the latest foreign weapons. At the time of Kikutarō's birth, the shogunal government has been marshaling its forces for a second military expedition against the rebellious Chōshū domain. The expedition will prove the shogunate's undoing.

But the blows to the shogunal system have not only come from the outside. In part, the system has been the victim of its own success in creating a favorable environment for economic growth and prosperity. As living standards have improved with the introduction of new commodities, and as the taste for luxury has flourished in Japan's major cities, the samurai have been unable to expand their incomes in tandem. This inability applies at all levels of samurai society, from humble foot soldiers on fixed stipends to the shogunal government itself. Increasingly, the shogunate, domains, and samurai have found themselves in debt to wealthy merchants, moneylenders, and even to peasant entrepreneurs.

At the same time, rural communities like Hashimoto have become increasingly riven by distress and conflict. Earlier population growth, and the more recent accumulation of wealth by successful families like the Aizawa, has created a stark divide between village haves and have-nots. More than two-thirds of the families registered in Hashimoto possess less than one *koku* of assets—a *koku* is normally considered the minimum amount of income needed to feed a single adult for a year. Most possess less than half a *koku*, clearly insufficient to make a living from farming activities alone.[10]

In the same register, Aizawa Yasujirō is listed with assets of seventy-two *koku*. His brother, Tashichirō, who was been set up as head of an independent branch household by their father, has twenty-seven *koku*. Other sources indicate that their combined landholdings are in excess of sixty hectares.[11] How did one family become more than a hundred times wealthier that the village average? The Tokugawa landholding system theoretically prohibited the alienation of land, so that unless a family's members reclaimed new land, it should be impossible for them to increase their landholdings. Yet such increases were the reality of Tokugawa village Japan. While land sales were not recognized, mortgages were. A lender could not deprive a delinquent borrower of his land; but he could make the borrower his tenant, owing permanent rent on the land he had once owned. Only in this way could the Aizawa have increased their holdings so substantially while many of the remaining villagers became all but landless. To a great extent, the Aizawa were the beneficiaries of an economy in which taxes and fertilizer must be paid for in cash. Inevitably, the constant need for cash put power and wealth in the hands of those who could supply it in time of need.

Cash is both the savior and the destroyer of the landless village families. Even without land, a family can purchase mulberry leaves, rear silkworms, and reel and sell silk. Its members can labor for cash, on the fields of the wealthier farmers or on the highway as porters. They can live through petty trade—in household necessities like soy sauce or sake, or in local handicrafts such as straw mats. But when the economic winds turn unfavorable, these families are forced to sell their assets, to borrow money however they can, just to survive another year. When the strains become intolerable, they are liable to erupt in rioting and protest.

. . .

Such an explosion was brewing at the time of Kikutarō's birth. The adjustment of Japan's currency to the international market had caused severe inflation for the last decade. Rice now cost nine times as much as it did a decade earlier.[12] The increases had been particularly steep in the past year. For those villagers who were dependent on cash earnings to buy their food, the price increases were disastrous. Although silk prices also increased with the general inflation, the increase was only a quarter that of rice and other food grains. Moreover the shogunal government, concerned at the loss of rice and grain fields to mulberry, had recently ordered strict new controls on silk production, bringing further hardship to those without the land resources to grow food crops. Rural protests erupted throughout Japan—141 separate incidents were recorded in the year 1866, a record for the Tokugawa era (1603–1868).

The closest came within a few miles of Hashimoto. Its leaders were from the hardscrabble villages of the mountain districts north of Hachiōji. Several thousand villagers descended from the mountains into the prosperous towns on the edge of the plain. They sacked the warehouses of grain merchants in Hannō, then moved on to Tokorozawa, where they attacked grain and silk merchants, sake brewers, and moneylenders. The rioters focused especially on merchants known to be engaged in foreign trade, since the opening of the ports to trade was held to be the main cause of the peasants' distress. The protesters worked in groups of a dozen or two up to several thousand, dressed in straw rain-capes tied with colored cords as they went about their business of smashing and burning. Although they destroyed enormous amounts of property, the protesters were strictly enjoined not to harm people. They carried only agricultural implements, and the leaders ordered them "only to chastise the unjust and give the public an object lesson."[13] Some groups made their way towards Hachiōji, intending to continue marching all the way to Yokohama where they would attack foreigners and "crush the root of the national malaise in order to bring peace of mind to the ordinary people."[14] If they had been allowed to proceed, their route would have taken them right through Hashimoto.

Before they could reach Hachiōji, though, they were stopped by well-armed village militias. The militias were organized by local land-lords—who also comprised the village leadership—seeking to protect their own assets. They were supported by their lords and by the sho-gunal authorities, who were deeply concerned at the breakdown of law and order in the countryside. For example Kojima Tamemasa, head-man of the village of Onoji, created an army of seventy-five village men equipped with spears, swords, and fifteen modern rifles provided by their feudal lord in spite of the strict feudal prohibition of weapons outside the samurai class. The army also obtained a makeshift wooden cannon, and the soldiers were supplied with uniforms, helmets, and other equipment. The village army even had a drum and fife corps to march in front.[15]

BUILDING A NEW NATION

In June of 1866 the nineteen-year-old shogun, Iemochi, died of beriberi while on campaign against the rebellious province of Chōshū, and the huge military undertaking, disastrous from the outset, was ignomini-ously abandoned. From that point on the shogunate quickly unraveled. The new shogun, Tokugawa Yoshinobu, formally renounced his title in November 1867, but his gesture failed to prevent the rebels from advanc-ing on the capital. By early 1868, a new government comprised mainly of samurai from Satsuma and Chōshū had consolidated its political position as caretaker for an imperial "restoration." The emperor was moved from Kyoto to Edo, which was renamed Tokyo, and installed in the former shogun's palace. Henceforth, all major political initiatives by the government were enacted in the emperor's name.

The death throes of the shogunate affected villages throughout Japan. Worst affected were those that lay in the path of the advancing armies. In the Kantō area, government officials and feudal lords called on villagers to support the tottering system, through contributions of money and labor. In the area around Hashimoto, the village of Tana was forced in 1859 to make a special loan of five hundred gold *ryō* to its feudal lord, the Toriyama domain. Suzuki Kazuma, a *hatamoto* with landholdings in fifteen villages close to Hashimoto, demanded special impositions in March, July, and December of 1867 totaling six hundred gold *ryō*. Once the imperial army took control of Edo and the surrounding countryside, the new government, too, demanded exactions of villagers. These were in addition to the economic and social distress caused by the upheavals—rising prices, supply disruptions, and widespread banditry.

The great upheaval of 1867 and 1868 was the starting point for a series of policies affecting the countryside where 80 percent of Japanese still lived. Some of the policies were minor but symbolic—for example the adoption of the Gregorian calendar and the "naming" of the Japanese peasantry. Others, such as the education and conscription systems, were major reforms that would come to affect the lives of a large percentage of villagers.

In June of 1869, the new government announced that all land formerly belonging to *hatamoto* retainers would now come under its direct control. In September, it created Kanagawa prefecture, composed mostly of former shogunal retainers' territory, including Hashimoto. Hashimoto was no longer divided between four different lords. The entire village was answerable to the prefectural superintendent in Kanagawa. Two years later, with the abolition of the *daimyo* domains, governors were appointed to head up each prefecture. Kanagawa's first governor under the new system was Mutsu Munemitsu, a Chōshū samurai and one of the leading figures in the new government.

In 1871—the same year in which the domains were abolished— the government also announced the abolition of the feudal system and the class system, and the removal of all restrictions on farmers' movements and activities. The measure also abolished the separate treatment of the "untouchable" groups known as *eta* or *hinin*. Until this time, status had been defined at birth into one of four major class groups: samurai, farmer, artisan, or merchant. The system left many gaps—priests, entertainers, artists, outcastes—and over time the groups increasingly tended to blur at the edges. Many farmers became engaged in trade, for example, while merchants were often granted or assumed the privileges of samurai status. But in principle, if you were born a farmer, you died a farmer. Moreover, the hierarchical relationship between these groups was also prescribed. Farmers were expected to show extreme respect for the ruling samurai class. The new system created a European-style aristocracy, and for a few more years the samurai retained their legal status. But samurai were now free to take up professions (including farming, which many did), and farmers and other classes were relabeled "commoners," with freedom of movement and occupation, and without the obligation to kowtow to the samurai. In practice, of course, most farmers stayed on the farm, and they continued to show considerable respect to the educated members of the ex-samurai class.

In the same year, 1871, the Japanese government—deeply concerned about its image in the West—outlawed the wearing of swords, and ordered its male subjects to cut off their topknots. The topknot had been an accepted part of self-respecting villagers' appearance for centuries. Many villages by the mid-nineteenth century had a hairdresser, who specialized in trimming, combing, oiling, and tying the hair. The waxy ointment *(bintsuke)* used to stiffen the taut sides of the hair had a distinctive scent that was a part of the very fabric of daily life. Many villagers chose to ignore the new regulations, and there is no indication that they were strictly enforced in the villages. Isabella Bird, an English visitor to Japan, wrote as late as 1878 that "most of the men of the lower classes wear their hair in a very ugly fashion—the front and top of the head being shaved, the long hair from the back and sides being drawn up and tied, then waxed, tied again, and cut short off, the stiff queue being brought forward and laid, pointing forwards, along the back part of the top of the head."[16] But it is very likely that Aizawa Yasujirō, who could not avoid being aware of the rule and who had an obligation to set an example, was among the first to have his topknot removed and his hair cut short. A popular ditty reproduced in the newspapers went: "If you tap a shave-head, you will hear the voice of indecision. If you tap a long-hair, you will hear the sound of imperial restoration. If you tap a crop-head, you will hear the sound of civilization and enlightenment."[17] That sound was beginning to be heard even in the villages of the Kantō region.

At the start of 1873, the government mandated the use of the Gre-

gorian calendar. The measure caused a good deal of chaos at first, especially as all but two days of December 1872 were "cancelled" (this was
for purposes of alignment, although some have suggested it was mainly
a measure to avoid paying civil servants a twelfth month's salary). The
sudden shift from a lunar to a solar calendar was undoubtedly a shock
for conservative Japanese villagers, many of whom vigorously protested
the change. But it would be misleading to suggest that the change radically affected the seasonal pattern in Japanese villages. Rural Japanese
had no agency in the old calendar, which was strictly controlled by the
shogunal government (even the printing of calendars required a government license). Moreover, the old system was strictly speaking not lunar
but lunar-solar, since it was adjusted periodically to stay aligned with
the solar year. The new system used the same twelve months as the old
(though without the need for intercalary months), and the weekdays in
Japan have used the same seven-day sequence of planetary names as in
Europe since at least the ninth century.[18] In spite of the adoption of the
solar calendar, many village holidays and almanacs remained tied to
the lunar cycle—as they do to this day.

At roughly the same time, the government began encouraging—
and finally requiring—villagers to adopt family names. During the
Tokugawa period, the public use of family names had been a privilege
granted to the samurai class, to those serving in public positions, and
to those granted the right as a special favor in exchange for money
or services. Theoretically at least, this amounted to a very small percentage of the nonsamurai population. In reality, a large number of
villagers used family names privately within the village community.
Sometimes these were "house names" (yagō), which identified the
family by a trade or a location within the village. At other times the
name was adopted to show the origin of the family—often, it was the
name of the place from which the family had originally immigrated
to the village. It is unclear how widespread these private names were,
since by law they could not be used on official documents. However,
records of donors to temples or shrines show that many had family
names under which they registered their gifts (for example, of a total of
2,345 families from thirty-three villages in the Matsumotodaira region
of Nagano who had their names inscribed on a votive tablet in 1830,
all but sixteen used family names).[19] Family names were also routinely
inscribed on gravestones in family burial plots. The prevalence of private family names may well have varied by region, but in the Musashi
and Sagami areas surrounding Hashimoto—close to the capital and

relatively developed commercially and economically—the use of private family names appears to have been widespread.[20]

Nevertheless, many families were reluctant at first to register their family names officially. One reason for this may have been the fear that registering a name would make family members more readily liable for the new conscription system. Another was that the adoption of official family names might upset the hierarchy within the village, which connected official names to a leading status in the village.

In April 1871 the government passed a law creating a family register system. This system, modeled on an ancient practice of the seventh century (the term *koseki*, or family register, dates to the Taika reforms of 646), was nevertheless a pragmatic measure aimed at establishing modern bureaucratic control over the Japanese population. Since the basic unit of the *koseki* was the family, the new measure would be ineffective without the use of family names. In February 1875, the government passed a law requiring all Japanese to adopt family names, and Japanese subjects were required to enroll in the *koseki* registers in the following months.

Although many villagers undoubtedly recorded names that they had already been using for some time, stories abound of villagers (usually those of lower status or those in remote regions) who had to choose family names to fulfill the new requirement. In many cases, they entrusted the choice of names to their village headman, landlord, priest, or another trusted leader. There were a number of tricky issues involved in choosing names. Villagers could not choose a name that might suggest superiority or otherwise give offense to the elite families of the village. They had to coordinate their choice of names with their close relatives, to prevent a proliferation of names within the same family (this effort was complicated by the difficulty many families had in communicating with sons who had gone to live in the cities or in distant provinces). And their names should preferably have some meaning or relevance.

Village headmen and other name-pickers adopted a number of methods for selecting names for the subordinate families in the village. Some bestowed variations of their own family names. In other cases, headmen picked names related to the occupation of the recipients. The Meiji ethnographer Yanagita Kunio interviewed villagers on the coast of Shikoku Island who told him that the headman had named their parents and grandparents after fishing tools, garden vegetables, and fish: Iwashi (sardine), Hirame (flounder), and Kabu (turnip).[21] In a small eel-fishing hamlet in Kagoshima prefecture, the entire population adopted the name Unagi (eel).[22] In another recorded case, the priest of the Kōkyōji Temple in Harumiya village near Osaka suggested names for his parishioners based on the direction of their homes from the temple. Those to the north were named Kitano (north field), those to the south Minamino (south field). Another account has a priest giving villagers the names of samurai warriors from the *Taikō-ki* (biography of Toyotomi Hideyoshi) he had just been reading.[23] In some cases, those in authority had to dampen the enthusiasm of villagers for grandiose or impractical names. There is a story (perhaps apocryphal) of a villager who wanted to adopt the name "Tennōheika" (His Majesty the Emperor). The village head persuaded him to stick with the *kanji* for "heika," using the alternative reading Hashigami.[24]

The registration of some seven million families and thirty-three million family members was an enormous undertaking. Although the class system had officially been abolished, the registers nevertheless recorded the family's social status, with separate entries for the imperial family, the aristocracy, ex-samurai, temple priests, shrine priests, nuns, commoners, and residents of Sakhalin. Commoners were of course by far the largest category, accounting for 93 percent of the total. The registers also contained annotations if the household was of the former *eta* or *hinin* (untouchable) castes. The registers were entrusted to the lowest levels of local government—in the case of villages, the village headmen. The names and ages of family members, and the occupation and assets of the family, were also recorded.[25]

The abolition of the feudal system was preliminary to a radical restructuring of land ownership. In theory, in feudal Japan all land belonged to the shogun and his feudal vassals, and the farmer held only cultivating rights. The legal basis for the exchange of land through sale or foreclosure had always been murky, relying for the most part on local custom and tacit consent. The Meiji government, however, put land ownership on a legal footing. Government officials conducted extensive surveys of land throughout Japan, and awarded title deeds to those villagers judged to have the best claim to the land. In most cases, they recognized the rights of landlords and mortgagors, and awarded them full possession of the land.

The new system was fraught with injustice for many. Because of the vagueness of ownership laws under the Tokugawa, even those who rented land often continued until the Meiji reforms to have many of the rights of ownership. Rental arrangements differed greatly from region to region, but in parts of Japan (including Hashimoto) permanent ten-

ancy rights were common—equivalent to a sort of encumbered ownership. The new system, though, ignored such rights, and placed full
control of the land in the hands of the landlord. In a survey, Hashimoto
acknowledged four traditional types of tenancy: permanent tenancy
(over twenty years), tenancy of land mortgaged to a creditor, tenant
cultivation of the landlord's fields, and "immigrant tenancy"—land
cultivated by those from outside the village.[26] Although these categories
continued to exist, each must now be separately negotiated and agreed
by contract, while existing arrangements were subject to arbitrary
revision.

The new landownership system also threatened the status of land
that had been considered communal. Most villages held some communal land for villagers to use for grazing, firewood, and fertilizer.
Sometimes this land was commercially viable, in which case it might be
an important source of income for the village. In other cases, it might
have been uncultivated wild or mountain land that no one had ever
troubled to claim—though it was still vital to the villagers as a source
of fertilizer and firewood. In the Meiji land reorganization, much of
this land was claimed by powerful villagers or the government.[27]

The corollary to the regularization of land ownership was the reform
of taxation. Previously, taxes had been imposed by feudal lords, based
on a variety of formulas. While there was no standardization, a large
percentage of the taxes were payable in kind—mainly in rice, which
was a de facto currency in Japan throughout the feudal era. And for
the most part, they were imposed not on individual households, but
on the entire village community, which was collectively responsible for
their payment. The priority of the new government was to establish
a uniform national taxation system, giving it a predictable income
stream sufficient to meet its obligations. It did so by establishing a
new land tax, payable by the individual land-holding family and not
by the village, and payable in cash and not in kind. The government
established a fixed percentage (initially 3 percent) of the value of newly
deeded land, payable annually regardless of land use, crop conditions,
weather, or the many other factors that had made the previous system
so unpredictable.

For rice farmers, this was in many cases a major transition, and
helped push those farmers into the commercial economy. Formerly,
their taxes had been paid in kind, and, since rice was also their main
item of consumption, they had generally been less involved in the cash
economy than commercial farmers like those in Hashimoto. Now, they

must sell rice even if they would have preferred to eat it, to pay the taxes demanded by the government. For the villagers of Hashimoto, though, the main question was: would the new tax cost more or less than the old feudal imposts?

The government's intention was to make the new tax system revenue-neutral—it should leave villagers paying no more or less tax than they had before. On average, the government intended farmers to pay about 40 percent of their farming income in national taxes. In addition, prefectural and local authorities were allowed to tax villagers up to a maximum 20 percent of the national tax. The total tax was thus expected to be about 50 percent of farm income. All these assumptions were based on 1870 price and land productivity data, as established through an exhaustive national survey. Over the following years, rice price and productivity increases tended to decrease the real burden of the tax.

The taxable land in Hashimoto was valued at a total of ¥30,000. Based on the 3-percent formula, this resulted in an annual tax payment of ¥900 for the entire village. It is hard to tell how much of an increase this represents, since feudal records are very incomplete. But an 1867 document indicates that the village only paid 131 *kan* combined to its four different lords. Exchange rates between the old copper coinage and the new yen currency are very uncertain, but in theory at least the *kan* and the yen exchanged at parity. This would suggest a substantial increase for the villagers.[28] Very likely, the new land surveys revealed productive land that had been hidden from the Tokugawa authorities. However, Hashimoto in the Tokugawa era may well have been subject to "off-the-books" payments to the feudal masters in the form of forced loans or additional imposts. Probably the most we can say with confidence is that the villagers did not get off any lighter under the new system.[29] Unlike rice farmers in other villagers, though, the villagers of Hashimoto were already accustomed to paying their taxes in cash, so that aspect of the reform affected them little.

. . .

Another major new initiative, quite astounding in its ambition, was the creation in 1872 of a system of universal education. Japan's young leaders were deeply impressed by the educational systems they saw in operation on their travels to Europe and North America, and they became convinced that a modern educational system was an essential part of creating a nation-conscious, patriotic citizenry. Japanese intellectuals were also deeply impressed by the principle of "self-help" embodied in the Scottish author Samuel Smiles's bestselling book of that title, which was first translated into Japanese in 1871.[30] In fact, the principles expressed in the book resonated strongly with the ideas of popular Confucianist educators and philosophers like Ninomiya Sontoku, who was to become the "patron saint" of the Japanese school system. A forward-looking educational system would, government leaders hoped, give Japanese children basic tools that they could use to turn themselves—and hence Japan—into success stories.

The government had nothing like the resources needed to finance an entirely new school system, so—following Smiles's principles—it devolved the responsibility for financing and implementing the new system onto the local communities. Villages were required to raise the sometimes very substantial sums needed to create new schools, preferably in Western-style buildings, and make their services available to all the children of the village, boys and girls alike.

Most villages already had a limited system of education in place: the so-called temple schools. Wherever possible, they used this foundation in the creation of the new government-mandated elementary schools. Often run by the priest of the local temple, or by a teacher affiliated with it, the temple schools educated up to one-third of the boys in village Japan, and occasionally they took in girls, too. To some extent, these schools were a response to the increasing commercialization of Japanese agriculture. As farmers became increasingly involved in trade, they developed a greater need for numeracy and literacy. Starting in the Tenpō period (1830–44), the number of temple schools throughout Japan increased dramatically. The districts of Kosugi and Mizunokuchi, some thirty kilometers from Hashimoto, had thirty temple schools by 1864, serving a total population of thirteen thousand. The schools typically met daily from eight in the morning until dusk, with holidays twice a month on the first and fifteenth (in addition to the New Year and mid-year holidays). The students were tested at the end of each month, with one major test each year. Students studied reading, writing, and arithmetic (with the abacus), using textbooks that were usually handwritten by the teacher. Payment for classes was often made in kind, depending on the agricultural activities and means of the students' families (though increasingly near the end of the Tokugawa period, payments were made in cash). Students were expected to help pay for maintenance costs including tatami, charcoal, and incense for the school altar, and they were expected to make small gifts to the teacher at the mid-year and year-end holidays.[31] Francis Hall describes a visit to a village school in 1860: "Each [child] had his little table on which was his copy book and writing materials. The copy book was made of some sheets of Japanese paper sewed together, the writing materials were the reed pens of the country, India ink, and a tablet to grind the ink upon. The desks were black with ink and hacked, not with Yankee prick knives, but with the paper cutting knives of the school boys. Their copy books were smeared with ink into one general blot, for it seemed that as each page was finished the whole was blacked over."[32]

The early elementary schools for the most part were built on these local school traditions. In the case of Hashimoto, the temple-school teacher at the time of the education laws was Yasuda Beisai. Yasuda was a monk, trained in the Zen tradition at Seisōji Temple in Tokyo while simultaneously studying the Chinese classics. In 1865, he moved to a temple in Tana village, and three years later he transferred to Zuikōji Temple in Hashimoto, where he began teaching temple school students.[33] When the new education laws were passed, the village quickly appointed Yasuda to the position of teacher, and moved him into new premises in a house rented from the Aizawa family.

It is not clear in the early years if the student population was much different from what it would have been under the old temple school system. The entering class on the occasion of the school's opening in 1873 consisted of twenty-one students: nineteen boys and two girls. The students ranged in age from seven to fourteen. The laws provided that students between six and fourteen were eligible to enter the new elementary schools. It is unclear why no six-year-olds enrolled. Most of the older students had probably already been studying under Yasuda. Among the entering class of seven-year-olds was Aizawa Kikutarō. Kikutarō entered the class alongside his brother, Kenjirō, who was eleven, and his cousin Jungorō, who was eight.

Apparently the leadership of Hashimoto village made a sincere effort to encourage more students into the school. But in the early years, the school suffered more losses than gains. Eight students quit the school in 1873, and although another three joined in 1874, two of those quit almost immediately. By February 1874, the school was down to only eleven students. Most of these were from the village elite. Of the 106 families in the village assessed in 1873 with assets of less than one *koku,* only four sent a child to the school.[34]

One obstacle to a wider enrollment was undoubtedly the cost of elementary school education. The Hashimoto school charged an average of 3.6 *sen* (one *sen* equaled ¥0.01) per month. At the time, a farm laborer might earn no more than ¥0.20 per day. If a family had several children, the cost of their schooling could come to one day's wages per month, in addition to expenses for paper and ink. Another was the perception that education was the prerogative of the wealthy. Children in poorer families were needed to work and contribute to the family's fragile economy. Even among those children who did attend the school, attendance at classes was amazingly low. According to school records, only one student in the school attended more than 60 percent of classes in 1875, while three students attended less than 20 percent of classes.[35]

In December 1876 the new Hashimoto elementary school graduated its first class. They had completed four years of elementary education in addition, for the older boys, to an unspecified number of years in the temple school. The would-be graduates traveled to Kamimizo village to take a prefectural exam that reflected the practical and self-help values of the Ministry of Education. The questions in the 1881 exam included:

1. A man owns a piece of land measuring 35 *ken* by 14 *ken*. One *tsubo* of land is valued at ¥0.80. How much is the land worth? [author's note: a *tsubo* is one square *ken* (1.82 meters × 1.82 meters)].

2. ¥143 is distributed among A, B, and C. A gets ¥9 more than B, and C gets ¥7 less than B. How much does each man get?

3. $13 + 44/22 \times 4 - 11 + (30-3)/9 + 12 =$

4. A cart has wheels of diameter 9 *shaku* [author's note: 1 *shaku* equals 30.3 cm, 6 *shaku* equals 1 *ken*]. The cart travels 120 *ken* down the road. How many times do the wheels turn?

5. What do you call a piece of land that is surrounded on four sides by water?

6. Who was the American leader who defeated the British in the War of Independence?

7. In what circumstances can a branch family be created?[36]

These questions reflect a relatively high standard of elementary education, after only four years of schooling. Was it really possible in four years to train a student in literacy and numbers, especially given the demanding nature of the Japanese writing system? Kikutarō was to be a prolific writer throughout his life, and his writing shows an extensive command of the Japanese writing system. Surely, the school system on its own could not have equipped him with these tools. Undoubtedly he received further education at home. The houses of wealthy farmers in the Kantō region were often well provided with books and educated readers. The house of Ishizaka Masataka, a wealthy farmer of Notsu village to the northeast of Hashimoto who would later become a Diet member and prefectural governor, was said to contain one thousand volumes, and in addition to his formal schooling, Ishizaka had private instructors in Chinese poetry, calligraphy, and Japanese poetry. The house of the Kojima family in Ono village contained no fewer than six thousand books of poetry, woodblock prints, fiction, Chinese literature, Nō plays, and, after the Meiji restoration, treatises on law, the economy, and politics.[37]

In addition to his formal schooling, Aizawa certainly benefited from his exposure to the many visitors who stopped at his house. The Hashimoto road was always busy with travelers, and those who had a claim to special attention might well stop at the home of one of the village's leading families. The politician Katayama Sen, who grew up in a wealthy village family, describes this frequent exposure to newcomers:

> When I was little, all sorts of people would visit with us, stay overnight, or request some help from us. My father was the *shōya* [village headman], and as such, it was his job to entertain visitors, or to give help to those who needed it . . . The visitors were from every walk of life. Artists, reciters of poetry, haiku poets, masters of judo or swordsmanship; these people would walk from province to province improving their skills. Among them were quite a number who were to make national reputations or leave their mark on history. If an artist stopped with a wealthy family and brushed some pictures, he could expect to receive a little money so he could continue on his journey. As they rested with us, they would tell us stories about the things they had seen and heard on their travels. I was fascinated, and begged my grandmother always to treat these travelers kindly.[38]

The creation of elementary schools on Ministry of Education guidelines was a very expensive proposition. For the most part, the schools were financed by subscription, with the village elites contributing the largest share. But middle-class and even poor villagers were also pressed to contribute, and most villages also imposed some sort of special tax to help pay for the schools. Hashimoto's school in its early years got away quite cheaply. While other villages purchased land and

built new (often Western-style) buildings, Hashimoto's school rented
an existing house. The total capital contributed by wealthy members
of neighboring villages averaged more than ¥1,000. The capital of the
Kamimizo school was ¥2,557, yielding an annual interest income of
¥256. Hashimoto, by contrast, had capital of just ¥148—the lowest
of any village in the area. Its interest income in 1875 was a mere ¥25.
Adding school fees to this, the total annual income of the school was
less than ¥40. Meanwhile, the school had expenses of more than ¥70,
including ¥54 for the teacher's salary, and ¥12 for rent. The deficit had
to be paid for by a special village tax.[39]

. . .

The other major reform affecting village life was the system of conscription. Throughout the Tokugawa period, military service was both the
duty and the prerogative of the samurai class. Commoners were strictly
prohibited from owning weapons. Nevertheless, in the waning days of
the Tokugawa some of the more forward-looking domains had begun
recruiting commoner soldiers and training them according to European
methods. Even in the conservative Tokugawa heartland, the authorities
allowed and sometimes encouraged peasants to create local militias.
After the Meiji restoration, the new leaders studied the military systems
of the Western imperial powers as they pondered how to create a unified nation able to resist both internal and external threats. The architect of the conscription law, Yamagata Aritomo, studied the military
systems of France and Prussia during their conflict in 1870 and 1871.
France had been the original pioneer of the conscript army, introducing
conscription after the French Revolution, and both countries relied on
huge armies of conscripts. The Meiji leadership came to believe that
modern warfare depended more on large armies of disciplined recruits
than on the swashbuckling ways of the traditional military caste.

The basic law initiating the new system was passed on January 10,
1873. The law required all males reaching the age of twenty to submit
to a medical examination. Those who passed the physical were entered
into a lottery, and those selected by lot would serve three years in
the military, followed by three years (extended to nine in 1882) in the
reserves. An imperial edict accompanying the new law emphasized that
conscription was not in fact a new system in Japan—it had been in
force throughout antiquity, and it was only because "idle and arrogant" warriors had imposed their power on the land (a veiled reference
to the recently overthrown shogunal system) that it had been allowed

to fall into disuse. Conscription was therefore held up as a symbol of a lost national unity in which all classes participated in the affairs of the state.[40]

In practice, in the early years of conscription a relatively low number of men—as few as 5 percent on average of those eligible—actually served in the military. Eldest sons were exempted, as were married men, household heads, higher-school students, and those with brothers already serving in the military. For those with the resources, it was also possible to purchase exemption, though the cost at ¥270 was far too high for ordinary villagers. Those who would not otherwise be exempt adopted a variety of measures to change their status, such as arranging their adoption as eldest sons into other families, or entering new "branch" households as household head. Such arrangements led the famous educator Fukuzawa Yukichi to remark on the increase in "sons who do not know where their fathers live" and in those "who call themselves the heads of families but have no family members to feed." According to one estimate, exemptions exceeded 80 percent of the total pool throughout the 1870s. Over time, the government tightened the loopholes, making it illegal for those under twenty to form new branch families, and exempting eldest sons only if the family head was over fifty (later increased to sixty) years old. But it took twenty years before the system was fully functional.[41]

Still, for villages, the conscription system meant a significant shift in the rhythm of the community. Just when young men were likely to be most active in hamlet institutions such as the youth association, fire brigade, and shrine festival, they were liable to be taken out of the community and placed in an institution whose orientation was not local but national. In most cases, they would enter a regiment stationed in their home prefecture, so they would never be too far away from their families. But for many, military service was the first time that they saw modernity in action: the first time that they used running water and flush toilets, traveled on trains, wore boots or even trousers, slept in beds, or ate meat. Although the basic diet of the soldiers differed little from that of humble Japanese urbanites, even this probably contained more variety and higher quality food than most peasants had eaten at home. In addition, field provisions included canned food, bread, and biscuits—all undoubted novelties for village men. From their (frequently urban) barracks, conscripted soldiers also participated in urban entertainments, including dining in inexpensive restaurants, visiting brothels, and theater going.[42]

The system also placed new burdens on the village administration. Villages were charged with keeping accurate registers of eligible conscripts, and delivering them to the annual medical examination, usually held in June. The examination center was typically in the school buildings of a town or larger village, and village mayors from the surrounding area would lead their eligible recruits for examination. The mayor would be held personally responsible for ensuring a minimum of malingerers or draft evaders. Once recruits were conscripted, the village authorities had to keep a benevolent eye on their families, who were often reduced to dire financial straits by the loss of their precious manpower.

HARDSHIP AND PROTEST

When the American journalist Francis Hall recorded his travels in the Kantō countryside in 1865, he wrote: "Again and again have I stood in their valley hamlets where there were no signs but those of peaceful industry and content, each hamlet to all intents a little republic by itself, knowing little and caring less for the outside world; to whom a change of rulers or revolution in the State would have no significance as great as the death of their own *nanooshi* or headman—people who know no oppression because they feel none, whose lives have fewer disturbing elements, perhaps, than any other people on whom the sun in its daily revolution falls."[43] Even after the Meiji restoration and its attendant upheavals, the countryside no doubt looked serene and unchanging as the farmers went about their annual cycle of planting and harvest. And indeed for much of the rural Kantō area, the reforms were implemented with little fuss and no protest. Hashimoto was one of the majority of communities that made the transition smoothly—at least on the surface.[44]

But surface impressions could be misleading. Lying just under the bland façade that villages like Hashimoto presented to the world were burning aspirations and seething discontents. Villagers of the Kantō area, as elsewhere, were by no means ignorant of or indifferent to the changes taking place in the outside world. In the 1850s, village leaders closely followed the negotiations between the shogunate and a succession of foreign intruders. Contemporary copies have been found in remote village storehouses of the foreign treaties of the late 1850s, as well as of seminal foreign ideas such as those in Rousseau's *Social Contract*. In the mid-1860s, fervently patriotic young villagers like Shibusawa

Eiichi (later to become one of the founding fathers of Japanese capitalism) resolved to give up their lives for the sake of reform: "Unless my friends and I mounted a rebellion that shook the country and purged the government of its evils," recalled Shibusawa in his autobiography, "Japan would never regain its power. We were, to be sure, merely peasants, yet so long as we were Japanese we could not stand idly by, saying it was not our duty. We might accomplish little, but at the very least we could gloriously offer up our lives as blood sacrifices and lead the way to rebellion."[45] Shibusawa lived just sixty-five kilometers from Hashimoto, in the Kantō village of Chiaraijima. In the 1870s and 1880s, members of village elites were fervent supporters of the People's Rights Movement, which was agitating for a constitution and an elected parliament. Villagers in the Kantō drafted proposed constitutions, based on extensive study of foreign models, and pressed for the adoption of a constitution even at the risk of imprisonment. As one member of a rural "Learning and Debating Society" wrote in 1880: "Those who grieve for their country and love their people must become the eyes and ears, the body and soul of the nation and dedicate themselves wholeheartedly to the task of establishing a national assembly to consider carefully what will prosper or harm the country in the days to come. They must debate whether or not a constitution will serve the people's interests. They must guarantee the people's rights, uphold justice, preserve freedom, and ensure happiness."[46]

The current of popular feeling in rural Japan was subject to many conflicting influences. As much as some villagers wanted change, others resisted it. Underlying much of the latent frustration in village communities was the smoldering discontent of the landless and tenant farmers who labored under an immense burden of debt and obligation. The insecurity and economic dislocation caused by the collapse of the shogunate, followed by a decade of dramatic reform under the new government, added powder to the explosive mixture of aspiration and discontent, and caused unprecedented outbursts of protest and violence in rural areas throughout Japan.

From the mid-1860s to the turn of the 1870s—a time when nothing was clear except for the impending, and then actual, collapse of the old order—almost 350 peasant protests erupted throughout Japan—about five times the average rate of the preceding three centuries.[47] Moreover, the protests were of greater magnitude and violence than the average.[48] The disturbances of this time were enormously varied in cause and outcome. They ranged from relatively minor complaints about local abuses of power or wealth, to organized, domain-wide insurgencies, such as the months-long rebellion that took place after the fall of the shogunal domain of Aizu.

In late 1867 and early 1868, peasants and poor townsmen in western Japan broke out into carnivalesque celebrations, said to have been triggered by showers of Buddhist amulets falling from the sky. Crying out a jumble of nonsense verse, often ending in the refrain *eejanaika* ("it's okay, ain't it!") villagers took to dancing their way through the streets in huge, sometimes frenzied crowds, wearing outlandish costumes or even pulling off all their clothes.[49] Some of the verses they sang were explicitly antigovernment or antiforeigner: "The gods will descend to Japan, while rocks fall on the foreigners in their residences. Ain't it okay, ain't it okay! Ain't it okay, ain't it okay! Ain't it okay, ain't it okay! Ain't it okay, ain't it okay!"[50] The villagers were calling for a new world, in which they would be emancipated from the care and toil of their daily lives.

While some looked to Buddha and the gods to liberate them, others took matters into their own hands. Unlike earlier peasant protests that had typically seen village communities—often led by their elite members—appeal to the benevolence of feudal lords in response to poor harvests or excessive tax burdens, the targets of these *yonaoshi* ("world-renewal") protests were often those very village elites: landlords, moneylenders, and village headmen. The characteristic act of protest was the *uchikowashi*, or "smashing," in which poorer villagers attacked the homes and warehouses of elites, appropriating or destroying food stores, burning homes, and destroying tax and loan records, and property deeds.[51] In the most extreme cases, protesters from many villages joined in regional movements that threatened the very structure of Japanese society. In such cases, villagers at times expressed a clear political vision in response to the upheavals that had undermined or destroyed the authority system they had been reared to think was eternal. In the Aizu uprisings of 1868 and 1869, for example, villagers not only attacked the homes, storehouses, and granaries of wealthy villagers, burning records of land ownership and debts owed by villagers; they also demanded the replacement of all hereditary village officials, the confiscation of land records and other village documents, the appointment of small-scale farmers as village headmen, the return of pawned goods, and the cancellation of interest and/or principal on loans. It was "a revolutionary movement by small proprietors and poor peasants who violently rejected the notion that the traditional political and economic hierarchy in the village adequately protected their vital interests."[52]

A second phase of protests, lasting roughly from 1872 until 1878, specifically attacked the modernizing reforms of the Meiji government. The protests targeted virtually every reform made by the Meiji government in its first five years: the adoption of Western hairstyles, the emancipation of the *burakumin* caste, the demise of the shogun and daimyō, the land tax, the education reforms, conscription, and the introduction of the Western calendar. Some of the protests even attacked rumored measures that were never in reality contemplated by the government—for example, the rumor that the revered Ise Shrine was to be moved to Tokyo.[53] Sudō Shigeo recalled in the 1920s his grandfather's stories of his induction into the military in the first cadre of conscripts under the new law: "In those days it was said that conscripts were selected for the 'blood tax' based on their excellent health. After their blood was drawn, it would be used to dye their uniforms and military caps blood-red. Everyone believed that, my grandfather included. However, since he was in such good health, he felt that even if a little blood was taken from him, he wouldn't be much harmed by it. So he willingly did his service."[54] Others, though, were less willing to play along. In Okayama, villagers went on a rampage in 1873, believing that the conscription law was part of a plot to drain youths of their blood and sell it to foreigners.[55]

The fantastic nature of many of the rumors, and the apparently reactionary nature of villagers' demands—that, for example, the repressive feudal system should be restored, the *burakumin* once again designated as outcastes, the new schools abolished, and the daimyō returned to power—suggest a blind antagonism to anything new, reminiscent of the Luddite Movement sixty years earlier in England. But like the Luddites, the villagers of Japan in the 1870s were not merely blind reactionaries. They were also motivated by real grievances at the economic and labor burdens of the new policies.

Indeed, comprehensive surveys have shown that the majority of protests were fundamentally economic in motivation, even when modernizing reforms were the overt cause.[56] The single greatest object of protest was the land tax, which was the greatest economic burden borne by Japan's peasantry. Resentment against this tax was well justified, for it brought upward of 10 percent of landowning peasants to ruin over the next fifteen years.[57]

Even the schools, built at village expense and ostensibly for the benefit

of villagers, came under attack. Hundreds of school buildings throughout Japan were destroyed. Destruction of schools was most commonly
only a part of more widespread "smashings" of all the institutions
that represented the new government and its modernizing reforms. As
with the other institutions, the villagers must have seen in the schools
a heavy financial burden, thrust on the villages in much the same way
as a new tax. Unlike the "temple schools," the new schools once built
were direct representatives of government authority. Their avowed aim
was to make good national subjects out of villagers whose loyalties had
hitherto been mostly local. Perhaps it is not so surprising that villagers
resisted this authoritarian vision of their place in a modern, militarized
state. Indeed, their experiences over the next century—indoctrination
into a coercive emperor-centered political system, and compulsory military service in increasingly deadly wars—in many ways justified their
initial resistance.[58]

The third wave of peasant protest, in the early 1880s, came in the
wake of severe economic hardship caused in part by the very reforms
that villagers had been protesting in the previous decade. In 1880,
shortly after Matsukata Masayoshi took office as finance minister,
Japan embarked on a new monetary policy of fiscal austerity and shrink-
age of government expenditures. The Ministry of Finance ordered the
withdrawal of a series of banknotes, amounting altogether to almost
35 percent of the currency in circulation. Partly as a result of this,
and partly due to a global downturn, prices began falling across the
board.[59] The price of rice fell particularly steeply, declining by more
than 50 percent between 1881 and 1884. Silk, too, declined in price
by close to 50 percent. The government also introduced new taxes, on
tobacco, soy sauce, and sake—forcing those villagers who had invested
in these products to retrench substantially, especially as the depression
also reduced consumption. Meanwhile, local taxes increased, as the
central government cut back on its expenditures. From 1880 to 1883,
prefectural taxes increased an average of 39 percent and village taxes
by an average of 19 percent.

Most sources agree that after the creation of the new landownership system in 1872 and 1873, the amount of land farmed by tenants
was about 30 percent of the total.[60] A variety of Japanese studies have
fairly conclusively shown an increase in tenancy during the years of the
Matsukata deflation, to around 40 percent.[61] By 1912, tenancy had
further increased to around 45 percent. The transfer of land spiked
sharply in the early 1880s. The crisis led the German economist Paul

Mayet, working as an adviser to the Meiji government, to comment: "Ten thousands of country people have . . . been ruined during the past years, and helplessly delivered over to the bloodsucking usurer, and hundreds of thousands will so fall into his hands during the next decades."[62]

The Hashimoto region did not escape the suffering. In July 1884, the county chief sent a message to villages instructing lenders to report to the police immediately if they were threatened with violence. Three Hashimoto villagers, citing hardship, applied in 1884 for permission to emigrate to Hawaii. In November 1884, five villages around Hashimoto petitioned the county chief for tax relief, citing the collapse in crop prices and their financial distress, as well as the previous year's drought and the current year's wind damage.

The administration of Kōza county (in which Hashimoto was located) was concerned enough to survey its villages in 1885 on the level of poverty, and the conditions of those living in poverty. Hashimoto reported that "more than half the villagers are poor." Asked the cause of the poverty, the village responded: "Since around 1877, prices increased rapidly, and from 1879 to 1880, new banks and lending companies appeared one after another, and money became extremely easy to borrow, making the lives of the people very easy. . . . However, from 1882, prices went into a decline, and then last year, the crops suffered wind damage, so now the poor people are barely eking out a livelihood. They are unable to repay their debts or pay their rent on the fields, and so the lenders and landlords are also suffering." The report added that the price of land had fallen to as low as half the tax valuation. "In this area, in eight or nine cases out of ten the lenders take real estate as their collateral. With the recent severe recession, the borrowers are unable to repay their loans and have had to sell their property. But they only receive from the sale about half of what they borrowed. So they still have no way to repay the loans. Thus, both borrowers and lenders are suffering."[63]

Villagers in Hashimoto were paying interest of 12 percent on secured loans and 30 percent for pawned items. The village estimated that the typical rent for a one-*tan* wheat field was ¥1.10 to ¥1.60. Income at current prices was only ¥5.10, and even that income depended on the farmer investing as much as ¥3.60 in fertilizer. The tenant was left with no more than ¥0.40 in cash income for his work.

In spite of all the hardship and misery caused by the Matsukata deflation, the crisis undoubtedly benefited the class of wealthier land-

owners to which the Aizawa belonged. These men were the buyers of
last resort for those landowners forced by their debts to sell part or all
of their land. And they were also the "usurious bloodsuckers" described
by Paul Mayet—moneylenders willing to advance loans to smaller-scale
landowners against the security of their land, which in many cases
would ultimately fall into the lenders' hands due to foreclosure. In spite
of or because of the economic troubles of the countryside during this
decade, the 1880s saw a decisive increase in the wealth and influence
of this class. By the end of the decade, journalists were talking of a new
golden era for the "country gentleman" *(inaka shinshi)*, similar to that
enjoyed by the British squirearchy. This upper echelon of the formerly
despised peasants was eclipsing the former samurai class as economic
and political leaders of Japan.[64]

In the mid-1880s, the pent-up feelings of oppression and poverty
arising from the Matsukata deflation exploded in violent protest. The
silk producing districts of the Kantō region were at the forefront. No
fewer than thirty separate protests erupted in the silk villages in 1884—
half the number in the whole of Japan.[65] The poor farmers and landless
laborers were experiencing to the full the double-edged sword of the
cash economy. Unable to rely on the land for their living, they had come
to rely on silk as their lifeline and their savior. Now, in response to
the movement of distant and uncontrollable financial forces, it became
their scourge.

The protests of the villagers of the silk region fed into a complicated
political situation in the Kantō area. For the past decade, educated
members of the village elites had been fervent supporters of the People's
Rights Movement, calling for liberal reform of the political system and
the early introduction of a constitution. Now that the constitution had
been promised, the People's Rights leadership had formed a political
party, the Liberal Party. Once again, the rural gentry were key supporters of the party, which was already placing its candidates in the
prefectural assemblies (regional deliberative bodies with very limited
powers, first established in 1878; assemblymen were elected by male
voters, twenty-five years and older, and paying ¥5 or more in annual
taxes). Among the platforms of both the People's Rights Movement
and the Liberal Party was the alleviation of rural distress. Indeed, in
the early 1880s, influential village leaders in the Kantō area joined to
create a Poor People's Party, with the goal of attacking problems of
rural poverty. At the same time, though, the village elites who made
up the leadership of the Liberal and Poor People's parties in the Kantō

area derived their privileged position from landownership, in most cases accompanied by money lending. Aoki Shōtarō, one of the leading Liberal Party politicians in the area, was also the president of the Busō bank, the major institutional money lender in the region. The would-be saviors of the village poor were also their creditors. In spite of their best efforts, the contradictions in this position made it very hard for them to mediate the escalating crisis.[66]

The most extreme of the protests in the silk-producing villages of the Kantō region was the Chichibu uprising of November 1884. Chichibu was a mountainous region, agriculturally marginal and heavily dependent on the silk trade. The villagers were thus hit especially hard by the financial downturn of the 1880s. Their protest had much of the flavor of a revolutionary political movement, and it has attracted both fascination and sympathy from subsequent generations.

The leaders of the uprising were mostly from the middle ranks of the village hierarchy: independent landowners and village tradesmen, many of them members of the Liberal Party. Some, like the movement's "General," Tashiro Eiichi, were from wealthy families. They were therefore not so far removed, in terms of social background or ideological orientation, from the landlord base of the People's Rights Movement. But the path they took was much more extreme than the basically conservative approach of the mainstream rural elite, who hastened to disavow them. Tashiro and his associates formed a plan to seize control of the entire Chichibu district, with the aim of establishing a revolutionary government. They raised a force of upward of ten thousand participants (though it is not clear how many of these were coerced), and they briefly took control of Ōmiya, the administrative capital of the Chichibu district, hanging a banner reading "Revolutionary Headquarters" from the district superintendent's office. The government had to send a strong armed force to quell the rebels, and it tried and punished more than three hundred of them, with a dozen sentenced to death.[67]

In the intervening century, the Chichibu rebels have come to be seen as martyrs, willing to die for the cause of freedom and popular rights. At the time, the government did its best to vilify them as gamblers, wastrels, and trouble-makers. What did the rebellion, and the unrest closer to home, look like to young Aizawa Kikutarō? Certainly there is no suggestion of a society in revolt in the pages of the diary that Aizawa began keeping in October 1885.

CHAPTER 2

From Farm Manager to Independent Landowner

1885–1894

A YOUNG MAN OF THE ENLIGHTENMENT

In February 1885 Aizawa Kikutarō turned nineteen. Already four years an adult in the eyes of the community, he had long been engaged in the grown-up world of farm management, field work, forestry, and property dealing. He went about his work with the energy, enthusiasm, and complacency of his youth. The village around him was not only a beautiful place containing bountiful fields and the friends and relatives he had grown up with; it was also the source of his family's present and future wealth, and Aizawa was doing his share to increase that wealth.

It was in these circumstances that Aizawa, on October 9, began to keep a diary: "I woke up at five, and went to the stable. I spread out wheat straw to dry, then until noon I cut bamboo in the grove, to use as flooring for the new shed. From one o'clock, I stopped work to honor the Yakushi Buddha and for the Mount Narita Festival. The weather cleared up at the end of the day."

Who was this young man, penning the first page of what was to become a lifelong project? The guardians of fate had dealt him one extraordinary piece of fortune and one slightly less welcome inheritance. His good fortune was to be born into the Aizawa family—the wealthiest landowners in the village and for several miles around, at a time when land was one of the few guarantors of prosperity. His lesser fortune was to be born a second son in an era when the eldest son took everything. Kikutarō's brother Yasuemon had, on the death of their father in 1879, inherited the largest house in Hashimoto, fifty hectares of farmland, in addition to large tracts of mountain forest, a roster of more than one hundred rent-paying tenants, and an assumed right to the leadership of Hashimoto village. Kikutarō, on the other hand, had nothing but the good graces of his brother. It is a tribute to his brains and energy that it was he, and not Yasuemon, who was eventually to become the leading citizen of Hashimoto and its surrounding villages.

Aizawa Kikutarō lived in his brother's house, and he worked on his brother's farm. His position was a mixture of foreman, independent businessman, farm laborer, and handyman. In the first months of the diary, we get a clear picture of a young man whose life was intimately connected to the rhythms of the agricultural cycle.

Because of the type of farming common in Hashimoto—which included winter crops of wheat, millet, barley, and vegetables—there were few slack times in the year. In January, right after the New Year celebrations, Aizawa and his helpers began harvesting the winter crops. The harvesting went on through much of January, as they cut the grain by hand and threshed it using a simple hand-powered machine—a revolving drum with spikes to catch the grain and detach it from the stalk. During the months of January and February, Aizawa and his helpers also harvested sweet potatoes and cut dry grass to use as fertilizer and feed for the one or two cows that he kept.

In March and April Aizawa tended the mulberry fields—planting new saplings, weeding out old or diseased plants, and carefully combing the leaves for insects (inchworms and caterpillars were a particular problem). He also found time to harvest the early season soy crop, selling the beans to a local trader.

From May, the busiest season of the year began. Beginning early in the month, the household began rearing silkworms. The family hired one or two female helpers to help with the worms. They were known as "May hires" and Aizawa grumbled constantly about their cost: ¥6 to ¥8 for the two-month growing season, plus food. This was the one time of year when hired laborers seem to have had a bit of bargaining power.

The silkworms took over the Aizawa house. As with most substantial houses in the area, the third floor was entirely devoted to silkworm rearing, with racks and trays built in. But that was not enough space for the enormous brood that the family raised each year. While the top floor was reserved for the most delicate operations such as the crucial cocoon-spinning, the silkworms in various stages of development were spread over every room in the house, after the tatami mats had been removed from the floor. There was barely room for the Aizawa family— Yasuemon, his wife Ai, Kikutarō, their mother Riu, the boys' sister Ei, the two "May hires," and one or two maids—to sleep. Silkworm season was an extraordinarily busy time. The worms had voracious appetites for mulberry leaves, especially as they grew. Family workers had to harvest leaves, carry them to the house, chop and prepare them, and feed them to the silkworms. They also had to keep the silkworm trays clean, periodically cleaning out the worms' feces and other waste such as sloughed-off skin, and manage the temperature and humidity by lighting fires in order to prevent the delicate insects from getting sick.

Nor were the silkworms the only major job during the two months of the silkworm season. As important economically as the silkworm rearing was the family's business selling surplus mulberry leaves to other rearers. The Aizawa had a large surplus of mulberry, and during the weeks of the breeding season, they made a substantial cash income by supplying buyers who came from as far as Hachiōji, some eight kilometers away over the Goten Pass. So valuable were the mulberry leaves, in fact, that in 1890 the mulberry farmers of Hashimoto organized themselves into night watches to prevent theft, since—as Aizawa recorded in his diary—many local farmers "have no mulberry bushes, yet they seem to have plenty of food for their silkworms."[1]

May and June were also the tea-harvesting months. After picking the leaves, Aizawa supervised the process of drying and roasting in the family compound. During May he would also plant another crop of rice (because the fields of Hashimoto were not amenable to wet rice irrigation, he planted a variety of dry-field rice). Then, in June, Aizawa and his helpers harvested the second grain crop of the year—including wheat, millet, rye, and barley. He also planted a second crop of soy beans.

In late June or early July, Aizawa and his brother sold their cocoon crop to merchants from Hachiōji. They usually sold the entire crop in one deal, to be carried away by horse and cart. Smaller cultivators reeled their cocoons into silk thread before taking it to market, but the Aizawa sold most of their cocoons to be reeled by contract workers hired by the silk merchants. The family kept some cocoons (often those of lower quality) for its own consumption, to reel using the wooden *zaguri*.

Once the cocoon crop had been sold, the whole family, including farm hands, held a celebration, inviting hired workers, family, and neighbors for rice cakes and sake. But this hardly spelled the end of the busy season. The work of plowing, weeding, harvesting, threshing, bagging, and hauling the grain harvest continued through the end of August. It was not for nothing that people said "even the cat and the ladle" were made to help during this busy time of year.

September was a relatively quiet month, giving Aizawa and his brother time to work on the tracts of hill land that the family owned. From now through the winter months, Aizawa would take gangs of workers out to the hills and have them plant large stands of pine, beech, and other timber. Usually they would plant upward of three thousand saplings at a time. On other occasions, the crew would cut wood for sale, or Aizawa would accompany a buyer to the woods, to negotiate a price for the buyer to cut and haul the wood.

In October and November Aizawa and his helpers harvested late fall millet and rice crops (they harvested both dry-field rice and the extra short-grain rice used for sticky rice-cakes). They also harvested the hemp crop, which was sold to local weavers who would process it into rough cloth. Finally, in November, Aizawa turned to planting the winter crop of wheat, millet, barley, and rye, to be harvested in January. This was a large operation, as the family had several hectares under cultivation. Hiring a team of fifteen workers, Aizawa supervised them as they plowed the fields, fertilized with rice bran, and seeded with the help of a pair of horses. They might complete one hectare, scattered over several fields, in the course of a long day.

As the year drew to a close, Aizawa harvested the vegetables that would see the family through the winter months. These included baby eggplant, which were pickled with salt or with fermented rice bran; and daikon, a crucial staple vegetable in the winter months. The family ate it fresh (they buried it in the cold earth) or preserved in the form of *takuan* pickle: the daikon were hung outside to dry for two weeks, then they were pickled in a barrel with rice bran and salt. The rice bran fermented and created a slimy liquid, penetrating the daikon and giving it a powerful, pungent flavor. The family also dried the leaves to use as an additive to winter soups.

This was also the time to harvest sweet potatoes, and to pick the bitter persimmon crop, from fruit trees scattered around the fields. The small orange fruit was so bitter to eat that it made the mouth and tongue pucker and swell as though full of cotton. But when pickled in alcohol, it softened, lost much of its bitterness, and took on a pungent sweetness—a perfect snack to go with sake. Aizawa personally supervised the laying down of the pickles in a wooden barrel. He added about a pint of sake, then—no doubt following a secret family recipe— he scraped some fragrant hair oil *(bintsuke abura)* into the mix, to add pungency.

The cycle of the fields was punctuated by the cycle of village observances and festivals. Until Kikutarō was four, this cycle had followed the phases of the moon. The New Year had started with the midwinter new moon, and the villagers had used government-authorized lunar almanacs to determine the correct times to plant, harvest, and rest. The Bon Festival of the Dead had been held at the full moon of the seventh month. After the government mandated the change to the Western calendar, the village had gradually adapted. Now the villagers celebrated the New Year on January 1, and the Bon Festival on August 15. The village also celebrated the official national holidays—National Founding Day *(kigensetsu)* on February 11, and the emperor's birthday on November 3. But they continued to celebrate many of the old holidays, too, including the old people's festival in February, the village shrine festival at the end of July, and the rest days occurring irregularly throughout the year.

Although the village still did not observe regular Sunday holidays (as government offices now did), the farm workers were able to rest at least two or three days per month on regular village rest days, as well as on rainy days. Aizawa himself rested at least one or two days a week on average, sometimes more. He was free to take the day off if he felt like it, whether to run errands, go visiting, make calls on families who had had a birth or a death, or just do nothing. He also took several days off if he felt himself even slightly under the weather—in spite (or perhaps because) of the toughness of life in nineteenth-century Japan, Aizawa made sure to take good care of himself.

. . .

On April 7, 1888, Aizawa noticed an article in the *Tokyo Denpō* newspaper on making money. The title was "One dollar of capital can create several millionaires." He was interested enough to transcribe the article in full in his diary. "It is hardly necessary to state that in this civilized world, the power of money has expanded without limit. It is even said that after death, one's condition in hell will depend upon how much money one has." The article went on to note that the crucial condition to make money in the modern world was to understand the compounding value of money. "Eighty or ninety out of a hundred people just blindly throw away the interest on their money; and it is very rare for someone to notice that they are doing so. According to a European proverb, if you want to know the value of a dollar, then you should borrow one. Then you will taste the value of that dollar in full." After transcribing the article, he noted: "I, too, should make it my duty to follow these precepts."

Throughout his life, Aizawa was interested in money. He came to maturity at a poignant moment in the economic history of the village. From the mid-1880s, enormous opportunities for money-making opened up as Japan entered a phase of rapid economic, infrastructural, and industrial development. For the time being, the opportunities remained centered on the countryside. Japan's major export products remained silk and tea, both produced in Hashimoto (though tea was mainly grown for home consumption). And for the money made in these products, there was ample opportunity for investment. A chronic shortage of capital led to extremely high returns: 15 or 20 percent was considered quite normal. For those who were accumulating money, the opportunities to increase their wealth seemed boundless.

In contrast, for the villagers caught in the pincers of the Matsukata deflation, the mid-1880s meant the end of the road, as they were forced to sell their land to repay the loans they had taken out or to make good on their taxes. For the majority of the villagers of Hashimoto, these were hard times indeed, and it is not surprising that Aizawa was, for much of the next two decades, so pessimistic about economic conditions—even as he personally benefited from them.

The Aizawa family business had four major components, all closely intertwined. First, there was the business of farming. For generations, the villagers of Hashimoto had grown commercial crops of wheat and mulberry, selling their produce for cash and buying rice and other consumables. The Aizawa family had the most extensive business dealings of any in the village. They gained cash income from the sale of wheat, barley, rye, soy beans, and mulberry leaves, in addition to their sales of forest timber.

The timber business was an important source of income. The trees that the Aizawa brothers cut and sold in the late 1880s had been planted by their father and grandfather, decades earlier. But the brothers also made sure that they left a similar legacy for their own children and grandchildren.

Throughout the silkworm season, Aizawa was dealing in mulberry leaves. Every day during the peak weeks in May and June, buyers would arrive from within the village, but also from surrounding villages and even farther afield, looking for mulberry to buy. The price was set by the horseload—¥1 was the base price, but when demand heated up the price could quickly jump to ¥3, ¥4, or even ¥5. Aizawa had to judge the market carefully: if he sold too soon at a lower price, he might miss out on the big price spikes; but if he waited too long, he might be left with unsold leaves at the end of the season. Over the course of a season, Aizawa would (on behalf of his brother) collect upward of ¥200 for mulberry leaves.

Second was the business of trading in local commodities. The business of silk was central to the economy of the region. Many farm families not only reared silkworm cocoons, but also reeled them into thread, to be sold in the local market or transported directly to Yokohama. Although the Aizawa usually sold their cocoons without reeling the silk thread, they occasionally acted as merchants, buying up locally produced thread, as Kikutarō's older brother did in 1891. Between July 6 and 8 of that year, he bought at the local markets of Machida, Kamimizo, and Hachiōji. On July 19, he sold seventy "cauldrons" *(kama)* of silk floss for ¥200. Later that year, on December 5, Aizawa's brother once again made the rounds of the local markets, departing on the seventh to sell the silk thread in Yokohama.

The family also engaged in other forms of trade. On January 27, 1886, Aizawa walked together with his farm worker, Shigezaemon, around the Yarimizu and Yugi districts, in the hills north of Hashimoto, buying straw mats (making mats and sandals out of surplus straw was a common winter activity for farmers, who hoped to earn a few extra coins from their sale). He contracted for four horseloads, stamping each mat with his imprint after taking delivery. In the following months, he sold the mats, delivering the last batch to his Aizawa cousins in mid-May. The Aizawa family also appears to have traded at times in rice-bran fertilizer and medicine. On July 20, 1886, Aizawa records buying sixty bales of bran (of sixty kilograms each) for just under ¥1 a bale. Although he does not record selling the bran, this was probably too much for the family's private consumption.

The third component was the business of renting out farmland for money. The Aizawa family gained a substantial cash income from farming, forestry, and trading in related products. But even though they had access to an almost unlimited supply of cheap hired labor, they only farmed a small proportion of their arable land themselves. Throughout Japan, landowners preferred to rent land out rather than consolidate and apply the cost-saving techniques of large-scale farming. A number of factors were responsible for this. During the Tokugawa period, the laws against the alienation of land had prevented such consolidation, and the tenancy system had become entrenched. In the Meiji period, some landlords did experiment with larger-scale farming, but due to the high labor-intensity of rice farming in particular, the experiments were generally unsuccessful. Most importantly, population pressures ensured an enormous demand—tenants would pay almost any price to gain access to farm land, because for many the alternative was to leave the village for a very uncertain future in the cities or even Hokkaido or Hawaii. As a result, the return on rented land was high.

Most of the Aizawas' rented land was in mulberry and wheat fields (though they also owned a sizeable number of rental houses). Unlike rice fields, where tenants usually paid their rent in kind, tenants had always paid rent on mulberry and wheat fields in cash. Given the differing productivity and special characteristics of each field, it is hard to say just how much of a burden this was to the tenant farmers. Calculations made by concerned observers of the Matsukata deflation indicated that tenants could barely survive on the profit of their farming—a report prepared by Hashimoto village, for example, suggested that a tenant would make no more than ¥0.40 annually per *tan* (0.1 hectare, see chapter 1). Aizawa himself, in an interesting analysis, suggests that renting could potentially be much more profitable. On November 19, 1894, he suggested that the village of Hashimoto should rent a one-hectare mulberry field, in order to raise money for its two annual festivals. He argued that the profit on a mulberry field rented for ¥20 per hectare would be about ¥30: using volunteer labor, the village would grow and sell sixty horseloads of mulberry for an average ¥1 each, and would pay ¥10 for fertilizer in addition to the ¥20 rent. This analysis was probably overly optimistic (perhaps Aizawa assumed a preferential rate on the rent). Aizawa himself rented out fields at a wide range of prices, from nothing (in the case of a small plot of wild land that the tenant promised to cultivate) to as much as ¥28 per hectare for well-established mulberry fields.[2]

The Aizawas' property rental business was intimately connected to the family's fourth major business activity: money-lending. They derived a significant part of their income from the interest on loans, ranging from casual short-term loans of a few yen to large financial transactions.

Through the pages of the diary, a constant stream of debtors and would-be borrowers come calling on Aizawa. After a while, it becomes evident that a sizeable proportion of the families in the village owed money to the Aizawa family. What was it like to be the creditor to most of the people eligible to be one's friend? Perhaps the relationships were smoothed over by the traditional concept of the landlord's "benevolence" to those less fortunate than him in the village—though this is not a word that Aizawa himself uses much at all. Perhaps Aizawa was thick skinned enough not to notice that the politeness of those he spent his time with—at village meetings, at festivals, or at drinking parties— might come from ingratiating self-interest rather than from genuine friendship. Perhaps he found enough companionship among members of his own class, both within the village and outside. But when it came to money, as the diary reveals, almost no one was immune from the urge to occasionally lean on the Aizawa family for cash—including other members of the Aizawa family.

A notable example is the debt of Aizawa's own first cousin, Aizawa Jungorō. One year older than Kikutarō, Jungorō was the eldest son in a "branch" family of the Aizawa (a family created by settling assets on a younger son, in this case Jungorō's father). He was also married to Kikutarō's sister Ei—making him both cousin and brother-in-law. In 1887 he had launched a business enterprise trading in mulberry and silk thread, with financial help from Kikutarō and Yasuemon. Jungorō had invested ¥1,500—borrowed from the bank, but equivalent to two-thirds of his family's assets—while the Aizawa brothers had chipped in ¥800, which they also borrowed.

In early 1891 Jungorō made some disastrous mistakes in his business and ended up losing nearly all his capital. His father, Tashichirō, was forced to sell about half of the family fields (luckily, values had increased and he could sell at three times the registered value of the land). But the Aizawa brothers were also forced to take a sizeable loss. After some negotiations, Jungorō offered to give the brothers land with a registered value of ¥124. This was an absurdly low compensation for the ¥800-plus outstanding loan. Aizawa commented rather bitterly: "This represents a 650 percent premium over the tax value. Moreover, we are borrowing the money ourselves from the bank, to which we must pay interest. We had only intended to lend the money short-term for the purchase of mulberry. Moreover, the current value of land is only three times the tax value." Aizawa goes on to express his contempt for his cousin's business failure: "Even when Jungorō was active in his business he was doing it half as though in play—there was no way that it was going to succeed. Looking at the way things were going, I remonstrated with him again and again, but he just answered me with pleasant words and carried on with his activities. So finally it ended in failure, and all I could do was say over and over again 'I'm so sorry.'"

Normally, money-lending was a much more profitable proposition. Interest rates were usually between 15 and 20 percent. Typically, loans were secured except for small, "casual" loans of under ¥10, which tended to be at a much higher rate of interest (though Aizawa often required a guarantor's signature even for these). On March 20, 1891, for example, Aizawa discusses a secured loan made to the Shitara family. This family lived in a village near Hachiōji, and the family head was apparently a friend of Aizawa's uncle, who lived in that village. The Aizawa lent them ¥150 for five years, with interest fixed at ¥30 per year (a 20 percent rate), payable in July and December installments. Late payments were to be charged a 10 percent penalty, and in the event of missed payment the collateral was subject to immediate foreclosure.

With payments as onerous as this, one might assume that only those in dire straits would resort to borrowing—and that for such people the path to eventual foreclosure was virtually assured. In many cases, this was indeed what happened—through the pages of his diary, Aizawa spends about as much time foreclosing on old loans as making new ones. But he seems to have preferred where possible to lend money to viable borrowers: those, for example, who were investing in a business enterprise (as in the case of his ill-fated cousin), or those who needed money for expansion of their farming operations. Indeed, Aizawa himself borrows money occasionally (usually from a relative), to meet short-term cash-flow shortages.

In a period of little or no price inflation (for example, wages for casual labor were stagnant at ¥0.25 to ¥0.35 per day), a 20-percent annual return on capital is staggeringly high. The high returns reflect in part the risk of lending to relatively unstable borrowers, though this risk was greatly mitigated by the availability of collateral. It also reflects the severe shortage of capital in Japan in the twenty years from 1885 to 1905, as new enterprises in a rapidly developing economy competed for capital for their expansion needs. These circumstances were highly favorable for the rural elite, who financed to a significant extent Japan's industrial modernization.

The corollary to lending was the acquisition of land. The Aizawa holdings were growing rapidly through the 1880s and 1890s, as the family foreclosed on loans (in many cases, hammering the last nail in the coffins of family fortunes ruined by the Matsukata deflation) and bought up land from willing, even desperate villagers who found themselves in one form or another of financial trouble. Their purchases included wheat, mulberry, and rice fields (the last in villages outside Hashimoto), mountain woodlands, houses and housing land, and unimproved land awaiting reclamation. On occasion, the brothers also made the rounds of village offices in the region, checking the land registers to identify unclaimed or uncultivated land, which they could offer to buy.

In most cases, the brothers put the newly acquired land to work as rental property. In the case of foreclosures, they usually allowed the former owner to stay on the land as tenant. His interest payments were replaced with rent payments—now payable in perpetuity. In several cases, Aizawa promises on the occasion of a foreclosure that if the debtor should repay the original loan in full, with interest, over the next five years, Aizawa will return the land to him. However, there is no example in the diary of such a post-facto repayment actually being made.

In this way, the Aizawa's money-lending and land-renting activities fed each other, resulting in rapidly increasing wealth for the family. Just how wealthy were they? Aizawa Yasuemon was listed with fifty-three *chō* (about fifty-two hectares) of land in 1884, and with his acquisitions of the following decade, this number must have increased substantially.[3] Certainly, they were not among the class of the very wealthy, who built mansions in Tokyo, traveled abroad, collected valuable art works, and purchased the very latest new technologies as they appeared in Japan. Kikutarō himself maintained a healthy frugality throughout his lifetime: he preferred to make consumable items rather than buy them (as, for example, when he made paper for his account books in March, 1886), and he continued to walk the eight hilly kilometers to Hachiōji whenever convenient, in order to save the ¥0.15 rickshaw fare.

. . .

Imagine traveling from Tokyo to Hashimoto in the late 1880s. You take a rickshaw along well-paved streets to the Kanda coach station. Around you are the sights and sounds of a modernizing city: the railway terminus at Shinbashi, with the Yokohama-bound steam train belching smoke; the horse-drawn carriages of the well-to-do, and the countless rickshaws pulling their passengers through the colorful streets; the gentlemen in English-style jackets and hats, and the ladies in silk clothes under elegant parasols; the new telegraph lines running through the streets. You leave Tokyo on the regular horse-and-cart service, run by the Teiseisha, from Kanda via Shinjuku to the market town of Hachiōji. As you leave Tokyo behind, you enter another world—the eternal world of the soil, where men and women dressed in hemp clothing labor their fields under straw raincoats. The profound silence is broken only by the panting of the horses and the curses of the driver as "he whips them up to speed through the mud."[4] The journey to Hachiōji takes three and a half hours.

From Hachiōji, you hire a rickshaw to take you up the narrow and muddy road to the Goten Pass. Because of the muddy conditions, you have to hire two rickshaw men—one to pull and one to push from behind. "Sometimes the rickshaw sinks into the mud up to its axles, and it's almost impossible to describe the difficulty with which we progress."[5] Finally you descend the hill into Hashimoto. The village is steeped in the deep silence of the unchanging countryside. Even the mountains that lend it its habitual dramatic beauty are barely visible through the misty drizzle.

The houses of Hashimoto are like a picture from an ancient scroll. The farmers at work in their fields are hunched from a lifetime of bending over their crops. Some of them still sport the feudal-era topknot hairstyle. There isn't a sign of the modern world that is so rapidly bringing Civilization and Enlightenment to the cities. Surely no one here has heard of John Stuart Mill, or of the harnessing of electricity, or of the siege of Paris.

But wait. All is not as it seems in this village. Enter the house of its leading citizen, Aizawa Yasuemon, and you will be surprised at the civilized greeting you receive. Aizawa and his younger brother Kikutarō have their hair neatly cut in the European style. Aizawa senior sports a jaunty mustache. They are eager for news of the city. When will the next industrial exposition take place? How are the people of Tokyo reacting to the expulsion of the leading campaigners for People's Rights from the capital? What news of the silk market? (But it turns out they know more than you about the latest prices in Yokohama). Have you visited the government's experimental farm in the Mita district of Tokyo? No? Why, they were there just last month, buying some of the latest imported agricultural tools.

In spite of their limited education and isolated location, the Aizawa brothers were part of a network of landlords and other elite villagers who were very much in touch with the trends of the times. Through frequent interaction with each other, through study groups and public lectures, through the reading of books, newspapers, and agricultural journals, through a range of activities to improve agricultural practices, through travel to the capital and throughout the region, and through political support for popular rights campaigners, these men were deeply involved in the Meiji enlightenment.

For the twenty-year-old Kikutarō, these activities were part serious, part play. Certainly, he had a deep interest in agricultural improvement. After all, greater crop yields and improved silk cocoon quality could bring direct financial returns. But Kikutarō was also a young man of relative leisure, with the time and means to enjoy himself. Travel to the provincial and national capital was as much about having fun as it was about self-improvement.

The first trip to Tokyo that Kikutarō recorded in the diary took place in 1886. On September 15 he and his brother traveled on foot to Tokyo together (a distance of more than forty kilometers). They went to the house of their fellow-villager, Yajima Seisai. Yajima, from one of the three distinguished Hashimoto families, had followed in his father's footsteps and trained as a doctor; he now had a practice in the Fukagawa district of Tokyo, east of the Sumida River.

After recovering from their journey, the next morning the brothers set off back across Tokyo to visit the School of Agriculture and Forestry, located on the western outskirts in Komaba. Unfortunately, due to an outbreak of contagious disease, the campus was not admitting visitors, so the two were forced to return to Fukagawa.

The next day was much more successful. In the morning, they visited the government's tool workshop and experimental nursery in Mita. The workshop was established to manufacture Western-style farm tools and to adapt them to Japanese conditions. The workshop's chief inspector, Mr. Hoshino, showed them round and explained the various tools to them. Aizawa bought a "garden trowel" for use on his family farm.

Later the same day, the Aizawa brothers went to Ueno and paid ¥0.05 to visit the new museum on the site of the second National Industrial Exposition of 1881. The museum occupied a handsome building designed by the English architect Josiah Conder. It was under the management of the Ministry of Agriculture and Commerce, and it contained an eclectic mixture of fine arts, and objects relating to Japanese history, geography, and natural history.[6]

Aizawa was deeply impressed. "On the first floor is a forestry section, an agricultural section, a fishery section, an engineering section, an antiquities section and a marine section. The emperor's palanquin with its accessories was also on display. It is truly hard to convey it all in writing." After the main hall, the brothers visited the museum's annex, where they saw an exhibit of famous Japanese houses and bridges, with information about their construction, and 1/30-scale models on display. There was also an exhibit on Japanese mines and mining.

After making the rounds of the museum, the brothers walked all the way back to Mita, to purchase a "side hill plough" and the equipment to attach it to a horse. This was exactly the kind of equipment that the Mita workshop wanted to promote, and the Aizawa brothers, with their enlightened approach to new farming methods and their ample fields to justify a new investment, were ideal customers.

Exhibitions and practical demonstrations were an important part of the culture of agricultural improvement for enlightened landlords such as the Aizawa, and they regularly participated in such exhibitions, as well as in study groups and lectures. Sometimes these were held in nearby villages, or, as in the case of the October 1887 Capital City and Nine-Prefecture Cocoon, Silk Thread, and Silk Weaving Prize Exhibition, in Hachiōji. An event like this was after Aizawa's own heart. It offered the chance for an entertaining excursion while at the same time promoting improved sericulture and allowing for the exchange of ideas. Aizawa attended with a group of friends from Hashimoto. They arrived shortly after noon and repaired to the Shiraiya Restaurant in the downtown Yokoyama district for lunch. Then they went to Ōwada Kawahara, a rural area to the north of the town on the banks of the Arakawa River. There they viewed a firework display, after which they went on to visit the Daizenji, a beautiful and isolated temple in the foothills of the mountains.

Finally they returned to Yokoyama in the center of town for the exhibition. "There is much here to awaken the ideas of the viewers," commented Aizawa. "The construction of the gallery is an extraordinary piece of work, exceeding my every expectation. Around the entrance way, electric lights were hung. Two wires stretched about fifteen meters from the generating machine to a pillar, from which the lights hung. At around six o'clock the lights were at last switched on, and the evening gloom was suddenly transformed into broad daylight. The spectators all looked up in wonder, and no one talked of anything but the beauty and strangeness of the sight."

Aizawa's interest in agricultural improvement led him to explore new methods in newspapers and agricultural journals, through government technical centers, and through the more traditional methods of correspondence and information exchange with other landlords. In October 1887 Aizawa planted two new varieties of wheat seeds that he had purchased the previous month on his visit to the Mita experimental nursery. They were a white-colored French variety called "Oosutorarii" (Australie) and a red-colored American variety called "Nyuuinkunto" (New England). Aizawa mentions that "many people living around here have begged some of these seeds from me." He reported a few days later that the red variety had produced more sprouts than the white, but he still did not know which would prove the better once fully grown. He also did not yet know the best mix of fertilizer for these two varieties, so for the time being he spread a mixture of rice bran and fish meal.

In January 1888 Aizawa entered into a lengthy correspondence with Inoue Yōtarō, a farmer who experimented with improved rice seeds. Inoue had been featured in an article in the *Agricultural Journal (Nōgyō zasshi)*, and Aizawa decided to write to him. In extremely polite language, Aizawa asked Inoue if he would be willing to send some seed samples. He comments that "if the word of these seeds spreads widely, then this will not only redound to your credit, it will also benefit the nation." Inoue replied by sending a few seeds, though he commented that he had received dozens of enquiries after the magazine article appeared, and he had only a few to hand out. He promised that if he had a good harvest, he would prepare more seeds. Sending thanks and payment, Aizawa mentioned in his reply that he lived on the main route to the Afuri Shrine at Ōyama, one of the major pilgrimage destinations of the Kantō region. If Inoue found himself on this pilgrimage, Aizawa hoped he would visit and offered hospitality.

Perhaps it was in response to the arrival in Japan of Western farming seeds, tools, and terminology, that in September 1886 Aizawa began studying English. On September 11 a traveling teacher, Mr. Kimura, set up a class in the village school building. He brought copies of a textbook series, National Reader, for which Aizawa and the other students paid ¥0.10 each. Aizawa records: "In the evening I read English."

The National Readers were, together with the Independent Reader series, standard textbooks in American schools, and they came to be widely used in Japanese schools (English was not taught in the four years of compulsory education, but it was a popular subject in higher elementary schools). There were five levels—National First Reader through National Fifth Reader. They were designed to be "beautifully

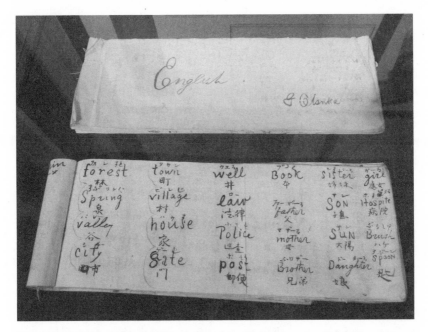

Figure 9. English vocabulary book kept by a Kantō area landlord (Courtesy Hachiōjishi Kyōiku Iinkai)

and copiously illustrated," with "variety as well as excellence, both in drawing and engraving." Aizawa's book started with extremely simple writing exercises, like "The boy and the dog run," but it soon worked up to short stories, such as the story of John and Dick, who tried in vain to catch a rat.[7]

Like many of Aizawa's self-improvement exercises, the classes were short-lived. Aizawa studied hard throughout September, doing little else in the latter days of the month. He persevered through October, beginning volume 2 of the National Reader in the middle of the month. For someone with only a few years of schooling and no background in foreign languages, it seems unreasonably ambitious to have worked through a lengthy text designed for native speakers in only six weeks. Perhaps that is one reason why, after the beginning of November, Aizawa's attendance at class became more and more sporadic, until by the end of the month he had given up altogether.

Not all of Aizawa's travel activities were directly aimed at self-improvement. There was a good deal of continuity between the activities of an "enlightened" man of the Meiji and his Tokugawa forebears. Travel to hot-spring spas and seaside resorts, visits to famous shrines and temples, poetry group meetings and sake parties, all remained a part of the leisure activities of the landlord class.

On April 19, 1887, Aizawa left his village together with two friends, and walked the thirty-seven kilometers to the town of Fujisawa. From there, they traveled downriver by boat to the resort island of Enoshima—a popular destination since Tokugawa times lying just offshore at the mouth of the Sakai River. The three friends climbed the low mountain that dominates the tiny island, then descended to visit the famous caves. Then they walked to the north part of the island to view the cherry blossoms and have lunch. In the afternoon they walked back to the ancient coastal city of Kamakura, where they strolled on Yuihama beach collecting shells, before walking up the wide avenue lined with cherry trees to the Tsurugaoka Hachiman Shrine. After their day of sightseeing, they left Kamakura and climbed up the grueling mountain road and down again to the port of Kanazawa, where they took a ferry to Yokosuka, home of the Japanese government's naval shipyard—one of the showplaces of Western technology.

The next morning, they toured the shipyard, then took a boat to Yokohama. After lunch they watched a reservoir under construction, then visited the Grand Shrine of Iseyama. Then, in what must have been the highlight of the trip, they rode the steam train to Tokyo, arriving at five in the evening. As luck would have it, they were able to see the emperor on his way back from an inspection of the harbor works. Aizawa comments: "We were able to see many foreigners from various countries." They stayed that night in a hostel dedicated to visitors from their area, the Sagamiya.

Their stay in Tokyo included a visit to an industrial exhibition in Ueno and a viewing of a *kabuki* performance at the Chitoseza Theater. Even in the midst of these relatively frivolous activities, though, Aizawa found time to stop at the Yūrindō Bookshop and buy an agricultural manual. Finally, the three friends hired seats on the new horse-drawn service operated by the Teiseisha Company between Shinjuku and Hachiōji, arriving at Hachiōji at three in the afternoon, and walking home from there.

Although he was lucky enough to have the opportunity (and good health) to make such trips now and again, Aizawa of course spent the vast majority of his time at home. Even in Hashimoto, though, Aizawa was able to stay in touch with the pulse of modernization through newspapers and journals, educational activities, and reading.

The Aizawa family appears to have taken a newspaper at least from the mid-1880s. In January 1887, Aizawa was reading the *Yūbin Hōchi* newspaper. Two years later, he seems to have switched to the *Foreign and Domestic Trade* newspaper *(Chūgai Shōgyō Shinpō)*. In his spare time, he would read agricultural journals, such as the *Japan Agricultural Association Report* (founded in 1881) and the *Agricultural Journal.*[8] Aizawa also read books, though he had only sporadic access to booksellers and seems to have borrowed most that he read.

On October 21, 1888, Aizawa mentions that he spent the day at home, reading a biography of Bismarck that his uncle Suzuki had lent him. This book was probably *The Story of Count Bismarck's Life: For Popular Perusal,* published in translation the previous year in Tokyo.[9] Prussian-dominated Germany was in high esteem in Japan in the 1880s, in part because of the parallels between Germany and Japan. Recently unified, Germany had attracted the admiration of the world through its military prowess, growing industrial might, and constitutional monarchy. The Japanese government was looking to Germany as a model in everything from constitutional affairs to military tactics. Bismarck was widely and admiringly reported in the press—the *Yomiuri* newspaper ran fifty-three stories about him during 1888 alone—and a regular newspaper reader would certainly be aware of him.

REACHING MATURITY IN MOMENTOUS TIMES

At the start of the Aizawa diary, Kikutarō was just nineteen years old, a young man with bright prospects and an eager appreciation for money, travel, and good fellowship. By the time he was granted an independent family headship six years later, Aizawa was a much more mature individual: married, the father of a son, and deeply experienced in the intricacies of agricultural cultivation, trade, and finance. Perhaps his brother recognized Kikutarō's maturation when, in 1887, he helped arrange his marriage to Ushikubo Sato, the Aizawas' close neighbor to the south.

Kikutarō had known Sato all her life. The Ushikubo were the other main landholding family of Hashimoto, and the two families had close ties dating back for generations. Sato was seventeen at the time of her marriage, and there can be no doubt that the marriage was based on deep affection, dating back to their childhoods. Aizawa was fascinated by the developments going on in the world outside his village, particularly the new technologies and ways of life arriving from Europe and America; but when it came to marriage, he chose from within the village.

The marriage took place on December 19, 1887. In spite of the Aizawa family's exalted position within the village, the event was relatively low key. For Kikutarō, perhaps the most striking feature of the ceremony was his decision to wear European clothes. Two weeks before the wedding, Kikutarō ordered a set of clothes from a Western clothes shop owned by relatives of his new in-laws, the Ushikubo family. The total cost was ¥16—a large sum, but not out of line for a set of men's wedding clothes (Sato's wedding costume undoubtedly cost a lot more). The clothes were delivered on the morning of the wedding. Was this the first time he had dressed in foreign clothing? Certainly there were few occasions for such attire, though Aizawa does record wearing Western clothes once again in January 1889, when he and two friends walked all the way to Yokohama at the invitation of a Christian acquaintance, to attend church. On this occasion, their Western attire was presumably out of respect for the foreign religion, though the villagers did put comfort over appearance in the matter of their feet: they wore straw sandals on the long walk.

The wedding day dawned bright after a night of rain. Aizawa got dressed in his Western clothes and went to the house of Ushikubo Nagayoshi, his new father-in-law. Accompanying him were a dozen close friends and relatives. At the Ushikubo house, Kikutarō and Sato drank sake and walked around the sake cups five times, as custom dictated. In the evening, once he had returned home, a succession of visitors from Hashimoto and neighboring villages came to congratulate Aizawa. They brought small gifts of money, which Aizawa carefully added up (they totaled ¥14.52). These gifts were on top of ¥15 he had received from his uncle, Suzuki Seiichi, a few days earlier—though he had given ¥10 of that to his younger sister, Ei. Aizawa summed up the day by saying: "We had good weather throughout, which made all the wedding arrangements both happy and successful." The next morning, Aizawa added up the cost of the wedding: ¥22 for sake, ¥58 for fish, and ¥20 for vegetables and other items. By the next day, he was back at work.

. . .

At twenty-one, Aizawa was married, well read for his level of education, well traveled for his status, well informed on agricultural affairs, and a highly experienced and shrewd farmer, moneylender, and property investor. The only thing that held him back from taking up a leading position in the affairs of the village and the region was his status as a younger brother. But he had already secured his brother's agreement in principle to set him up as head of a new branch family of the Aizawa clan. Over the next several years, his involvement in village, prefectural, and national affairs gradually deepened, until at the age of forty he was the natural choice for mayor of Hashimoto's successor village, Aihara.

The political climate in which he reached his years of maturity was changing. The startlingly young upstarts from the distant western provinces, who had commandeered the reins of government in the wake of the Meiji restoration, were now (those who survived) venerated senior statesmen. The upheavals of the mid-1880s were the last major challenges to the new order in the wake of the fall of the shoguns. Certainly, there was still political dissent; but henceforth it was to be channeled through new institutions: the political parties, the military and oligarchic leadership, and the new Diet. The instability that had haunted the countryside ever since the mass protests of the 1860s had now settled down into a new status quo—by no means an equitable one, but powerful enough to stave off protest for at least two decades to come. Its most salient feature was an alliance between the village landlord class, Diet politicians, and regional bureaucrats. The alliance harnessed the growing power of the state to protect its class interests and maintain a semblance of peace and stability in the villages.

The first major step in the establishment of this new status quo was the launch of a new parliament (the Diet) under the auspices of Japan's Meiji Constitution, promulgated in 1889.

The constitution was presented to the people of Japan as a benevolent gift from the emperor, and dissent or criticism was strictly suppressed. Aizawa, living as he did near the heart of the rural People's Rights Movement, and knowing personally the local leaders of the Liberal Party, such as Aoki Shōtarō, must have been aware of criticism that the new constitution was a façade that preserved bureaucratic power even as it impressed Western nations with its veneer of civilization and democracy. But he gives no hint of such criticism in the diary. Indeed, he does not seem very interested in the political aspects of the promulgation. Rather, he is clearly fascinated by the symbolism of the constitution, representing as it does Japan's advance into the comity of civilized nations.

The constitution was promulgated on February 12, 1889—Japan's Founding Day, a national holiday commemorating the mythological founding of the nation by Emperor Jinmu. The newspapers reported fulsomely on the pomp and ceremony surrounding the promulgation, and Aizawa clearly caught some of this tone in his long entry on February 14:

> Celebrations are being held all over the country. This great ceremony of the promulgation of the constitution is being celebrated not only in our country but even abroad. His majesty the Emperor has held a special ceremony and pardoned those in jail. And he has even restored the good name of the deceased Saigō Takamori [a former member of the government—ment who had led a major rebellion in 1877—he was enormously popular both in life and in death], and bestowed on him the rank of courtier third class, since Saigō's deeds were originally motivated by deep concern for his country. . . . Moreover, by imperial proclamation, all those throughout the country who are over eighty years old are to receive gifts of money based on their age. Those over eighty will get ¥0.50, those over ninety will get ¥1, and those over one hundred will get ¥1.50.

Aizawa went on to praise Japan's technological progress, which seemed even to be filtering through to the area surrounding Hashimoto:

> Every year our world is becoming more civilized. This year, the railway opened between Hachiōji and Tokyo, and railways are being built in every region, so that throughout the country large towns are becoming linked to small, creating a new freedom of movement. Now even in the countryside you see not only rickshaws but also horse-drawn carts and carriages, and the number of hand-pulled carts is declining as nowadays everyone carries their produce on horse-drawn carts. Moreover, the trade in goods has changed. Nowadays the buyers no longer buy from the retail seller, but rather they go directly to the manufacturing location, sending telegrams to make their purchase contracts, and the money is paid by bill of exchange or by check, so everything has become much more convenient. And when the price of rice is high in one area, then it is possible now to send cheap rice from another part of the country by steam train and thus the demand will be met. Now several hundred *koku* of rice can easily be refined using a steam machine in a matter of one hour, and rice which has been roughly hulled by hand is no longer accepted.

If Aizawa had reservations about the promulgation of the constitution and the progress it represented, they were centered not so much in the political compromises, as in the threat to what he saw as traditional human ties of mutual respect and responsibility. His views must have been influenced by the hardship he saw around him every day in Hashimoto, and by his own occasional difficulties as landlord and moneylender:

As a result of all of this development, human feelings are under threat and becoming weaker. People no longer worry about others. Everyone is now dedicated to the accumulation of wealth. Starting in 1884, we had a very poor economy, and people were living in a state of emergency. Those who borrowed money no longer repaid it; if they could, they would let the days go by without saying a word. And in these circumstances, money stopped circulating, and lenders no longer wished to lend. However, this year economic conditions have finally improved, and the circulation of money has also become a little better. But still, the reverence for money above human feelings continues (I am not talking about this in a legalistic sense, but about what I actually see today among farm families). Clothing is progressing every year: even when they're just going next door for a minute, people wear white *tabi* socks and silk clothes. At least half of them do this. Even if they go out for one minute they will carry a watch and wear Western clothes. This started in the towns, but now even in the countryside you can find beef (the price is ¥0.15 for one *kin* and 120 *momme* [660 grams]), and sake is readily available too. Quite a few people will eat and drink these all the time. Somebody who is hired as a laborer for one year will earn only twenty-five yen in that year. But even someone with such a low income has come to know that kind of way of eating, and he will do whatever he can to raise his level of income. And talking of clothing, even among laborers there is hardly anyone that does not own some silk clothes. And their farm work clothes are also freshly dyed at the indigo shop—that has become a standard now . . .

It seems that Aizawa analyzed the tendency to a higher standard of living not as desirable material progress, but as an unsustainable love of ostentation and luxury even in the face of poor economic conditions. As a lender, he must have worried that he was financing such luxuries—even as he sometimes denied them to himself. Aizawa concluded: "Starting in April, it will be possible to travel by steam train from Tokyo all the way along the Tokaido to Kyoto and Osaka. It will be easy to travel back and forth in one day. However, no matter how convenient these machines may be, the development of human beings is slow."

. . .

In 1890, the Imperial Diet opened, bringing with it a new world of political parties and national elections (the franchise was very limited, however: only males over twenty-five and paying ¥15 or more in annual taxes were eligible—about 1 percent of the population in 1890). In the same year, the Home Ministry implemented a major overhaul of the administration of Japanese villages. The new administrative system brought an end to the ad hoc modifications to the Edo system of village governance and introduced a modern approach to regional bureaucracy. The changes had major consequences for Hashimoto—indeed, they spelled the end of Hashimoto's existence as an independent political entity.

The reforms implemented by the Home Ministry called for the amalgamation of small villages into larger administrative units, comprised of anything from two to ten former villages, and Japan's seventy thousand villages were reduced in number to only twelve thousand. Villages that formerly had independent status now became hamlets within the administrative village. These reforms inevitably resulted in a weakening of the social and political structure of the hamlet community. The village head was no longer the hereditary representative of the leading family: now he was an elected leader who might not even come from one's own hamlet.

To some extent, the goal of these village administrative reforms was the creation of a modern system of regional government. The village head was the lowest echelon in the hierarchy of bureaucratic administration going from village to county to prefecture to the central government in Tokyo. Above the level of village head, all of these positions were appointed by the central government. Thus, the new system created a direct administrative hierarchy leading right into the village community. That said, there were other compelling reasons for the reform, not least of which was the dismal financial position of many smaller villages, which had proved unable to meet the administrative demands of the modernizing state. Amalgamation of the villages allowed for economies of scale in schools, village offices, and village employees.

Hashimoto was integrated into the new administrative village of Aihara, which consisted of four former villages: Hashimoto, Aihara, Oyama, and Hara Shinden. Hara Shinden was a relatively new community, developed through reclaimed land just fifty years earlier by the father of Hara Seibei, who was now the richest man in the combined village community. But for Hashimoto, Aihara, and Oyama there was a good deal of déjà vu about this amalgamation. The three villages had actually been a single unit until 1664, when they were separated by administrative fiat. They had been temporarily brought back together in 1828, when the Shogunal government created "village groups" throughout the Kantō for the purpose of maintaining law and order.[10] The amalgamation of villages was by no means a new idea, nor was it always clear what constituted a "natural" village—in many cases, villagers' loyalties focused on even smaller units, such as the *aza* or neighborhood. Although Aihara hamlet gave its name to the new village, Hashimoto was its nerve center from the start, since it was situated on the main road to Yokohama and thus had the best communications with regional authorities. The village office was placed in Hashimoto, on land owned by the Aizawa family.

The reforms meant a tightening of ties with the county and prefectural authorities. The former villages—henceforth to be called "hamlets" *(ō-aza)*—that made up the newly constituted Aihara were located at the far north of Kōza county, a long and narrow county stretching almost to the coast. The county seat was in Fujisawa, almost forty kilometers from Aihara—a seven-hour walk, with no other convenient mode of transport available. In contrast, Hachiōji—the county seat of Minami Tama county—was less than two hours' walk away. The villagers of Aihara had close ties to Hachiōji, both cultural and economic. Fujisawa, on the other hand, was alien territory. As the leaders of the new administrative village contemplated this situation, they resolved to petition the Kanagawa prefectural governor to move Aihara from Kōza county to Minami Tama county. Kikutarō's elder brother volunteered to go to Hachiōji to talk the matter over with the Minami Tama county chief, and enlist his support if possible.

A few days later, the village leaders sent a petition to Asada Tokusuke, the governor of Kanagawa:

> This village is at the northernmost point of Kōza county. Our customs and feelings are the same as those of the people of Minami Tama county. . . . If the village remains in Kōza county, then we must travel a distance of ten *ri* [38 kilometers] to get to the county seat. Clearly this makes it very hard for us to carry out official business. . . . It takes three days for mail to travel between us and the county office—that would be too late in the event of an emergency. This results in the back-up of our official business, and it is inconvenient for both officials and people. Our customs are the same as those of Hachiōji, and we have to sell our produce—silk thread, silk and cotton cloth, grain and fruit—in Hachiōji. The distance to Hachiōji is less than two *ri* [7.7 kilometers]. . . . If you consider the question from the standpoint of both our moral life and our commercial life, it is easy to see the advantage of merging with Minami Tama county, and that is why we are making this petition.[11]

But all of these efforts appear to have been unavailing. The village of Aihara was born in Kōza county, and it remained in Kōza county until the entire county system was abolished in 1921. Aizawa himself was to taste in full the inconvenience of this distant but vital relationship as he worked as deputy mayor and then mayor over the next two decades.

. . .

If the distance between Hashimoto and Fujisawa remained inconveniently great, that between Hashimoto and Tokyo became dramatically less with the opening of the Hachiōji-Tokyo railway line. The diary indeed opens at a key moment in the history of transportation in the area. Until the early 1880s, more or less the only way to get from Hashimoto to Tokyo or Yokohama was to walk (those who could afford it might ride on horseback or be carried in a palanquin). However, improvements on the roads made rickshaw travel possible during the 1880s. Then, in November 1886 service began on a horse-drawn line between Hachiōji and Shinjuku. Aizawa traveled on this in April 1887.

In March 1887 Home Minister Yamagata Aritomo authorized construction of a railway between Shinjuku and Hachiōji, and the Kōbu Railway Company began surveying the route later in the year. This was one of a host of new railway lines that began construction from the latter half of the 1880s. Indeed, the railway boom was both symptom and cause of the economy's recovery from the depression of the first half of the decade. This particular line was considered high priority by the government, perhaps because the emphasis to date had been mainly on coastal railway lines.

In April 1889 the line opened between Shinjuku, in Tokyo's western suburbs, and Tachikawa; on August 11, service was extended to Hachiōji. The railway company initially ran four trains a day on the line, of which one connected to Shinbashi. The journey to Shinjuku took only an hour and fifteen minutes. Tokyo, which had been the best part of a day's journey away, could now be reached in time for breakfast. The one-way fare for the thirty-seven-kilometer journey was ¥0.28 for third class, ¥0.56 for second class, and ¥0.83 for first class. Aizawa gives no hint as to which class he traveled, but given his views on economy, one may assume it was not first.

The train quickly became a part of everyday life for Aizawa. But for the ordinary villagers of Aihara, it remained a novelty, and an expensive one at that. The return fare to Tokyo (even in third class) cost the equivalent of two full days wage for a day laborer. Nor, given the centrality of Hachiōji to the village economy, did most of them have strong reasons to travel to Tokyo. In 1894, Aihara village conducted a survey of travel by its inhabitants. All trips outside the village were surveyed. Two things are striking about the result. One is the very large number of trips taken by the villagers: a total of 31,700—or more than

sixty trips per family for the year. The other is the continued prefer-
ence for foot travel over all other available means of transportation.
For example, of the 450 trips taken to Tokyo in that year, 285 were on
foot. Given the availability of the train, this must surely have been for
economic reasons. The most popular destination was Hachiōji (eight
thousand trips, three thousand on foot), followed by the nearby villages of Mizo, Nakano, and Kawajiri (each four to five thousand trips,
mostly on foot).[12] Since most of these destinations were not accessible
by rail, the alternatives were either horse-drawn cart or rickshaw. The
latter cost about ¥0.02 per kilometer, the former about ¥0.8 per kilometer (though it could be shared). Both remained prohibitive for the
lower class of villagers.

TOWARD INDEPENDENCE

On September 20, 1890, Sato gave birth to a baby boy. She was attended
in childbirth by her mother and a local midwife. The neighbors quickly
came over to offer their congratulations. Aizawa himself was enormously excited at the birth of a son and heir. The next day, he traveled to Hachiōji to tell all his relatives there of his good fortune. These
included Sato's father, who was working at the Busō bank; the owners
of the Okabe shop, who were both relatives and business associates of
the Aizawa; and Aizawa's uncle Suzuki in Asakawa village. Suzuki gave
him medicine for Sato to prevent any kind of poisoning after the birth.

On the twenty-fourth Aizawa went to the village office and registered the birth of his son, announcing that the child would be called
Shigeharu—a name chosen by Sato's father, after consulting various
auguries. A month later, the family held a formal celebration for the
birth of Kikutarō's heir. They spent ¥23 buying fish, wheat, soba, rice
cakes, sake, rice, tofu, *yuba* (tofu skin), charcoal, and soy sauce for
a big crowd of guests (they also sent rice cakes to those who could
not attend). Married, and now a father: Aizawa was quickly taking
on new responsibilities, together with the quiet joys of adulthood and
family life. Now all that remained to confirm his status as a mature
and independent member of Hashimoto (now Aihara) society was his
own home. That was to come very soon.

On January 12, 1892, Aizawa heard from his Ushikubo brother-in-
law of a fine house for sale in Yarimizu village, a thirty-minute walk up
the road toward Hachiōji. The two of them, together with Ushikubo's
father, immediately set off to inspect the house. It was just what Aizawa

was looking for. The house had originally been the home of the leading family of Yarimizu, but the present family head, a very wealthy entrepreneur, now lived in Hachiōji. He operated a sake factory in the house, but he wanted to build a new, specialized facility on the site. For ¥208, he agreed to sell the house to Aizawa, who would dismantle and transport it to Hashimoto. The deal closed just two weeks later.

Over the next three months, Aizawa hired teams of workers to disassemble and transport the house the three kilometers to Hashimoto, and in early May work began on the site for the new house, on a prime piece of land purchased for Aizawa by his brother. The ground had to be leveled and a foundation prepared. A gang of ten workers labored through the first part of the month. Finally, on May 13, work began rebuilding the house. On that day, the first pillars were raised, and the contractors celebrated together with Aizawa, who broke out a bottle of sake.

Once started, construction went quickly. Teams of from ten to twenty men worked on the construction site. On May 19 no fewer than fifty people (those currently working on the site, and all those who had worked on it in the past) raised the ridgepole. Afterward, Aizawa held a party to celebrate this symbolic step in the building process. The following week, work began thatching the roof.

By mid-June the construction work was essentially complete. This was by no means a case of buying an old wreck on the cheap. The materials in the house were of the highest quality—so good, in fact, that the house still stands virtually unchanged today. There was still plenty of work to do on the details—installing doors and windows, and ornamental woodwork for the alcoves, laying down tatami on the floors, and painting. The work continued through June and July, although without the big crews that had been coming through June. Aizawa settled up with the contractors. The diary does not contain a full accounting for the house, but Aizawa comments several times that the costs were lower than he expected (the cost for professional roofers, for example, was just ¥6.30). Aizawa paid the three main contractors ¥40 for 120 days of work. Probably the whole project cost him less than ¥100. Adding the original cost of the house and his brother's purchase of the land, the entire cost was in the range of ¥500.

Aizawa slept for the first time in the new house on July 31. But it was a very hesitant move. For the next several months, he was coming and going as he furnished the house and gradually put everything in order. In particular, he had a lot of work to do in the garden, where he planted trees (many of them gifts from friends and family members).

Figure 10. The house Aizawa rebuilt

The house was built of *keyaki* (Japanese zelkova), an exceptionally dense hardwood that has contributed to the house's long life. When Aizawa rebuilt it, the spacious entry hall opened onto a pair of reception rooms, each twenty-five square meters in size. To the right of these rooms was an earthen-floored kitchen, leading to a dining area in the center of which was an *irori* hearth. The kitchen contained ample storage space for the various preserved foods that the family made or bought for the winter months—*miso,* pickled plums and persimmons, soy sauce (usually purchased), and pickled vegetables. In the back of the house was another earthen-floored room containing the wooden bathtub.

Upstairs, the house had four tatami-floored bedrooms as well as a substantial storage area. The third floor was devoted entirely to silkworm rearing. It was equipped with racks to shelve the dozens of trays of silkworms that the family reared each season. Instead of tatami mats it had disposable rush mats on the floor, for easier sorting and storage of mulberry and silkworm cocoons.

The garden covered about 0.1 hectare (large by Japanese standards), and included, once Aizawa had finished developing it, an ornamental pond and a bamboo grove. Amidst the trees were several outbuildings:

an earthen-walled storehouse (this was probably there before Aizawa bought the property); a small detached house, for visiting relatives or for Aizawa himself to retire and enjoy peace and quiet; and a pair of storage sheds. Later, Aizawa was to add an Inari shrine—dedicated to the fox god—with a handsome red *torii* gate.

It was not until October 23 that Aizawa, his wife, and infant son formally and permanently moved into the new house. They held a party that day to celebrate the move, inviting all of their cousins and neighbors. Aizawa was now formally an independent family head, although he had yet to receive his share of assets from his older brother. Aizawa continued going to work most days at his brother's house.

. . .

On June 26, 1893, Sato had her second baby. Her delivery came at a desperately busy time for the family. They were in the final stages of the summer silkworm season and about to boil the cocoons to kill the larvae growing inside them (by this time, boiling rather than sun-drying had become standard practice). Although Aizawa himself was not yet cultivating silkworms in his new house, he was heavily involved in his brother's enterprise. When he got home, he found that Sato had already gone into labor. Her mother had come to take charge, and she had summoned the local midwife, Mrs. Motogi. They had made all the preparations, and were sitting around the hearth waiting for matters to come to a head. At eleven in the evening, Sato delivered a baby boy. Carrying his other son Shigeharu on his back, Aizawa walked back to the main house to tell his mother, who came back with him to stay the night.

The next day, Aizawa went back to work at his brother's house, leaving Sato and the baby in the hands of Sato's mother, the midwife, and four or five visitors. That evening a wet-nurse, Naka from the Yoshidaya family, came to give milk to the baby. A few days later, Dr. Yajima came to examine Sato and gave her some medicine.

Two days later, Sato's brother's wife had a daughter. It seemed that the family was full of good tidings. On June 30 Aizawa went to the village office to register the birth of his son. He chose the name Kiyoshi. Since the birth of Kiyoshi, Shigeharu had been staying with his Aizawa grandmother, away from all the commotion in the house. But "I was woken up in the middle of the night by the arrival of my mother with Shigeharu." The little boy's world had fallen apart with the arrival of this presumptuous newcomer, and he was screaming for his mother and father. Although his grandmother took him back to her house, it was only for a while: at 2:30 in the morning they were back at the Aizawa house. Finally, "I took him in my arms and we went to sleep together." From that point on until Sato was well enough to take care of him as well as the baby, Shigeharu went everywhere with Aizawa, accompanying him to work at the main house on Aizawa's back.

On July 3 the family held the "seventh evening celebration," making rice cakes and handing them out to their relatives, friends, and neighbors. They decided that since Kiyoshi was only a second son, he should not receive the customary gifts. Instead, they had a small family party where they broke out the sake and ate rice cakes. The event was marred by Aizawa's mother having a sudden onset of spasms, with intense pain. Aizawa quickly called for a masseuse, Kino, who was able to relieve the symptoms somewhat. It was oppressively hot, "hard to endure," and thunder and lightning were playing in the distance. That night, while Kiyoshi was being given a bath, his umbilical cord dropped off.

The heat that summer was oppressive. Through July the temperature hovered in the high nineties and low hundreds—as Aizawa recorded from the thermometer in his house. On July 17 when he went to Kamimizo to register a land purchase, Aizawa had to travel by rickshaw because he could not stand walking in the intense heat (he makes no mention of how the rickshaw puller felt). That evening there was a huge thunderstorm. A bolt of lightning struck a tree at the Daijingū Shrine, splitting it in half.

In the middle of July, elections were held for the prefectural assembly. Because Aizawa had not yet formally received his allotment of land, he was still not eligible to vote. But he recorded the details of the election.

> Since the tenth, both the Liberal and Reform parties have been contesting the prefectural assembly seats. As the election will be in a day or two, the activities of the *sōshi* [organized groups who supported one of the parties, often through threats and intimidation] have been at their most intense. Both the Liberal and Reform parties are trying to grab voters by force. This evening, word came that a gang of Reform Party *sōshi* were going to come and threaten us. Tomorrow, a group of opponents will go and intercept them, to stop them going to the polling office. The Liberal Party side is warning us to be on the lookout. Tonight, a group of twenty *sōshi* under the leadership of Okabe Yoshitarō was dispatched from the party headquarters in Kamimizo to protect us in Aihara. They have divided up and will be stationed in Oyama and Aihara hamlets. Here in Hashimoto, forty volunteers have taken their stand at Higasa, and they are still there

at ten o'clock. Tomorrow my brother will set off as an official observer (at the county chief's request). Starting at five A.M., a hundred and fifty voters and their escort will come to Kōfukuji Temple. There they will rendezvous with voters and the escort from Oyama, and the whole group will total over two hundred people. They are saying that more *sōshi* sent from Kamimizo headquarters will also accompany them. Truly, this kind of tumult has become an everyday thing in Kanagawa prefecture. Supporters of both parties are descending on the prefecture from all sides, and the *sōshi* do nothing but confront each other. On this occasion, the home minister has requested the army minister to send a first lieutenant and five other officers, together with ten soldiers and five or six military police, to police the proceedings. In addition, seventy or eighty policemen have been sent from Yokohama police headquarters to accompany my brother, Yajima, and Ushikubo [all official observers] to the polling station.

The next day, Aizawa reports on the election:

In the morning I awoke at four and checked the eel trap. There were seven small eels in it. Then I went straight to the main house, where my brother was making his preparations to depart. I had breakfast with him, and the two of us set off together. While we were eating, the voters and their escort arrived from Aihara—there must have been 240 or 250 of them, including Ogawa, Shindō, and a number of other gentlemen who stopped at my brother's house. At five o'clock we departed, and together with over a hundred voters and their escort, we set off for Oyama, where we met the group from that hamlet. Then we went on to Shinden hamlet, and picked up that group too. Then the entire group of over five hundred men set off via Higanezawa, and by seven o'clock we arrived at Ikedaya in Kamimizo. The voters were directed by the five policemen on duty there to the polling station, where they voted. My brother Yasuemon, accompanied by policemen, arrived at the observers' seats, and then seven hundred and more voters and their escorts arrived from Ōno village. Kamimizo was jammed absolutely full. . . . The election finished surprisingly peacefully, and at three o'clock I, Jungorō, and several others waited for my brother to finish his business, and then we all repaired to the Ikedaya. There were ten or more people waiting for us, and we bought them sake, then we set off for home.

Neither Aizawa nor his brother was formally a member of the Liberal Party, in spite of repeated efforts by party representatives to get them to join. But there is no doubt that their loyalty lay with the Liberal Party candidates—particularly with Aoki Shōtarō, a local man from the neighboring village of Aihara (confusingly, this was a different Aihara from the Aizawas' village: it was adjacent, but across the county line in Minami Tama). Aoki was a powerful local leader, a wealthy landlord and the founder's son and current president of the Busō Bank. He had been involved in the People's Rights Movement, and was now a prefectural assembly member. A few years later, he would run for the national Diet.

And so, amidst the heat of summer and the excitement of politics, August arrived. Aizawa's home had still not settled down to a new rhythm after the birth of Kiyoshi. On August 3 Aizawa fired Kiyoshi's nursemaid. "She is lazy and no good at taking care of the children." After consulting with his mother, Aizawa summoned the girl's guarantor and told him of her dismissal, giving her a gift of an unlined cotton kimono as a severance payment. Aizawa continued taking care of Shigeharu, while Sato devoted all her attention to the new baby.

The oppressive heat persisted. The summer heat of the Kantō is debilitating: so humid that the slightest movement brings sweat pouring from one's body. The cicadas screech their terrible chorus, while people sit on their verandas in their lightest cotton garments, fanning themselves with wand-like paper fans, and trying to catch any stray breeze that might disturb the oppressive stillness. During the daytime, the sliding doors of the Aizawa house were opened wide to let in the occasional waft of freshening breeze. But they also let in hordes of vicious mosquitoes, which attacked the residents mercilessly in spite of the sticks of mosquito-repelling incense left to burn in the living areas (these sticks, using the powder of the pyrethrum plant, were a recent invention of the Wakayama-based entrepreneur Kamiyama Eiichirō—until the turn of the 1890s, the only remedy was to light a bonfire [kariya] in the yard to create as much smoke as possible—and to sleep under mosquito nets).[13]

At night, the family closed the wooden shutters tightly to keep out burglars—but they also kept in the unbearable still heat, together with the mosquitoes and other insects, which combined to make the night a restless interlude of tossing and turning in sweat-soaked nightclothes. The children broke out in scabs as they scratched at their tormenting stings and bites. Dysentery and typhoid lurked in the unwashed corners of the village. Sudden epidemics swept the hamlets. Food that was not eaten immediately quickly sprouted fungi and threatened to poison anyone who tried to eat it—but there were families who could not afford to throw a scrap away.

On August 6 disaster struck the market town of Hachiōji. A fire broke out in the commercial district, and, fanned by a rare summer wind, quickly spread. Within an hour, the center of the town was burning fiercely. By chance, the Aizawas had a visitor from Hachiōji that day—the merchant Okabe Senpachi, with whom they had close business and family ties. Yasuemon walked with him on his return up the mountain road from Hashimoto, as far as the top of the Goten Pass. At the pass they could clearly see the fire raging in the town below. Yasuemon rushed with Senpachi to the scene of the disaster. By the time they got there, more than a thousand houses had burned to the ground.

On August 14, just two days before the village was due to celebrate the Bon Festival of the Dead, Kiyoshi suddenly fell ill.

> In the morning, Kiyoshi appeared to have caught a cold. His color was a strange blue-green. Toward evening, he started crying. We thought that it was because he couldn't suck the milk with his nose blocked. He didn't seem to be terribly ill, so we all went to bed. Then soon after midnight, he began screaming. We quickly sent for Sato's parents to come and help. Then we sent for Dr. Aoki from the Kaishundō clinic. He came together with his assistant, and immediately pronounced that Kiyoshi was seriously ill. He gave Kiyoshi a little medicine dissolved in water, but it had no effect, and his breathing rapidly became shallower, until he passed away as though he were falling asleep. The doctor said that the illness was called "tetanus."

This tragedy struck a powerful blow to the Aizawa family. The deaths of children were a common event (on average, 20 percent of rural Japanese children died before their tenth year), but this was the first time that Aizawa had personally experienced such a tragedy. The family rallied round and dozens of them came to visit, staying for the funeral the next day. Within a week, Aizawa's diary entries were back to their matter-of-fact normality. But something had changed, too. The bright-eyed youth who six years earlier had set out so optimistically to see the sights of Enoshima, Yokohama, and Tokyo was no longer the same person he had been. Aizawa, the child of good fortune, had been touched by tragedy.

. . .

Aizawa had to wait more than two years before receiving his share of the family assets and becoming fully independent as a branch family head. On March 27, 1894, Aizawa and his brother conferred and finally decided which assets he would receive. The land amounted to some twelve hectares and would have a total tax value of ¥1,475. By this time, actual market values were from three to five times higher than tax values, so the actual value may have been in the region of ¥5,000, enough to make Aizawa a man of some means, although by no means one of the region's wealthiest.

Aizawa formally took possession of his assets on February 3, 1895. On that day, his brother presented him with a list of his land holdings, and, using that as a reference, Aizawa proceeded to make a tenancy ledger, as well as a cash ledger. Aizawa always enjoyed record-keeping activities, and this must have been a particularly pleasant task. His brother also gave him a seal engraved with the family name and an ink-jar, both of which had been passed down in the family for generations. The day happened to be the *setsubun* festival, one of the divisions of the Chinese calendar, coming just before the lunar new year, and said to divide the coldest phase of winter from the beginnings of spring. Japanese families traditionally throw dried beans to ward off any ogres who might be lurking in the house. It is a wonderful occasion for children, and Shigeharu—an only child once again—was just old enough to enjoy it. After throwing the beans, "we celebrated our safety with sake."

Aizawa sent out notices to sixty tenants whose fields were now under his ownership. With the change in ownership, all prior rental contracts were rendered null and void, and Aizawa received a stream of visitors over the next few days, seeking to renegotiate their contracts. For the most part, he agreed to do so under similar terms. For example, on February 10, Aizawa renewed a contract with a tenant called Sōkichi. The contract was for about one *tan* (0.1 hectare) of land planted with mulberry, for an annual rent of ¥2.50. The rent was a little lower than the going rate (the same tenant was renting a 0.15 hectare field from Yasuemon for ¥4.20 a year), but "the tenant promised that he would increase the amount of mulberry under cultivation." The contract was for five years, and if the two parties agreed to extend the contract, the rent would remain the same ("except that if prices fall due to recession or rise unduly, then we will follow that trend"). The discussions with other tenants were complicated at times, as some fields were split between the two brothers, and the tenants would now need to make two separate rental agreements. In one case, Aizawa refused to renew the contract unless the tenants paid all of their outstanding rent from the previous year.

On February 23 Aizawa registered the new ownership at the Kamimizo registry office. He did this by borrowing his brother's official seal, and taking his brother's officially executed deed assigning the land to Kikutarō. Since it was problematic for him to represent his brother when he himself was the beneficiary, he requested the head of the registry office, Mr. Kiryū, to act as his brother's legal representative (he paid Kiryū an official fee for this service, as well as giving him a tip). The Hashimoto portion of the transfer amounted to ninety-five separate pieces of land, with an assessed value of ¥1,450. Aizawa had to purchase a revenue stamp (a form of registration tax) for ¥8. In addition, he received one piece of land in Aihara hamlet, with a tax value of ¥25.

The next year, Sato had another baby, a son. He was born on September 18, Shigeharu's fifth birthday. Aizawa named him Yasuo. Although no one could replace the child they had lost, the Aizawa branch family once again had two healthy sons, and the continuation of the family line seemed assured. All in all, Aizawa had a more than satisfactory situation. He lived in a fine house in which he could rear silkworms; he had a wife he loved and sons to inherit the headship of the newly established family; he had a delightful garden to potter about in; and he had sixty tenants to bring him rent and support his lifestyle. In spite of the tragedy of his son's death, Aizawa had every reason to feel satisfied. He did not neglect to thank the gods for his good luck.

• • •

Like all the villagers of Hashimoto, Aizawa inherited from his forebears a complex set of spiritual allegiances. The Aizawa family had a wide variety of loyalties—institutional, financial, and spiritual—to religious institutions both inside and outside the village. Probably the most important was their membership in the Kōfukuji Temple. This was where their ancestors were buried, and the family graves, together with the mortuary tablets kept by the temple, were indeed an essential part of the family's constitutional structure—as important in some ways as the family home and property. The family was in a very real sense a trust, presided over by the current family head, but transcending the generations. It must be preserved and nourished not only for the benefit of future generations, but also as a mark of respect to those who had struggled for it in the past.

Since the Aizawa were a wealthy family, a large part of the burden of maintenance of Kōfukuji fell on their shoulders. They were a part of a small committee of leading member families, which met periodically to look after the temple's assets (the temple was itself a landowner, with its own tenants), and to ensure maintenance of the temple buildings.

Figure 11. Kōfukuji Temple, 2006

The temple "belonged" to the Aizawa and other member families, very much in the same way that a church might be held to "belong" to its congregation.

The family also supported the Jinmei Shrine in Hashimoto. The shrine paid homage to the tutelary deity of the village, and it represented in many ways the spirit of the village. In this sense, it was a much more public entity than the temples (Kōfukuji and Zuikōji), which were more about the family and the individual. The shrine had an annual festival, in which the entire hamlet participated. The Meiji government was highly aware of the ideological significance of the Shintō shrines as it developed the notion of the "family state." Just as the shrine with its local deity represented the village community, so the emperor, as the descendent of the sun goddess Amaterasu and Shintō "chief priest," represented the national community. Shintō was held to represent the intangible essence of Japan, personified in the figure of the god-like emperor.

Probably the nationalistic aspect of shrine worship had not, in the early 1890s, yet found its way into the soul of the village. The shrine was above all an integral component in the customary practice of the village—in the cycle of the seasons, the times of celebration and festival, and the warding off of disasters and prayer for good harvests.

Because of the importance of the annual festival—when the shrine's deity would be paraded in a palanquin to the accompaniment of dancing and drums—the shrine was primarily the concern of the young. The village "youth group" *(wakashū)* was in charge of the festivities, and the young men of the village displayed their strength and prowess in the festival parade. When, in the summer of 1888, the village youths decided to build a grand new vehicle on which to mount the *mikoshi* portable shrine for the festival parade, Aizawa was deeply involved in the building project, to the exclusion of almost any other work.

Did these connections together constitute a "religion"? Certainly, each had their function in Aizawa's spiritual life. In times of drought, he did not hesitate to call on the shrine priest to lead prayers for rain.[14] And in the aftermath of his son's death, he certainly found comfort in the sutras chanted for his son's spirit by the priests of Kōfukuji. Perhaps it would be more accurate, though, to suggest that Aizawa's spiritual home lay in the village community, and that the temples and shrines— with all the rituals and obligations that they brought—were an integral and ancient part of that communal life.

In addition to the temple and shrines, Aizawa also belonged to a neighborhood based religious group *(kō)* that was responsible for raising money for Buddhist causes, including prayers for the dead, and pilgrimage. Villagers frequently went on excursions (perhaps "pilgrimage" is too solemn a word for these visits that combined sightseeing and entertainment with an element of worship)—whether to local sites such as the Hachijōji Tenman Shrine, or further afield to the temple-shrine complex atop Mount Takao, the Afuri Shrine atop Mount Ōyama, or to Mount Fuji. Aizawa himself went on a pilgrimage in September 1893, a month after the death of his son. Together with three friends, he set off at dawn from Hashimoto, for the rugged climb up Mount Ōyama to the Afuri Shrine.

The friends took it easy at first, traveling by rickshaw from Hashimoto to the banks of the Sagami River at Tana village. From there, they walked to the town of Ōyama, at the base of the mountain. This was no country stroll. Ōyama lies deep in the mountains, accessible only by a long and difficult trail. The next morning they left early to climb the mountain. The silence and majesty of the 1,250-meter mountain must have inspired feelings of deep awe, perhaps mitigated in part by the chat and laughter of fellow-pilgrims on the trail. The shrine sits near the top of the mountain, surrounded by deep forest, and with spectacular views of gorges below. Aizawa prayed for "the safety of my family," noting that he donated ¥0.25 for incense and prayers.

From the shrine, the pilgrims continued their climb, emerging near the summit at Minoge, before descending to Tōkaichi. After lunch, it began to rain, and, perhaps losing the edge of their fervor, the four pilgrims took to rickshaws to ride the last leg of their pilgrimage to the temple at Mount Dōryū, where they once again lit incense (another ¥0.25 each). By now it was raining heavily, and the pilgrims were soaked. Climbing back into their rickshaws, they chatted while their pullers struggled through the mud and rain down to the town of Matsuda. From this town on the Tōkaidō line, they were able to catch a steam train to Tokyo and then back to Hachiōji and Hashimoto.

In spite of his overtly religious activities, Aizawa clearly still felt a need for spiritual and moral solace that the temples and shrines could not, it seemed, provide. Part of the reason, perhaps, lies in Aizawa's deeply pragmatic personality. For Aizawa, the life of the spirit was intimately connected to his worldly activities—land ownership and money-lending, village affairs, and nurturing friends and family. In his pessimistic comments on the decline of human nature, one can detect a search for a moral philosophy that could combine a morality of human relationships, a philosophy of business and money, and a nod to the transcendent nature of the human spirit. For a while, he found this philosophy in the teachings of the Tōkyū school.

Aizawa first came across this teaching in 1888. The Tōkyū was sweeping through the village elites of the Kantō region at the time—it seemed to contain a magical spark that ignited the devotion of influential men throughout the region. Yokoyama Marumitsu, a low-ranking samurai of rural origin, developed Tōkyū teaching in the 1830s. His new system was one of many being created in the late Tokugawa period, to offer practical programs of self-improvement for townsmen and educated villagers. The underlying premise—that through moral self-cultivation one could improve both oneself and one's lot in life—was deeply rooted in Confucian thinking. Another variant was the teaching of Ninomiya Sontoku, the agriculturalist whose notions of self-reliance were so influential that before World War II, every Japanese school had a statue of him in its yard.

At the heart of the Tōkyū teaching was a system of divination: the reading of one's fate in order to try and improve it. People were endowed at birth with personalities based on the configuration of the twelve zodiacal realms. Marumutsu worked out a complicated statistical formula for assessing the influences on one's personality at birth: the "three rings," which could be calculated based on the twelve zodiacal signs, the "ten stems," and the "twelve branches." These rings were in turn influenced by environmental factors, such as the rings of one's own parents (known as the "field"), and one's physiognomy, which Tōkyū teachers liked to try and analyze.

Once understood, one's "material endowment" of attributes coming from the alignment of the three rings could be used to work on rooting out undesirable character traits. As Marumitsu put it, "one can improve the shape of a tree if one prunes it correctly."[15] He called for the nurturing of the goodness in the tree's "trunk," while pruning the branches of one's inherited traits, which were often out of balance with one's material endowment. The emphasis of his teaching was practical, not philosophical—as such, it was well suited to the rural elite, with their limited education and constant desire to improve their economic lives. Disciples were encouraged to work on improving their attributes, in order to influence the direction of their own lives. To help them, the teaching called for regular meetings, at which members would share their experiences with others, and seek support in their efforts at self-improvement.

Aizawa seems to have joined the group more or less as a gesture of politeness. His interest was clearly not very profound at the time, as he seldom mentions the group during the following months. However, at the end of 1891, Aizawa's interest suddenly picked up, and the group started to become a much more important part of his life. He helped initiate his brother, his cousin, his brother-in-law, his wife, and his mother. The Tōkyū was becoming as interconnected within his family as were his business activities.

From the beginning of 1892, Aizawa began attending group meetings at least once a week and sometimes every day, often spending a large part of the day in Tōkyū-related meetings. In the early days, the meetings Aizawa attended were usually in the home of a respected elder from Hashimoto or one of the neighboring villages (for the first several months, they were held in the home of Amino Teisuke, who lived in the next-door village). But as Aizawa became more involved, he began offering his own home for meetings. In January 1894, Aizawa traveled to Tokyo with several of his fellow Tōkyū followers, to attend the ceremonies held by the sect's headquarters in Kanda. The morning "purification talk" session was attended by over two hundred people, and by afternoon the crowd had grown to three hundred and fifty. When the formal proceedings ended at four, over a hundred people stayed behind to drink sake and talk more. The Tōkyū leaders served a feast of foods that would have been hard to get in Hashimoto: sashimi (assorted raw fish), grilled fish, and a whole large snapper. At the end, everyone carried home a portion of red-bean rice (symbolizing celebration), and one of fish. In the evening the companions from Hashimoto went to a *yose* (vaudeville-style) music hall in Kanda, the Shiraume.[16]

The next morning the companions called again on their Tōkyū teacher, Sano Masanori. After some talk, they repaired to the Kanda Myōjin Shrine, where they climbed to the Kaikarō Restaurant, at the top of a three-storey building with splendid views over Tokyo.[17] After lunch, they went to the Sarugakuchō district to visit another teacher, Mr. Yoshikawa, to offer their new year's greetings. They performed a "seating" with Yoshikawa, who then gave Aizawa a small book of poems celebrating the year of the horse. Aizawa copied one in his diary, by "Manpuku":

When you take the strength from my vile body,
Then do I truly know the precious taste of nature.

Later in the evening, the party went back to Sano's house and once again had a "seating" with Ms. Hizuki, after which three of their number caught the last train home, while the other four (including Aizawa) stayed to play some more. The next morning, the twenty-fourth, they checked out of their lodging and took a horse-drawn cart down to Kudanshita, where they visited the Kankōba Shopping Center—an early version of a department store.[18]

Aizawa's interest in Tōkyū teaching tailed off in 1894, perhaps because he became so much busier with his new responsibilities as deputy mayor. His wave of enthusiasm for the Tōkyū reflects in part his relatively leisurely life as a well-off landlord. In the coming decade, as his responsibilities to family, village, and nation multiplied, he would find it harder and harder to take time for such pleasures.

CHAPTER 3

For Village and Nation

1894–1908

THE NATION COMES OF AGE

What did the "nation" of Japan mean to Aizawa, and how did that meaning change over the first two decades of his adulthood? At least by the 1880s, as Aizawa came of age, he was clearly aware of both the nation and emperor. Perhaps one reason for this was the proximity of his village to the capital—a very different story from an isolated mountain village in the far north, for example. Another was his privileged position within the village, which gave him the opportunity to travel to the capital and to read newspapers.

There are a number of patriotic references to the emperor and country even in the early years of the diary. In 1887 Aizawa was clearly excited to see the emperor in his carriage in Tokyo, and he was quite aware of the correct honorifics to refer to the emperor (*shujō* for the person of the emperor; *miyuki* for an imperial visit). In 1888 he argued that the spread of an improved variety of seeds "will benefit the nation." In 1889 he commented at length and with great pride on the new constitution and its significance for Japan's position in the world, as well as on the emperor's benevolence in pardoning criminals. On March 9, 1894, when the village of Aihara observed a one-day holiday in honor of the emperor's silver wedding anniversary, Aizawa and other prominent citizens displayed the Japanese national flag at the entrance to their houses.

But these gestures to emperor and nation did not require any special commitment or sacrifice on Aizawa's part. The one time he was asked to do something specifically for the sake of the country—on the occasion of his conscription exam on December 25, 1886—he commented in his diary that "of course I am expecting an exemption, but until that happens I must wait anxiously." Clearly he did not wish to serve his country in this way.

During the decade from 1894 to 1905, Japan fought two wars. Both were fought entirely on Asian soil. Both were victories for Japan— the Sino-Japanese War (1894–95) an unqualified victory, the Russo-Japanese War (1904–5) a much more costly and less-rewarding affair, but a victory nonetheless. Aizawa reacted to each of these wars differently. His response to the Sino-Japanese War was one of unqualified support and exuberance over Japan's apparently easy victories. His response to the Russo-Japanese War was much more reserved; by this time, he was an official of the village and therefore a functionary in the war effort. He felt the burden of this war personally, and he saw its deleterious effects on the economy and social structure of the village.

In early September 1894 Aizawa records: "From May or June of this year, there has been discord between Japan and China, and now it has led to the outbreak of war. On July 25, there was a battle at the mouth of the Nikawa River [Incheon]. It was a major victory for our forces. Then on August 30, the army fought a battle at Seikan [Sonhwan], and routed the Chinese, capturing the fort of Kibasan [Mount Hyondea]. Our army had seventy-five killed and wounded, while the Chinese casualties numbered five hundred."

Although he did not write this first entry till almost two months into the war, Aizawa began following the war in the pages of the diary with intense interest. His entries are stirringly patriotic. On September 25: "A heroic spirit of loyalty is thriving in our country. The current issue of war bonds has been subscribed to the tune of more than sixty-seven million yen." On October 31 after the Japanese crossing of the Yalu River: "Since the arrival of His Majesty the Commander in Chief [in Hiroshima, to take personal command of the war effort], the decisions of the commanders have providentially made no mistakes, and the troops overseas have enjoyed victory after victory. The same is true for the Navy. Ah, I can hardly bear the joy! Reverently, I pray for long life for His Majesty the Commander in Chief, and I rejoice in grateful celebration." On the occasion of a Korean embassy to Japan: "The Ambassador was surprised at the beautiful scenery, and at the

Figure 12. Aizawa's drawing of the war situation
near Pyongyang (Courtesy Aizawa Family)

enlightenment of Japan." And when the final peace treaty was signed at Shimonoseki, Aizawa wrote: "Long live the Japanese Empire!"

Nevertheless, Aizawa recognized that the effects of the war were not all beneficial when it came to his village. In his entry on October 31, Aizawa commented: "Nowadays Tokyo is in a recession, while Hiroshima is booming. In the state of things today, the fancy restaurateurs and high-class merchants of Tokyo's fashionable districts are quick to cry out about the recession. . . . And in the countryside too, it's the same situation. The people are crying that they may be next to be conscripted. They worry about those they will leave behind, and the difficulties that they may face. And they worry about whether Japan will win or lose the war against China."

The outbreak of war did indeed lead to a flood of conscription orders, although nothing like on the scale of the Russo-Japanese War a decade later (the Sino-Japanese War put 150,000 conscripts in the field with 15,000 casualties, most from disease, while the Russo-Japanese War fielded 960,000 conscripts, with more than 150,000 casualties). Aizawa mentions only one conscript from Hashimoto hamlet by name: Matsuura Aisaburō, the son of the miller. Matsuura heard a rumor that he was to be called up on the evening of August 30, 1894, and Aizawa kept him company until the early hours of the morning, when the notice did indeed come.

The next morning, Aizawa joined much of the rest of his hamlet in preparing banners to send off Matsuura and the other soldiers from Aihara who were to join their regiments immediately. Aizawa inscribed three banners, and then walked to the Jinmei Shrine, where he and the other villagers toasted Matsuura and his comrades with some forty liters of sake. Then the entire company of several hundred villagers set out on the eight-kilometer walk to Hachiōji station. Aizawa describes the scene at the station:

> Three officers had come from Tokyo to marshal the conscripts. There must have been a hundred well-wishers for each conscript—there really was no space even to stand; it was truly an unprecedented crowd. Even the officers were moved by the loyalty and courage of the conscripts. The cries of *banzai* for the emperor and the Imperial Japanese Army sundered the heavens. The soldiers departed on the 6:30 P.M. train, and they all leaned out the windows and shouted in brave voices, while the well-wishers filled the station and shouted their *banzai*s to the soldiers with thunderous voices, so loudly that they whipped up a wind on the platform. Truly the Japanese spirit was gushing forth and could be heard by the heavens. The steam train disappeared into the distance, and everyone set off for home in an orderly fashion.

The villages were a vital part of Japan's war effort, in both the Sino-Japanese and Russo-Japanese conflicts. They were the major provider of conscript troops (the better-educated and physically weaker city dwellers were more likely to be exempted), and they were also the provisioners of grain, meat, and horses. The wealthier villagers were also a source of finance for the war, to be tapped through post office savings and the issue of war bonds. During the Sino-Japanese War, the Japanese government established a pattern of demands on the villages that was to be repeated in the Russo-Japanese War, and then again with greater severity in World War II.

On August 16, 1894, the leading villagers of Hashimoto met in Zuikōji Temple to raise money to provide financial support to serving troops. Aizawa pledged a ¥1 contribution. The village of Aihara had been assigned by the county a quota of ¥125, of which Hashimoto's share was to be ¥25. Of the total, ¥50 would be donated to the county office's general fund, and another ¥50 would be added to a county fund to give ¥3 to each departing soldier within Kōza county. The remaining ¥25 would be used to provide additional support to soldiers from Aihara village, in the form of gifts of money on the occasion of the soldiers' departure, and support for their families while they are serving.

On August 21 Hashimoto canceled its annual shrine festival in recognition of Japan's national emergency. A few days layer, on the twenty-fifth, the county chief, Emori Hozon, came to Aihara and summoned the leading citizens of the village, including Aizawa's brother. He asked the village leaders to take on a quota of ¥2,000 of the new war bonds that the Japanese government was to issue the following month. These bonds were to be issued with a coupon of 5 percent interest—much lower than the yield available from lending in the local area. Aizawa does not record the outcome of this request, but quotas handed down from the county were taken very seriously, and we may assume that this one was met.

On June 13, 1895, Matsuura Aisaburō returned from the war. A crowd of seventy, including Aizawa and all the children in the Hashimoto village school, walked to Hachiōji to greet Matsuura at the railway station, arriving at 10:00 A.M. They had a long wait: Matsuura's train did not arrive until 3:00 P.M. But the crowd returned home cheerful nonetheless (the children no doubt happy to have missed a day of classes) and repaired to the village shrine, where a barrel of sake was broached. In the evening the Matsuura family held a party and invited Aizawa. Matsuura showed Aizawa some Chinese money, as well as several fine scrolls, an inscribed fan, and a woodblock print that he had purchased from a famous Chinese calligrapher while on active duty in China. It was much as though he had returned from a sightseeing trip.

. . .

The war shifted Japanese citizens' attention away from their local communities, and focused them instead on the possibilities of empire. As a result of its victory over China, Japan gained its first formal colonial possession, Taiwan (Okinawa and even Hokkaido had some of the characteristics of overseas colonies, but they were considered an integral part of Japan). Japan also strengthened its stranglehold on Korea, which opened up the possibility of expansion into the vast Manchurian hinterland. This was not only a matter of national pride. Japanese in all walks of life looked to the ways in which they might personally profit from Japan's new empire, whether through emigration, trade, or investment.

For Aizawa, too, the expanding empire brought new opportunities. In spite of his increasing wealth from local sources—through land acquisition, money-lending, and farming—Aizawa increasingly looked outside the village for investment opportunities. As a result, by the time of the Russo-Japanese War he was reaping dividends from a variety of new sources, both in Japan and overseas.

The new investment opportunities to some extent opened Aizawa's eyes to the limitations of his local environment. Farming and land-ownership were profitable activities, but they were subject to considerable uncertainty caused by the weather and by the economic difficulties under which many tenants labored. In many ways, Hashimoto was fortunate. The Kantō area was known for its generally mild climate, and Hashimoto's elevated position protected it from the floods that sometimes afflicted rice-growing villages lower in the plain. But agriculture is a risky proposition at best. The crops are subject to disease and insect damage, as well as the vagaries of the weather.

On May 15, 1899, an extremely unusual frost gripped the Kantō. As Aizawa describes it:

For the past three or four days the weather has been very unsettled. First the wind was from the south, with heavy clouds. Then it changed to the north, and a cold rain occasionally fell. Then last night it became extremely cold, and very clear as the sun went down. This morning, there was a great frost, and bitter cold. I went to inspect the damage to the mulberry leaves at ten in the morning. It was nothing but disaster. Depending on the location, some places had almost no damage, but on average more than thirty percent of the leaves were lost. This year, perhaps because of all the rain in March and April, the leaves came out early, and they were just at their stage of greatest growth. Moreover, we had just cleared off all the insects on May 5, and I was looking forward to a really good crop. . . . This will be a cause of great anxiety to the silkworm growers, and surely will cause much suffering.

Later that same year, a typhoon struck. Just a week earlier, Sato had given birth to the couple's fourth child, a girl. On September 4 the family held a "seventh-evening celebration" for their new daughter, Asako—"Morning Child" (the addition of *ko*—child—at the end of her name was a middle-class pretension: most village women, including Sato herself, made do with plainer names, usually written in the phonetic script—Asako was written in *kanji*). Then, on the sixth, the weather took a turn for the worse. It rained heavily all day, and the wind became stronger and stronger. On that day Aizawa went to the Kōfukiji Temple to meet with fellow landlords. Their tenants were requesting reductions in rent due to the May frost damage, and the landlords needed to develop a coordinated response. "There was much discussion but no decision," as Aizawa succinctly puts it. As evening drew in, the wind and rain grew stronger and stronger. "It was getting very dangerous. From eleven in the evening it rained and blew extremely heavily. It's the first time this year it has been so violent, and will certainly damage houses, trees, and crops."

The typhoon blew itself out around three in the morning, and by dawn the sky was clear. But still the weather felt heavy and humid, and in the evening they could hear thunder in the distance. The reports of damage began coming in. In the three hamlets of Oyama, Aihara, and Hashimoto, five houses had been destroyed, while a large number of roofs had been damaged. Trees were torn down everywhere, and—most important for the villagers—some 30 percent of the crops were estimated ruined. "The warm weather had made us think it would be a bumper crop and we were all joyful. But now in an instant, it has been changed into a crop failure. One can only call it the will of heaven." Aizawa went on to assess the situation:

In the spring last year there was hail damage, and then this spring there was the frost. Last September 8 there was typhoon damage, and now this year the same has happened again, and everyone has suffered severe damage to their crops . . . . Last year, because of the failed harvest everyone was eating Chinese Nanjing rice (you could get seven or eight *shō* [about eight to ten kilograms] for one yen). As a result, money was pouring out of Japan to foreign countries, and banks raised interest rates to try and attract more money. Then, the railways and other industries were flourishing, and attracting huge investments, and that, too, squeezed the supply of money. So the farmers were left with no crops and no money. Truly, it is a world of suffering. . . . Then, the government has increased taxes because of the shortage of money, and so the suffering has spread from the lower to the middle-level farmers, who are crying at the high taxes. The junior officials have had their salaries reduced, and they can hardly put food on the table. Moreover, the poor people who make their living from day labor can get only ¥0.30 to ¥0.50 a day for their work, and they are right on the edge between being able to eat and going hungry. And yet, in spite of their circumstances these people are often living lives of excessive luxury, eating white rice and wearing fine clothes. They have no assets, and they just live from day to day. Surely they are heading for tragedy. All is the result of these cruel conditions.

On the eighteenth, the landlords met once again, and decided to reduce rents by up to 20 percent. It is the first occasion in the diary where Aizawa records across-the-board reductions. But as the years went on, his pessimism about local conditions if anything deepened. His appreciation of the difficulties faced by the villagers of Aihara— and his frustration at their apparent thriftlessness—must have been heightened by the constant effort required to squeeze rent and interest out of his recalcitrant debtors. Indeed, there must have been times when he wondered if it was worth the effort of browbeating his fellow villagers. Perhaps—although there is little hint of this in the diary—he was even dimly aware that it was landlords and moneylenders like him who were in large measure responsible for the suffering and hopelessness of large numbers of villagers, by squeezing out of them any little surplus that they were able to accumulate.

On September 13, 1903, Aizawa let some of his frustration show, as a series of deadbeat debtors knocked on his door.

> This morning Bunkichi and Ryūzō came, and asked for an extension on their rent payments. I refused to listen to this, and demanded that they bring the money. Then I summoned Tōjirō and discussed his rent payment. He promised to bring last year's rent by the end of this month, and I agreed. Then Mr. Oshida of Ōfuna [a hamlet in neighboring Yokoyama village] came, and the other people left so I could talk to him. Oshida asked me to please buy Kōjirō's land [in settlement of his debt]. But I refused. Oshida said that if I would buy the land, Kōjirō would be happy to pay me ¥10 or even ¥11 in rent, but I told him that I do not like buying land. I want my loan repaid. It's only in case borrowers can not repay their loans that I make sure I have ample security when I lend money.

This response seems disingenuous, as foreclosure was a key component of Aizawa's strategy of wealth accumulation. And indeed, a few
days later, Aizawa formally took over three plots of land totaling 0.17
hectares from Kawabe Kōjirō, in lieu of the ¥87 owing to Aizawa (in
order to save on stamp tax, he cheated on the deed of sale and registered the purchase price as ¥65).

Aizawa also found the returns on farming to be increasingly less
attractive compared to other investment opportunities. In 1898 he
decided not to bother with silkworm cultivation—in spite of the fact
that this was considered the backbone of the local agricultural economy. He explained:

> It costs more than ¥8 per month to hire a helper, and if you take into
> account the need to provide seven shō [a measure of volume equivalent
> to just over one kilogram] of wheat, the total cost will not be less than
> ¥13. You also have to consider that you will use about twelve horseloads
> of mulberry leaves, which if you assume a price of ¥1 per horseload brings
> the total cost up to ¥24-¥25. In addition, the consumption of tools and
> charcoal comes to about ¥3, plus there is the cost of the silkworm eggs—
> even though there may be some return from the use of mulberry branches
> and silkworm feces as fertilizer. Assuming a total crop of ten kan [about
> 37 kilograms] of cocoons, the income would be less than ¥35 (and there
> is the risk of loss from a failed crop). Deducting the costs of about ¥27,
> we would be left with ¥8 at best, as the payment for our family labor.
> My wife is pregnant, and I have my work as a village official, so rather
> than working for this ¥8, it would be better just to sell the mulberry
> leaves—at the very least I should get ¥15 for them.

Rather than lend small sums to villagers he must meet in the street
every day, Aizawa also increasingly aimed his lending activities at
regional business—such as the ¥1,200 that he lent at 15 percent to the
Saitō family of Hachiōji on October 18, 1898. And rather than waste
time on marginally profitable farming activities, he focused increasingly
on the wholesale businesses of mulberry leaf sales (he reaped ¥200 to
¥300 per year from seasonal sales of mulberry leaves) and forestry.

From the turn of the twentieth century, Aizawa increasingly looked
to investments in joint stock companies as a way to benefit from the
rapidly modernizing economy. The first such investment that he made,
in October 1898, was in a company in his own hamlet. The Naigai trading company was created to provide services to local agriculturalists.
Aizawa was a founder shareholder. The company was officially opened
on January 19, 1899, with one hundred shareholders in attendance.
Since Hashimoto had only one hundred families, we may assume that

shareholding was fairly widespread (presumably investors participated from the surrounding villages, too). In addition to transportation services, the company also sold agricultural implements from a store in the village. Although its business was relatively simple, the company was a part of the modernization of business practices that was taking place throughout the Kantō region. As the silk industry expanded, and as foreign exporters in Yokohama increasingly demanded a uniform quality of silk thread, it became profitable for modern enterprises to buy cocoons, reel thread (an activity centered in Aihara and Hachiōji), and transport and sell the goods in wholesale volume.

The Naigai trading company seems to have been profitable from the outset. At the end of its first full year of operation it held a general meeting (on January 31, 1900) in the Zuikōji Temple. The shareholders resolved to pay themselves a dividend of 5 percent on their paid-up stock. By the company's seventh annual general meeting in 1905, the company was achieving profits of ¥2,000 and more on its capital of ¥8,000, allowing it to pay a 10 percent dividend and still reinvest capital into the business.

The Naigai trading company was just one of the modernizing companies that opened in the area in the 1890s. In Aihara, the Ekishinsha opened in 1892, to purchase locally spun silk thread. The company re-reeled the thread using hand-powered machinery, thereby increasing the uniformity and making the thread better qualified for export. In 1909 this company was merged, at the urging of the county chief, with the Zenshinsha in nearby Ōyama village.

Meanwhile, Aizawa was also becoming interested in joint stock company investments beyond his immediate community. Early in the morning of April 15, 1903, Aizawa hired two rickshaws to carry him and his elder son, Shigeharu, to the Hachiōji railway station. Shigeharu, now twelve years old, had graduated from the village elementary and higher elementary schools, and he was to start his new school life as a boarder at Tachikawa middle school. Only families with considerable financial resources were able to finance an education for their children beyond elementary school. Aizawa himself had not had the opportunity for any formal education beyond the elementary level. It is a mark both of his increasing fortune and of the opportunities offered by modern Japan, that all of his children, including the girls, received an education at least to the high-school level.

Kikutarō and Shigeharu carried with them huge bundles containing bedding, clothes, and other items that Shigeharu would need for the school year. After arriving at the school, they attended the beginning-of-year ceremony from ten until twelve. In the afternoon Aizawa took his son and his nephew Chōichi (also at the same school) by steam train to Koganei to view the cherry blossoms as a farewell treat. Then the boys took the train back to Tachikawa, while Aizawa went on to the village of Kichijōji, where he stayed with Tachibana Seisai.

Tachibana appears to have been a stockbroker of some sort. After a side trip to Fujisawa on village business, Aizawa returned to Kichijōji on the seventeenth and asked Tachibana to help him buy shares in the Keifu Railway Company. The Keifu line was built to connect Seoul, in Korea, to the southern port of Pusan. It was to become, and still is, Korea's major trunk line. Japan's undertaking to build the line was a significant step in its imperialist strategy on the Asian continent. At the time, Korea had only one railway line, connecting Seoul to the port of Chemulpo. This short line was being built by American business interests, but financial difficulties prompted them to sell it, together with the rights to the Seoul-Pusan line, to a Japanese company led by the prodigiously energetic Shibusawa Eiichi.

Shibusawa's company began construction in 1901, but the prospect of war with Russia highlighted the strategic importance of the project, and in 1903 the Japanese government intervened, effectively turning it into a semipublic enterprise. The railway, covering 230 miles, was a major undertaking requiring large amounts of capital. The Japanese government created a new semipublic company, the Keifu Railway Company, to manage the project and raise the needed capital from Japanese investors. The Keifu Railway Company's initial capitalization was ¥25 million, making it among the largest companies in Japan in terms of capitalization. The government facilitated fund-raising by offering various guarantees, including a guaranteed dividend of at least 6 percent.

When Japan declared war on Russia in February 1904, the still-unfinished railway immediately became a key artery in Japan's line of advance onto the Asian continent. Because of its strategic importance, in 1906 the government transferred the company to the Korean Residency-General, buying out the shareholders at a generous premium.[1]

In addition to railways, banks were another attractive investment opportunity for rural landlords with surplus capital. In the case of the Agricultural Industries Bank (Nōkō Ginkō) of Kanagawa prefecture, Aizawa was able to combine a modern joint-stock company investment with a more traditional landlord's concern for agricultural improvement, as the bank's mandate was to invest in improved sericulture and other agricultural activities within Kanagawa prefecture. Similar banks were founded in most prefectures following the passage of the Agricultural Industries Bank Law in 1886. Their parent institution was the Tokyo-based Kangyō Bank (now part of the Mizuho bank group: in 1944, Kanagawa Nōkō Ginkō was merged into Kangyō Bank). The government's aim in encouraging the creation of these banks was to provide financing for modernizing farming activities. The banks made loans to agricultural groups (for example, village companies like the Naigai Trading Company) and wealthier landlords. To some extent, therefore, the brothers' investment was a patriotic act, and a state-ment of faith in the future of farming in their district. The banks did not accept deposits, but raised money through the issue of long-term bonds. Aizawa and his brother were founder shareholders, attending the bank's opening ceremony in Yokohama on February 20, 1898.

POLITICS ON THE KANTŌ PLAIN

It was not only in business affairs that the local elite's attention was increasingly focused on nation and empire. In politics, too, with the opening of the national Diet, influential villagers became increasingly involved in national campaigns. When Aizawa acquired his share of the family estate in 1894, he became eligible to vote in national elections.

The most influential politician in the area was Aoki Shōtarō. Aoki was from Sakai village in Minami Tama county (just across the Sakai River from Aihara). Born in 1854, he was the son of a local agitator for people's rights, Aoki Kantarō. Both father and son were active in the movement for people's rights, calling for the creation of a parliament, and participating in the formation of the Liberal Party. Aoki's father was a founder of the Busō Bank, one of the major financial institutions of the Hachiōji region. On Kantarō's death in 1884, Aoki took over as its chief executive. His ties with the bank (seen by many as an oppres-sor of the poor) soured his relations with the Liberal Party in the 1880s, but in 1896, the party nominated Aoki as one of its two candidates for the special election to replace lower house member Ishizaka Masataka, who had been appointed governor of Gunma prefecture. The other candidate was Morikubo Sakuzō.

It was in this campaign that Aizawa himself became a *sōshi*. The *sōshi* emerged in the wake of the People's Rights Movement, which in its early years was a hotbed of discontented samurai. They were a ubiquitous element in political campaigns of the 1880s and 1890s, and they contributed significantly to the dirty reputation politics acquired during the 1890s. The word *sōshi* means literally "young man," and for some time it existed side by side with the similar term *shishi,* meaning "man of purpose." The *shishi* were active in antiforeign agitation in the 1850s and 1860s, and had their apotheosis in the failed Satsuma rebellion of 1877, when thousands of spirited young samurai were cut down on the field of battle by the conscript troops of the new, technocratic government.

The *sōshi* had the same overtones of high spirits and willingness to fight. However, perhaps because of government efforts to paint them (and the political parties they represented) in a bad light, the *sōshi* had by the 1880s come to have a much less salubrious image. Rather than the pure patriotic spirit attributed to the *shishi,* the *sōshi* were more generally associated with gang-like confrontations, rowdiness, and intimidation on behalf of electoral candidates. Given this association, it is surprising that Aizawa would have identified himself as a *sōshi,* as he did in a diary entry on October 11. Perhaps the government's smear campaign had not yet filtered through to the countryside, or perhaps Aizawa wore the label with pride precisely because of the government's opposition to the Liberal Party with which he identified.

In fact, there is no evidence of overt violence in the diary, although the suggestion of gang-like activity and intimidation is clear. The political parties fielded gangs of *sōshi* to protect their candidates, to cheer them at speeches and rallies, and to persuade voters to support them. They were recruited from the villages that supported one side or another in the campaigns. Although involved in election campaigns, the vast majority of *sōshi* were not qualified to vote. Probably, their motivation in joining the campaigns was not political idealism so much as local loyalty (to a village leader or his preferred candidate) and the excitement of the rowdy campaigning around the countryside—in addition to the money that candidates distributed in payment for the services of the *sōshi.*

In the case of Aoki's campaign, both sides were running for the Liberal Party, so the *sōshi* were recruited based not on party but on personal loyalty. Aoki was a local figure, and it was natural for the hamlets of Aihara village to support him.

On September 30, 1896, Aizawa was approached by a local organizer to become involved in Aoki's campaign. Aoki was frantically mobilizing local support, sending out rickshaws by the dozen to pick up local notables and take them on campaign-related missions. On

October 7, for example, Aizawa's brother Yasuemon was picked up by rickshaw and taken to Hachiōji to work on persuading a voter there to come over to Aoki's side. Meanwhile, the two Ushikubo family heads had gone (in rickshaws sent by Aoki) to make sure their relatives across the Sakai River would vote for Aoki.

Early on the morning of the eleventh, a message came from Aoki requesting the support of a party of young men from Hashimoto. Aizawa immediately conveyed the news to his cousin Jungorō, as well as a number of other young villagers from leading families. Each of these called on his friends in the village, and in no time they had rounded up a group of forty young villagers. One of them, Mankichi, broached a keg of sake in his garden, and then the young men set off for Aoki's house. Jungorō was appointed their general. On their way, they were met by a messenger from Aoki's younger brother Genjirō, who had instructions to guide them instead to the house of Hayashi Soeshige, a local campaign organizer in Koshino village. Hayashi sent some of the Hashimoto *sōshi* on to Hachiōji to help staff the campaign office there, while the other twenty-four, including Aizawa and Jungorō, stayed the night at Hayashi's house.

The next morning they set off at five for Ochiai village, where they went the rounds of the voters, asking them to vote for Aoki. At nine they returned to their headquarters at Hayashi's house. They had a big breakfast, then set off again to campaign with voters to the west of the village. They returned to the Koshino campaign office at noon, and stood guard there until three in the afternoon.

The next morning, the Hashimoto *sōshi* were sent to campaign in Tama village. Aizawa and Hayashi's brother Kakutarō visited a house in the hills behind the village, where they met a party of twenty villagers. There, they handed out bean cakes and talked to the local voters, "with excellent results." But then, word suddenly came that a group of *sōshi* from the opposing camp was approaching the house. The owner urged them to leave by the back door. Aizawa remonstrated at first, but in the end discretion was the better part of valor, and Aizawa and Hayashi slipped away. On emerging from the house, Aizawa saw twenty *sōshi* from the opposing side approaching with a roar of cheers. Quietly, they slipped back to their headquarters at the Hayashi residence.

The Hashimoto *sōshi* drifted back in during the afternoon, increasingly bedraggled as a steady rain set in (although the campaign manager sent out to all corners of the village to borrow umbrellas, all that most of the *sōshi* had to ward off the rain were their straw farmer's hats). In the evening the whole party set off back to Aoki's house, where they stayed the night.

Aoki lost the election on October 17, but on the twenty-first an envelope arrived from two of Aoki's local organizers, containing ¥12 to be used to buy sake to thank the *sōshi* supporters from the village. A few days later, on November 13, the villagers received an additional ¥30 from Aoki himself. It seems they were to be paid at least at the going rate for day laborers for their contributions to Aoki's campaign.

THE MANTLE OF RESPONSIBILITY

By the middle of the 1890s, the new village administrative system had become well established in Kanagawa prefecture. The villagers no longer referred to Hashimoto as a "village" *(mura)*, but as a "hamlet" *(ō-aza)* within the larger village of Aihara. The status of the hamlets was ambiguous. They retained some important areas of independence: for example, most retained at least some common land as a source of resources or income, most had their own "village" shrines with independent tutelary deities, and most had some form of local authority, usually an elected committee of leading families, who bought their place by financing the major undertakings of the hamlet community. But they had no formal status as political entities, nor in the case of Aihara was there a fixed system of hamlet representation in the village government. Instead, the mayor had to do his best to ensure that the composition of the village council and its subordinate committees balanced the interests of the hamlets. Members of the village council were certainly not supposed to put hamlet interests in front of village interests. But the ambiguities inevitably led to strains that, during the course of Aizawa's long service as deputy mayor and then mayor, were occasionally to flare up into real crises.

In December 1896 Aizawa Kikutarō was elected by the village council to the post of deputy under the village's long-serving mayor, Kiryū Zōbei. There were two deputy mayors according to the village's rules of governance. They were elected by the council of eight prominent villagers, who in turn were elected by a two-tier electoral system in which most, but not all, villagers had the opportunity to vote. Tier one, which elected four of the village councilors, consisted of the 15 percent of villagers who collectively paid half of the total tax burden of the village. Tier two, which elected the other four, consisted of the remaining voting members of the village community—males over twenty-five with over two years' residence in the village, who paid ¥2 or more in national taxes. The system gave wealthier villagers a significant political advantage in selecting their favored candidates. Aizawa's brother Yasuemon had been elected under this system earlier in the decade.

Why would Aizawa undertake what turned out to be onerous duties, when he was already financially secure and busy with his own business and farming projects? Service to the village community was, as it always had been, a necessary companion to the privileges enjoyed by the Aizawa family. It seems that Yasuemon was more attuned to the life of cultured leisure that his income afforded, so it was left to the younger brother to take on the burden of family service. Of course, this service was in itself a two-way street: as deputy mayor and later as mayor, Aizawa had considerable influence in the direction of village affairs, in which he could be counted on to support his family's interests.

It took Aizawa a year or so to settle down into his new position. It is clear from the early period that he found the job burdensome. His starting salary was derisory—only ¥2.50 a month (though this was raised to ¥5 on May 29, 1897). And the duties were clearly heavy. The biggest difficulty in the administration of Aihara village was the village's distance from the county office, in Fujisawa. A trip to Fujisawa was a major undertaking. Aizawa's first such trip was on April 9, 1897. Waking up before dawn, he took a rickshaw on the eight-kilometer journey to Hachiōji, and caught the 8:06 train to Shinjuku, changing trains and traveling on to Shinagawa (he traveled in the company of two fellow villagers). After lunching with his companions in Shinagawa, he caught an early afternoon train to Fujisawa, arriving at 2:30. On this particular occasion, he managed to turn the trip at least in part into a pleasure outing. On his return from Fujisawa to Tokyo, he stopped at the officer cadet school, where two villagers were enrolled. The cadets gave him a tour of the school, showing him an imperial throne that was housed there. Afterward, Aizawa went to meet another military villager, Lieutenant Yoshikawa Iwatarō, with whom he drank sake and stayed the night. And the next morning he stopped at Koganei on his way home to enjoy the cherry blossoms.

But in June, Aizawa went to Fujisawa on the second (traveling by rickshaw all the way, a seven-hour journey) and returned the next day, only to have to go there again on the seventh—this time leaving home at 4:00 A.M. and catching the train from Hachiōji. This trip seems to have worn him out, and from June 10 to June 26, he did not go to the village office once (he was sick with a cold from the thirteenth to the fifteenth, and he was busy with silkworm cultivation the rest of the time).

Aizawa did in fact try to quit twice in his first three years as deputy mayor. The first time, in July 1897, he felt overwhelmed by his job on the village health committee in the midst of a dysentery epidemic—Aizawa was expected to personally visit the houses of contagious patients and supervise their disinfection. The second time, in March 1899, he sent in his resignation because the village council overturned his decision to pay ¥30 in medical expenses incurred by a sick villager in a neighboring village hospital (Aihara did not yet have its own clinic), forcing Aizawa to pay the money out of his own pocket. In each case, Aizawa was persuaded back by delegations of leading villagers, and after his second return, he remained in village office as deputy mayor and mayor for the next twenty years.

Aizawa's duties as deputy mayor reflected the role of the village administration in both local and national affairs. He divided his time between tax collection duties, agricultural promotion activities, education, conscription, and health and hygiene. The village was responsible for the collection of all taxes—village, prefectural, and national. Paying taxes had always been an immutable duty of Japan's farmers—part and parcel of the cultivation of land. The national tax was only a part of the burden. The village of Aihara depended to a great extent on local taxes for its finances. For example, in 1902, ¥4,900 of Aihara's total expenses of ¥7,500 came from the regular village tax (for an average of about ¥9 per family); less than ¥100 came from government subsidies; and the remainder came from other sources within the village—primarily donations from wealthy residents and special taxes on villagers. This money was used for education (¥4,200), staff and office expenses (¥1,050), hygiene (¥350), road works and other construction (¥350), as well as miscellaneous expenses of about ¥1,400.[2] These miscellaneous expenses were often related to health emergencies: during the 1890s Aihara had several outbreaks of dysentery, forcing the village to spend a large amount of money on disinfection and other prevention measures.

In spite of its cost-saving intentions, the implementation of the new amalgamated village system resulted in sharply increased taxes for villagers. With the introduction of that system, the prefectures transferred many services—such as road maintenance—to the villages, without offering any financial compensation. The continued improvements in educational facilities also greatly increased village expenses: for example, Aihara's spending on education increased from ¥619 in 1890 to over ¥4,000 a year in the early 1900s. Moreover, a law of 1901 prohibited villages from charging school fees—which had previously contributed a portion of the school budget. Overall, Aihara had to increase its budget by more than 500 percent between 1892 and 1902, from ¥1,200 to ¥7,500.[3]

The basic village tax was the *chikawari* or proportional land tax, based on the same land valuation system used for the national land tax. But villages were forced by law to limit this tax to no more than 20 percent of the national land tax. This was seldom enough to meet the financial needs of the village. Aihara supplemented its tax income by taxing local businesses, but business taxes were also limited by government-imposed ratios. The remaining needs were met by assessing a special "household tax" (*kobetsuwari*, also known by the traditional name of *kosūwari*). The village authorities were very hesitant to impose new village taxes, in the knowledge that many poorer villagers were hard-put to pay their regular taxes. But in most years they were forced to make such an assessment. In 1891, for example, Aihara charged its villagers a household tax ranging from ¥0.23 for the poorest villagers to ¥8.06 for the wealthiest. Altogether, the village raised ¥340 through the tax.

The village administration was responsible for collecting village, prefectural, and national taxes, and delivering the latter to the county office in Fujisawa. Through the early 1900s, this entailed physically carrying the money to Fujisawa, although by the end of the Russo-Japanese War it was becoming more common to send the money by bank transfer. Because it was responsible for collection—including forcible collection from late- or non-payers—Aihara's role was not so different from that of Tokugawa era villages, which were held collectively responsible for the villagers' tax contributions. Collecting the taxes was by no means a gentle activity—especially the household taxes, which were imposed even on very poor villagers. For many, the taxes—particularly if they had accumulated back-taxes—were an impossible burden, as onerous as unpaid debts to landlords or money-lenders. And the village had to resort to similar methods—the threat of foreclosure, and actual foreclosure—to collect. For those who were seriously delinquent, the village had to resort to seizure (*sashiosae*) of the villager's property. Aizawa spent a part of his work time knocking on the doors of delinquent taxpayers, even as he spent his personal time accosting delinquent debtors.

As deputy mayor, Aizawa was also deeply involved in the expansion and consolidation of the village school system. Shortly after Aizawa took up his post as deputy mayor, the village council resolved to build a central elementary school for the entire village and fold the existing hamlet schools into it. The school was to be built on a much grander scale than any of the existing hamlet schools. In order to turn the plan into reality, the village leadership had to deal with a host of issues, from choosing where to locate the school to purchasing an appropriate plot of land, designing the school buildings, and financing the entire project.

After some initial negotiations, the councilors decided to build the school in Hashimoto. Even with the nod to Aihara in the naming of the village, Hashimoto with its location on a major communications route remained the natural choice as lead hamlet within the village. The problem of how to obtain a suitable plot of land was solved by the Aizawa family: Yasuemon owned a suitable plot near the center of the hamlet, which he was willing to make available to the village on a long-term lease on favorable terms. The village also rented an adjacent plot from another landowner to make up the needed space.

Because the school was in Hashimoto and on family-owned land, Aizawa's involvement in the school was particularly close. He undoubtedly took a personal pride in its completion as a project that would redound to the credit of his family. Aizawa was, for example, closely involved in the design of the school buildings, which he and the mayor mapped out in general, before handing them on to an expert draughtsman provided by the county government. The school was much larger than its predecessor. It contained both a regular elementary school (now called Aihara Elementary School) and a higher elementary school. Combined, the schools would offer six years of education to a growing student body.

Even with its greatly increased size, the school could not house all of the eligible children in the village. The existing Hashimoto elementary school was closed down and its pupils sent to the new school. But Oyama, Aihara, and Hara Shinden retained their existing schools, in which they offered schooling from the first through third grades. The village purchased the land and buildings from the hamlets, and—in the case of Oyama and Aihara—refurbished the school buildings. For the fourth grade, all students from throughout the village attended Aihara Elementary, and those with the ambition and family resources continued at the school for the higher elementary curriculum.[4] The school opened in April 1892, with Zama Shinjirō as its principal.

Another duty of Aizawa as village official was the creation and support of the village Agricultural Association. The creation of such associations throughout Japan was a major initiative of the Ministry of Agriculture and Commerce from the mid-1890s. In response to this policy, Kanagawa prefecture, Kōza county, and Aihara village all created their own agricultural associations in 1895. The mission of the Aihara association was to provide a communal outlet for the purchase and sale of agricultural products, as well as to promote agriculture through the dissemination of knowledge, utilizing in particular the research and extension services of the national Japan Agricultural Association. This was not so different from Aizawa's own activities as an enlightened farmer. However, in practice the Agricultural Association acted to some extent as a tool of government. Membership was made compulsory for those farming more than one hectare of land in 1899. The national association, with the support of legislation sponsored by the Ministry of Agriculture and Commerce, increasingly regulated the organization of farming activities in villages—with the eventual creation of hamlet level "industrial associations" charged with cooperative activities such as providing credit to farmers and the creation of "five-man groups" (goningumi) charged with a variety of block-level responsibilities (see chapter 4).

Aizawa's other main concern as a village official was health and hygiene. In some ways, Aihara village was comparatively blessed in terms of medical facilities—the village had three doctors, while many villages had to get by with none—but still the pages of Aizawa's diary are strewn with early deaths. The causes were many: tuberculosis, beriberi, typhoid, diphtheria, venereal disease, and smallpox, to name a few. In spite of their heavy toll, there was little the village administration could do about most of these (smallpox was kept under control by twice-annual vaccination drives, administered by the village). However, the village authorities—with prefectural support—took vigorous measures when confronted with epidemics of contagious diseases such as measles and dysentery, which periodically ravaged the village.

One such outbreak occurred in 1897. On August 5 Aizawa wrote in his diary: "The dysentery is spreading widely—very busy." On the thirteenth he wrote: "At home. Today, once again no tenants brought their payments. The dysentery epidemic has made everyone scared to leave their houses. No one is rearing silkworms either [this was the time for the fall rearing], so many people have empty purses." Aizawa, too, would doubtless have preferred to stay home. But his duties forced him out. On August 14, "Although I feel under the weather, a messenger from the village office came to fetch me, and I had to act as chairman of the Village Council."

On August 25 Aizawa wrote: "The dysentery epidemic is in full swing. Up to yesterday, there were forty-three patients in Oyama hamlet, twenty-five in Aihara, and eleven each in Shinden and Hashimoto, for a total of ninety patients. Of these, fifteen have already recovered, but fifteen have died. In Oyama, the number is likely to increase still further." The village had no in-patient clinic, so victims had no choice but to suffer and die at home. The village's four-member hygiene committee was going round the village every day disinfecting the houses of patients and inspecting others for cleanliness, together with Dr. Yajima. But the disease raged on unabated. The committee set up three command posts, in the village office and at the temples in Aihara and Oyama. They hired five or six workers every day to help disinfect houses and burn the infected feces of the victims. In addition, the prefecture dispatched two policemen to the village to help with inspections. Aizawa notes that the cost to the village was at least ¥10 per day.

The infections continued and by the beginning of September they reached 120. By this time, the village's plight was receiving attention from throughout the prefecture. On September 3 the governor himself arrived in Aihara, together with the head of the Jūzen Hospital, the prefecture's chief health inspector, the county chief, the county secretary, and the police chiefs from Fujisawa and Kamimizo. As a result of their visit, the village resolved the following week to build an infirmary for patients with infectious diseases. The facility, a seventy-four-square-meter building placed amidst wheat fields in the Hachigafuchi area of Hashimoto, was completed the following year.[5]

Village officials met several times to discuss what to do about the cost of the epidemic. The village turned to the county for help, and on December 18 two county officials came to Aihara to discuss possible compensation. Early the following year (March 23, 1898) the village assessed a special household tax of ¥0.35 for each taxable household "unit," to cover part of the cost of the epidemic. These units were the smallest division of the household levy. A poorer household would be taxed based on one unit, but wealthier households qualified for several units: Aizawa had to pay eight units' worth, or ¥2.80. It is likely that the village raised a little over ¥400 through this measure. This tax imposition, burdensome as it must have been for poorer villagers (¥0.35 represented about a day's wages for a farm laborer), shows how the amalgamated village was able to withstand emergencies better than the hamlets might have done on their own. For Oyama, the hardest hit hamlet, the dysentery epidemic might have been ruinous.

THE HOUR OF NEED

On January 13, 1904, Sato gave birth to her fifth child, a son. A week later, Aizawa registered the birth with the village office. His son's name was to be Yoshihisa. Aizawa was so busy with village business, and Sato still so weak from the birth, that the family delayed the traditional "seventh-night celebration" until January 23.

The birth of Yoshihisa found Aizawa in very different circumstances from when his previous children had been born. Now almost forty, Aizawa was a man of responsibility, busy with village affairs, with much less time for his family. But he was still able to enjoy the mature pleasures of a growing family, a substantial house and estate, and flourishing business interests. There were few clouds on Aizawa's horizon.

For Japan, the outlook was much more troubled. A decade after its successful war against China, Japan was still beset by insecurity on the Asian mainland. The political collapse of the Korean monarchy and its antiquated institutions of government had been hastened by Japanese aggression. A decade earlier China had been Japan's major rival for influence in Korea. Now, Russia posed an even greater threat. The decade following the Sino-Japanese War had seen an extraordinary expansion of Russian interests in Northeast Asia, starting with its lease of the Liaodong Peninsula in 1897. Just two years earlier, Russia had—with Germany and France—thwarted Japan's takeover of that same peninsula in the humiliating "triple intervention." During the following decade, Russia completed and opened sections of the Trans-Siberian Railway, connecting European Russia to East Asia. With the opening of the line through Manchuria connecting to Liaodong, Russian influence increased enormously, even as the Chinese government teetered on the brink of collapse. To the Japanese government, it was increasingly apparent that if Japan did not fill the power vacuum in Northeast Asia, then Russia would.

The tension came to a crisis point in the winter of 1903 and 1904, as negotiations over the withdrawal of Russian troops from Manchuria broke down. Russia had used its new transport network to send troops into China at the time of the Boxer uprising in 1900. In spite of pledges to remove them, it still had a sizeable army inside Chinese borders—considered by Japan to be an intolerable threat. Indeed, the sentiment that a war against Russia was inevitable had been growing for some time within the Japanese government.

The war began on February 9 with a surprise Japanese attack on Port Arthur, the main port of the Liaodong Peninsula. Although the war began auspiciously, with Japanese military successes fulminously reported in the Japanese press, Japanese citizens recognized from the outset that this was to be a much harsher and more demanding struggle than the war against China.

Aizawa's perspective was different, too. During the Sino-Japanese War he looked on as an enthusiastic supporter, but with no personal commitment or sacrifice required of him. Now, as a village official, Aizawa was called on to oversee his community's contribution to the war effort, providing soldiers, wheat and horses for the army, organizing funerals to bury the dead, and contributing money through the purchase of war bonds.

Altogether, Aizawa processed thirteen separate call-up orders during the fifteen months of the war, each order naming several conscripts. From surviving records, it appears that fifty-two villagers served in the military, with eight deaths. The call-ups were different from the regular conscription process, in which only a few medically fit twenty-year-olds were summoned each year for basic training. The call-up process summoned those villagers who had already completed their basic military service and were now in the reserves, or those who had been found unfit for front-line service in the conscription exams, but were now required for support services such as transport or supplies. The pool of eligible villagers was thus far larger than it was in any given year for regular conscription.

For Aizawa, the call-ups required rapid processing of the paperwork needed to deliver each conscript to his regiment. The call-up order might arrive at any time of the day or night, and Aizawa had to drop everything to process it immediately. In fact, the orders frequently arrived in the dead of night. One reason for this might be that they were sent from the county headquarters in Fujisawa by runner (Aihara was still not connected to the telegraph network, and the materials were considered too urgent for the regular post), who would take seven hours to cover the distance between Fujisawa and the village office in

Hashimoto. Another might be that midnight call-ups made it harder for the conscript to flee—for, as we will see, there was a strong element of coercion in the nation's cooption of villages and villagers into the war effort.

Shortly after the processing of each call-up order, the village would give the conscript soldiers a send-off. Since this was a semiofficial occasion, Aizawa usually attended. In most cases, the send-off included a brief ceremony at one of the village shrines, followed by a procession of friends, well-wishers, schoolchildren, and volunteers from the Women's Patriotic Association, part or all of the way to Hachiōji station. Close relatives would accompany the conscript on the train, often as far as his barracks.

While there was celebration in the raucous send-offs given by the village to its departing soldiers, there was also a strong element of sympathy. Like many villages, Aihara set up a fund to provide financial support to conscripts and their families. On several occasions, Aizawa supplemented the money provided by the village relief fund with personal gifts. On January 24, 1905, for example, the village fund gave a departing soldier, Kiryū Takesaburō, a gift of ¥5. Aizawa and a dozen others pooled funds to make an additional gift of ¥7.50 (Aizawa's share was ¥0.50). Later that same day, Aizawa went to another send-off, for Matsuura Aisaburō (the same Matsuura whom Aizawa had sent off to fight in the China war ten years earlier). On this occasion, Aizawa donated ¥0.30.

Contemporary records and subsequent scholarship widely attest to the hardship the war caused the rural lower classes. The Russo-Japanese War took a total of eighty-one thousand lives—perhaps twice that number were wounded, many of them crippled. A high proportion of these casualties were village laborers or small-scale farmers (whether owner-tenant or tenant), who tended to be physically strong (hence more likely to pass the physical), less eligible for exemption or deferment, and, due to their lack of specialized skills, more likely to be serving in the front-line infantry.

Removal of an able-bodied man from a tenant farmer family meant loss of income and loss of manpower for the all-important cultivation of crops. The majority of tenant farmers supplemented their farm work with paid labor of one sort or another. A day laborer at the lowest echelon of village society could expect to receive from ¥0.30 to ¥0.50 a day in addition to meals. By contrast, the army paid only ¥3 per month to its conscripts. This was not even enough to cover the expenses of barracks life. Ayase village in the neighboring county to Aihara commented in a 1903 report: "It is very hard indeed for those left behind by the conscript to continue the work of the house without trouble. Moreover, it is necessary to send to each conscript a minimum of ¥30 per year in spending money. In spite of the fact that the household is short handed and its income declines, they must pay these expenses. Truly it is hard for them."[6] Many conscripts had heavy obligations: the payment of rent to landlords, debts incurred by themselves or by their parents, wives and children to feed, and parents to care for. To be taken away from their work was indeed a severe hardship. Through the 1890s available records indicate that large numbers of conscripts— upward of six thousand a year—fled rather than submit to conscription. In 1897 a total of forty-eight thousand conscripts were on the run from the military authorities.[7] Village families are known to have prayed at temples and shrines for exemption in the lottery that decided who actually served in the military (Aizawa's family was no exception). By the time of the Russo-Japanese War, outright evasion was probably comparatively rare—there is certainly no mention of it in the diary. But there were many reports of cheating by men, both rural and urban, who tried to beat the physical exam by various forms of self-injury. A popular ruse was to inflict damage on one's right index finger—a relatively light wound for the victim, but effective in making him unable to shoot a rifle. Others rubbed tobacco juice in their eyes to imitate trachoma or drank soy sauce to imitate a weak heart.[8]

The village also responded dutifully to the call to buy war bonds. These bonds were one of several government initiatives to mobilize savings in support of the war (others included drives for the donation of materials and money, and extensive tax increases).[9] The villagers of Aihara contributed between ¥4,000 and ¥5,000 to each of the six bond issues. Although this represented an average cumulate investment of over ¥30 per household in the village, actual investments varied widely depending on economic circumstances. In the first bond issue, for example, the Aizawa family alone invested ¥500.

Undoubtedly the villagers' purchases of war bonds were motivated in part by patriotism and the desire to support the war effort. But there were other factors. One was the economic incentive: although not on a par with the 10 percent dividends offered by railways and other modern companies, the bonds offered attractive returns for a gilt-edged security (the return, including discount, was around 6 percent for the first three issues, slightly higher for the next three). Another, and perhaps more significant, motivation was the system of quotas that was widely used throughout rural Japan. Prefectures assigned fund-raising quotas to county governments, and the counties in turn assigned quotas to villages. Villages would then divide up their quota among hamlets, and even among neighborhoods. Villagers were motivated to contribute so as not to bring shame on their neighborhood or force their neighbors into taking on higher burdens.

The system of quotas was also used to press villagers to make "voluntary" contributions to the war effort. On April 23, 1905, for example, the county chief arrived in Aihara to request the village to contribute money to a "volunteer fleet" (giyūkantai) of warships. He assigned the village a quota of ¥860. As deputy mayor Aizawa had to divide this quota up between the hamlets of Aihara; then, as Hashimoto's leading citizen, he had to ask for funds from the villagers of his own hamlet, which was to contribute ¥156. The village's quota eventually contributed to the purchase of a warship, launched after Aizawa became mayor in 1908.

In addition to the summoning of conscripts and the requests for financial contributions, the military authorities, through the county seat in Fujisawa, also called on the villagers of Aihara to provide food for the army. In August 1904 the county authorities commanded Aihara village to furnish an overall requisition of 543 koku (a measure of volume, equivalent to about sixty-one metric tons) of wheat for military consumption, at a fixed rate of ¥3.375 per half-koku bale (the market price at this time was about ¥5.50 per bale). On Sunday August 14, while the villagers were celebrating the Bon Festival, the members of the village council met in the early evening, and agreed on the quotas to be met by each hamlet. Hashimoto's share was to be 162 bales of fifteen kan (56.25 kilograms) each, with two bales taken to be equivalent to one koku. That same evening, Aizawa used the occasion of a Bon Festival celebration at his house to consult with other leading members of the hamlet. They agreed to ask the farmers of the hamlet for quotas ranging from half a bale (about 28 kilograms) to fifteen bales (about 845 kilograms). Aizawa's own quota was to be six bales (about 340 kilograms).

During the following week Aizawa made the rounds of the hamlet, agreeing on quotas with farmers and inspecting the wheat to be delivered. In addition to verifying the quality of the cut wheat, Aizawa also supervised its baling. With the help of a pair of hired laborers, Aizawa verified the weight of each bale, and then inserted a wooden tag certifying its inspection. On August 26 the county secretary arrived in the village to inspect the wheat ready for delivery. On the twenty-ninth and thirtieth, the villagers delivered their quotas to the railway station at Hachiōji. Aizawa hired a driver to take his quota, but many villagers carried their own over the mountain pass to Hachiōji. Aizawa comments in his August 28 entry: "All the villages around here have many loads to haul, and for the most part people are traveling at night when it is cooler. Every night, people have been on the main road without pausing to sleep, hauling loads with hand carts or horse carts."

Unlike the fulsome outpourings he penned during the months of the Sino-Japanese War, Aizawa's comments on the conflict are surprisingly reticent. Aizawa does not once mention the emperor during the entire nineteen-month span of the war. Indeed, there are very few comments overtly celebrating the war effort. On the occasion of the fall of Port Arthur on January 3, 1905, Aizawa contented himself with the brief and rather clichéd comment: *medetashi medetashi* (oh, happy event!). Aizawa greeted the signing of the Portsmouth Treaty ending the war with the comment: "Unsatisfactory conclusion. The distress of the people knows no bounds." Aizawa is no doubt referring to popular demonstrations over the meager gains secured by the treaty—the worst incident of rioting in two decades. It is hard to interpret Aizawa's silence on the progress of this conflict that was so vital to Japan's imperial future. Was he just too busy with his official activities? Yet he found time to comment at length on the ill consequences of the war for the village and national economy. Was he, then, critical of this conflict in a way that he had not thought to be a decade earlier? Was he resentful at the demands it made on him and on his fellow-villagers? In spite of his participation in official activities such as conscription and fund-raising, Aizawa seems to have retained a healthy skepticism, based in large part on his pessimistic assessment of the financial consequences of the war.

On August 26, 1904—six months into the war—Aizawa comments at some length on those financial consequences:

> Financial affairs are out of order. This is the result of the military expenditures for the Russo-Japanese War; in addition, the silk industry is not doing well, and many farmers are abandoning agriculture. Food and clothing are daily becoming more luxurious, while people neglect their fundamental source of livelihood. Concern for others is disappearing, and people don't take seriously the need to repay their debts. Tenants use what they make from the fields they rent simply to feed themselves, and if that is not enough, they borrow more as a stop-gap measure, thinking that they can put off repaying both sets of debts until sometime in the

future. The wealthy thus tend to be on their guard, while the poor do not yet seem to have awoken to the reality of the situation. People have got into the bad habit of not keeping to what is proper to their station. It is said that the more developed the country, the greater the gap between rich and poor. Japan seems to be on the path to becoming a developed country, and the gap between rich and poor is sure to expand rapidly.

As a landlord and fellow-villager, Aizawa apparently both commiserated with the poorer classes for their declining livelihood and lamented what he perceived as their declining morality. His comments show a dim awareness of the strains imposed on the village community by the financial inequities within the village. However, Aizawa chose to blame these strains on the war, on tenants, and even on modern "civilization." He does not seem to have had a clear understanding of the enormous hardships imposed on tenant families by the landlord system itself.

More than anything, it was rising taxes that prompted Aizawa to make gloomy comments in his diary. In response to the vast expenses of the war, the government introduced consumption taxes for salt and tobacco, and increased them for soy sauce and a variety of other consumer goods. In addition, the government increased the land tax. On January 30, 1905, Aizawa comments: "The house tax has increased by 2.5 percent from 5.5 percent, making a total of 8 percent. The tax on miscellaneous land has increased by 2.5 percent from 3 percent, making 5.5 percent. It is an enormous burden. Until last year the total of national land tax, village tax, village land tax supplement, and other taxes was around ¥10 for every ¥100 in land value. But this year it has increased to ¥15." An annual tax of ¥15 on ¥100 of land value sounds like an enormous amount, but the land appears to have been undervalued for tax purposes by a factor of four to five—thus, the tax was equivalent to about 3.3 percent of the market value of the land.[10]

Aizawa's righteous tone is a little self-serving, perhaps, in the light of his response to the tax increases. On January 30, 1905, Aizawa and the handful of other landlords in Hashimoto village—including his elder brother and his Ushikubo relatives—met in the Tankōji Temple to form the Hashimoto landlords' association. The manifesto of the association attributed the problems landlords were facing not to the war, but to tenants:

Recently there has been a tendency to increasing division between landlords and tenants. There are many reasons for this, but we may say that one reason is the lack of sincerity on the part of the tenants. As a result, the administration of the village is suffering, and agricultural production is declining, and thus our economic strength is becoming weaker. We have arrived at the point where we can not endure our anxiety. . . . The landlords can not take their duty lightly or forget their sincere desire to protect the land that they love . . . . The truth is that the relationship between landlords and tenants has a strong impact on the productivity of the land, and clearly we must improve it. Thus, we believe that a land-lords' association is necessary, and we have created this plan to present for the approval of the county Agricultural Association and the prefectural Agricultural Association.

The first action of the Hashimoto landlords' association was to increase rents sufficiently to recoup the war-related tax increases. The landlords agreed that rents (which for the wheat and mulberry fields of Aihara were generally payable in cash) should be pegged at 30 percent of the assessed value of the land, or around 6 percent of its market value. In Aizawa's case, this represented as much a 50 percent increase: he records several contracts in previous years at 20 percent of assessed value. In the following weeks Aizawa began writing letters to his tenants announcing the increases. He found this a painful task: several times, he had to remind himself of the justification for the increase—the war and the tax increases.

The successful implementation of these rent increases relieved Aizawa of the burden of the government's increased tax levies. Aizawa's burden of tax as a percentage of total income actually *declined* during the years of the Russo-Japanese War, from 15.2 percent of income in 1903 to 13.4 percent of income in 1905. In 1906 some of the extraordinary taxes were reduced or removed, but Aizawa (and presumably the other landlords in Hashimoto) notably failed to pass on these reductions to the tenants. In 1906 Aizawa paid only 8.8 percent of his income in taxes.[11]

Indeed, for Aizawa personally, the economic consequences of the war were by no means all negative. The Aizawa family's investment of ¥500 in the first issue of Japanese government war bonds seems to have been made for economic as well as for patriotic reasons. The family could offer patriotic support in meeting the village quota, while at the same time investing some of its capital in a gilt-edged security with a fair rate of return.

Aizawa was also able to profit from the sale of his large wheat crop. Although the official price of wheat purchased through the government requisition of August 1904 was fixed at a rate of ¥3.375 per bale, Aizawa only had to contribute six bales to this requisition—less than

10 percent of his semiannual crop. The rest he could sell on the open market for ¥5 to ¥5.50 per 56-kilo bale—a price that was inflated due to the massive government demand for wheat, which forced private buyers to bid up the remaining supplies. Those villagers of Aihara who had surplus supplies of wheat were able to benefit handsomely from the high prices. On August 26 Aizawa commented in his diary: "Recently, the price of wheat has been high, and many farmers have been selling their wheat and buying Rangoon [i.e., inexpensive imported] rice. They can sell white wheat for about nine *shō* [roughly 10 kilograms] to the yen, and then use the money to buy eight and a half to nine *shō* of white rice. Since it's already refined, they don't have to pay for the hulling, and the measure is almost the same, so they are exchanging wheat for rice on an equal basis." Aizawa himself purchased imported rice several times during the course of the war, both "Rangoon rice" and "New Japan rice" from Taiwan, commenting each time on the wonderful cheapness of the rice, and on the high price of wheat that he was exchanging for it.[12]

THE RAILWAY COMES TO HASHIMOTO

Through the months of the Russo-Japanese War, the major concern of the leadership of Aihara village was as much local as it was national and international. A momentous opportunity had opened up for the village. Amidst a boom in railway construction throughout Japan, a company was formed in March 1904 to construct a railway line between Yokohama and Hachiōji.

This line had been under discussion for almost a decade. As early as October 1896, surveyors were in Aihara reviewing alternative routes. The favored route went right through some of Aizawa's fields, but what he and his fellow village leaders saw was the enormous benefits that a railway line, and more particularly a railway station, could bring to the village—not least of them a substantial increase in land values. After an initial flurry of consultations, the topic was dormant for the next several years, as the organizers in Yokohama struggled to raise financing for the project. The Yokohama Railway Company was by no means the only group to put forward a plan for constructing a line between Yokohama and Hachiōji. Indeed, there were at least five separate proposals for such a line in the preceding years. But the economic environment for railways was dramatically different compared to a decade earlier, and the railway company had excellent prospects for financing. The organizers received permission to form a company and build a line in December 1902, and began construction at the railhead in Higashi Kanagawa in June 1906.[13]

The line would run along the transport route for silk, connecting the mountainous areas north of Hachiōji through the cloth-producing communities around Hachiōji where the railway line was to begin, and on to the export market in Yokohama. The quantity of silk produced and transported along this route had been growing rapidly for the past fifty years, and there was still no sign of a decline. In addition, Hachiōji was emerging as a sizeable regional market, an economic focal point for the northwestern Kantō region.

The route of the railway line was clear in broad terms. It would follow the road that went through the market towns of Machida and Fuchinobe, through Hashimoto and up to Hachiōji. But the details could make or break a community. Although in earlier times some communities had been leery of allowing railway lines to go through them, nowadays most communities recognized the importance of being connected by modern transport systems.

The original plan for the railway, approved by the Home Ministry in 1902, called for a station in the town of Fuchinobe (six kilometers south of Hashimoto), followed by one in the hamlet of Aihara, in Sakai village. The Aihara station was only two kilometers north of Hashimoto. The hamlet (and, before that, the village) of Hashimoto had long enjoyed a prominent place on the silk route from Hachiōji to Yokohama. To its villagers, it was intolerable that they should be passed over for the chance to be connected to the transport medium of the future. Even before the creation of the Yokohama Railway Company, Hashimoto's leading villagers, led by Aizawa Yasuemon, had formed a committee to persuade the railway company to open a station in Hashimoto. Throughout 1904 and 1905, this group worked feverishly to develop a winning plan to ensure a station in Hashimoto. The leaders met almost weekly in the Zuikōji Temple. Sometimes these meetings were to discuss hamlet or village strategy; sometimes they were to host representatives of the railway company, who visited frequently to survey land, draw up detailed maps, and negotiate terms with the village leadership.

Ultimately, Hashimoto had to offer to underwrite virtually the entire cost of the station. Early in the negotiations, Aizawa Yasuemon offered to donate the large parcel of land that would be needed for the station. The preferred location was in the midst of the mulberry fields to the southeast of the traditional village center. But that on its own was not enough. The railway company also demanded a large donation toward the cost of constructing a station building. The villagers agreed to donate ¥1,000.

With these concessions from the hamlet leadership, the railway company agreed to add a railway station in Hashimoto. The station in neighboring Aihara would remain, so the line would have two stations barely two kilometers apart—much closer proximity than was normal for railways of the period. On September 24, 1905, the governor of Kanagawa prefecture and the chief of Kōza county came to Hashimoto to inspect and confirm the choice of location for the new Hashimoto station. The location was still in cultivation, and all around there were nothing but mulberry fields. The inspection party repaired to the shade of a nearby persimmon tree and came to a final agreement on the site.[14]

On February 6, 1906, the village leaders signed a contract with the railway company committing to donate the land and make the cash contribution. The village of Aihara appears to have made gifts in excess of ¥5,000 to the railway company in order to secure the privilege of a station in Hashimoto. Most of this contribution came from Hashimoto. The wealthy villagers of Aihara and Shinden—the Ogawa and Hara families—had little incentive to contribute, so the weight of the burden of giving fell on the main families of Hashimoto—the Aizawa and Ushikubo.

A part of the contribution was in the form of cash. But the larger part seems to have been in the form of gifts of land, both for the station area and for the railway line itself. Aihara village appears to have purchased the land from its owners in both Hashimoto and neighboring Sakai village. The purchases from residents of Sakai amounted to almost ¥3,000, and those from Hashimoto villagers amounted to some ¥700 (presumably the Hashimoto sum was less because much of the land was donated). The village paid for the land by issuing promissory notes, at an interest rate of 7 percent and for a term of five years. The value of this transaction was included in a list of "gifts" to the railway through June (reported in a diary entry of November 21).

But it was the cash portion of the gift that was the real burden for the villagers of Hashimoto. On February 28 Aizawa borrowed the sum of ¥1,000 on behalf of the hamlet from the Zenshinsha of Ōshima village. Over the next several months, the villagers refinanced this loan again and again, at rates varying from 12 to 16 percent. On June 20 the leading villagers of Hashimoto borrowed ¥1,000 from Ogawa of Aihara, and repaid the Zenshinsha loan. Although the loan was only for a few days, Ogawa seems to have charged a rate of 16 percent annualized. The loan continued to hang over the Hashimoto villagers for the next several years. As late as 1909, the villagers were still continuing to refinance the loan, without any real prospect of getting it repaid. Indeed, in July 1913, Aizawa notes that the leaders of the railway initiative still owed a total of ¥2,089 to the Seya Bank for the railway station. Seven villagers were guarantors for the loan, including the two main families of Hashimoto (Aizawa and Ushikubo) as well as their branch houses (including Aizawa himself).

It is not clear what made the villagers think they could repay a loan for such a large amount of money, when there was no immediate—or even medium term—prospect of any direct income return on their investment. For them to have taken out month-to-month loans under these circumstances seems quite reckless.

The railway project was carried out in the name of Aihara, but it was really about Hashimoto. It was Hashimoto that was to benefit the most from the opening of the station, and it was Hashimoto that brought the commitment and the financial resources to make the transaction happen. The one-sided nature of the dealings around the railway underscores the tension within the village, twenty years after the amalgamation of its four constituent hamlets. On September 22, 1908, the notables of Hashimoto met in the Zuikoji Temple, to discuss sharing the burden of the railway station subsidy. The elite of Hashimoto felt that since the railway project was being carried out in the name of the whole village, the other hamlets should take on a heavier share of the financial burden. They resolved to demand a larger contribution from the other hamlets, and to back up their demand they made an extraordinary threat. If their demand was not met, Hashimoto would secede from the village.

It is hard to say how meaningful this threat might have been. Any attempt to break up the administrative village of Aihara would have had to gain the blessing of both county and prefectural authorities. It is likely that both county and prefecture would have exerted strong pressure on Hashimoto to change its mind, and the evidence is that such pressure was usually effective. Even as a symbolic threat, though, it is striking.

The elite villagers of Hashimoto also invested in the Yokohama Railway Company. The railway appears to have guaranteed them an allotment of shares at a favorable rate—apparently they were able to buy one hundred shares at the nominal rate of ¥6 per share, even though the market price of the shares had already risen to close to ¥15 per share.[15] But Aizawa also seems to have bought a few additional shares at the market rate: on July 10 he paid an intermediary from the company ¥29.50 each for shares with a nominal value of ¥12.50—a substantial premium, but Aizawa notes that even at that price the shares "have very good prospects."

Construction began on the Hashimoto section of the railway in early 1906. On July 8 Aizawa took two of his sons, Yoshihisa and Yasuo, to the railhead in Sakai village to watch the construction work. The railway was changing the landscape of Hashimoto indelibly. In November, Aizawa watched the iron bridge being built over the Sakai River, putting the finishing touch on construction in the area.

Finally, in the fall of 1908, the construction was finished and the railway ready to open. The big day was September 23, when service opened between Higashi Kanagawa (near Yokohama) and Hachiōji. It was a banner day, both for the railway and for the people of Hashimoto. The railway offered half-price tickets for its first ten days of operation, and "the trains were packed from morning till night" (Aizawa himself had received a free round-trip ticket valid till October 31, as well as a guide to famous places along the route, and a timetable and fare chart). The crowds were all the bigger because the twenty-third was a national holiday, celebrating both the fall solstice and the spirits of the imperial ancestors *(kōreisai)*. The initial schedule called for seven round trips per day, but in the first week the railway put on extra trains to accommodate the crowds of people who wanted to try out the new line. By this time, Aizawa was mayor of Aihara village, and in that capacity he went to the new Hashimoto station in the morning and delivered a message of congratulation to the president of the railway, Asada, and seven other executives who were stopping at all the stations along the route. Aizawa commented that "the area round the station was extremely crowded from morning till night." He also notes that several foreigners rode the train up from Yokohama, and got off at Hashimoto station, where they "walked off to the south."

The opening of the station was also big news for the local businesses. Early in 1908, the Naigai Bussan Company opened a new stone-built headquarters by the station, with its employees smartly decked out in *hanten* livery coats emblazoned with the *marusan* crest (the character for *san* [of Bussan] inside a circle). After the opening of the railway, the station area would become a central focus of the company's business, as it shifted to rail freight. Another trading company, the Nisshinsha, also opened in the station area, as did a large restaurant, the Daikokuya. The Naigai Bussan sent off its first consignment of freight on the first day of railway service: ten freight cars packed with lumber, to be unloaded in neighboring Tsukui county. Bussan also brought in loads of sugar, paraffin, salt, rice, and rice bran, and exported wheat, silk, sweet potatoes, and silkworm cocoons. The Nisshinsha also sent off a load by rail freight on the first day: three hundred bales of wheat, to be brewed into beer by a brewing company in Ōsawa village. Bussan celebrated its new incarnation with a lottery held on September 24 and a *kagura* drama staged the next day.

In front of the station, up to a dozen rickshaw pullers were drawn up, waiting to bid for the business of the incoming passengers. They were fighting for a limited business. The ¥0.80 round-trip train fare to or from Yokohama was equivalent to two days' wages for a farm laborer and was only within reach of the village elites and their business associates.

Aizawa himself rode the new railway line for the first time on October 1, when he took the train into Hachiōji to deposit village money in the bank, and to go shopping for a new silver watch for his eldest son, Shigeharu. After getting his alarm clock mended and buying an umbrella and a pair of *geta* clogs, Aizawa returned to Hashimoto by train in the early evening. The journey that had taken an hour and a half by rickshaw or on foot could now be accomplished in fifteen minutes.

Even more significant for Aizawa as a village official, he could now conveniently travel to the county seat in Fujisawa by train. He did so for the first time on October 3, leaving on the 7:45 train, changing at Higashi Kanagawa, and arriving in Fujisawa at 10:15 in the morning. The journey that had taken no less than six hours by train from Hachiōji or by rickshaw now took only two and a half hours. Aizawa was to benefit from this convenience more than most, as he made the trip to Fujisawa an average of three or four times a month for the next fifteen years.

In the end, Aizawa was not to own his shares in the Yokohama Railway for long. In 1910, as a part of its nationalization plan, the government leased the railway line, and in 1917 it purchased all the outstanding shares.[16]

CHAPTER 4

The Mayor of Aihara

1908–1918

MAYOR OF AIHARA

Since the creation of Aihara village in 1889, its mayor had been Kiryū Zōbei. Kiryū was from one of the leading families of what was now Aihara hamlet, and he was an experienced and capable administrator who enjoyed the respect of the entire village. He was also remarkably hale for his age. On February 2, 1906, at the age of seventy-one, the mayor walked the seven hours to Fujisawa rather than employ the more normal means of rickshaw or train from Hachiōji. In this gesture, we see a man who had reached adulthood during the feudal era.

But in late 1907, Kiryū became ill. In February 1908 he was hospitalized. When he returned, he knew that he was dying. On March 28 Kiryū took Aizawa aside during a quiet moment in the village office (the school principal was in the office but had gone to the bathroom, and Tamada Sukeroku was in the front room updating the register of houses) and told him: "As you know, I'm not well. I'm going to resign as mayor soon. I'd like you to be my successor."

It was not Kiryū's prerogative to select his own successor. The mayor was elected by the village council, who in turn were elected by qualified villagers. Since the council was composed of elite members of the village community, some of whom had strong views about the administration and direction of the village, there was potential for discord. But for an important decision like this, the mayor's responsibility was to ensure that consensus had been reached before the formal vote. Aizawa responded to Kiryū that he would need to see which way the council vote went, but that if the consensus was that he was the best person for the job, then "although it's a heavy responsibility, I know that I must be your successor."

Why did Aizawa, a wealthy man with a profitable estate to manage and a flourishing family that he loved (in 1906 Sato had borne the couple's fifth surviving child, a girl named Hanako), want to take on a burden like this? The diary offers no explanation, but we may assume that Aizawa felt a deep commitment to his village community, based on loyalty and a strong sense of public service, but also to some extent on self-interest. No one could better defend the interests of the landlord class than a landlord mayor. Similar considerations had motivated his ancestors to accept the position of village headman. Aizawa, a second son with a much smaller income than his brother, may also have found the regular salary appealing. In spite of his relative wealth, Aizawa continued to take money—even quite small sums—very seriously.

The election took place on April 6, the day after Kiryū handed in his formal resignation. All eight members of the council were present for the vote, including Aizawa. Aizawa records that seven members voted for him—presumably he either abstained or made a token vote for someone else. And so, at the age of forty-two, Aizawa Kikutarō became mayor of the village of Aihara, with a salary of ¥140 per year plus ¥65 in expenses.

Aizawa's first order of business was to properly recognize the retiring mayor. The village council voted to grant him a retirement gift of ¥100, payable from village funds. Concerned about the former mayor's declining health, Aizawa hastened to hand over the money to him, although this meant borrowing ¥65 of it from the village Agricultural Association. The village council also held a farewell party for Kiryū. Aizawa led the speeches, and rounded off the event by calling everyone to rise and shout "*banzai* for the Japanese Empire, *banzai* for Aihara village, and *banzai* for Kiryū Zōbei."

Coincidentally, the prefectural government announced on April 8 that Kiryū Zōbei was to be awarded the Order of the Rising Sun, seventh class, for his services during the Russo-Japanese War (1904–5). Aizawa, too, was commended, receiving the Order of the Rising Sun, eighth class, with white paulownia leaves. Aizawa traveled to Fujisawa to collect the award both for himself and Kiryū. The medals were presented at a ceremony at the county office. Aizawa was given the medals themselves, as well as an official commendation from the emperor, and a guide to wearing his medal.

Early the next year, on the occasion of National Founding Day (February 11), Aizawa gave a speech to the village council at which he summed up his aspirations as mayor:

> Today is National Founding Day, and it is also the twentieth anniversary of the opening of the Diet, so it is even more a joyful day. It goes without saying that as the organ of Aihara village, you participate in all the affairs of the village, great and small. As the village's central functionary, I will consult with you on many different matters, and I beg you to give me your advice and help me manage the affairs of the village smoothly. In particular, there are times when opinions will differ due to hamlet affiliations. But this will be very damaging, as outsiders will not see us as a single united village. Thus, I ask your advice as mayor, and although I am inexperienced, I will not hesitate in my work as mayor, and with your help we can look forward to the continued prosperity of the village.

. . .

Aizawa's comment on hamlet unity was prescient, as this was to be a key point of contention at times during his term as mayor. Among the most contentious issues was the question of shrine amalgamation. The Meiji government elevated Shintō to a central place in national policy shortly after the Meiji restoration. The reasons for this were complex, but they seem to have been grounded at least in the early stages in a desire, inspired by the popular "national learning" movement, to restore Japan's native traditions—including the supremacy of the emperor, who, as a supposed descendent of the sun goddess Amaterasu, occupied a unique position within the Shintō pantheon. Confusingly—given this desire to reassert native roots—the elevation of Shintō also accompanied the creation of a new "department of rites" in imitation of the Chinese government practices adopted by Japan in the seventh century.

By the end of the nineteenth century, Shintō had become a key tool in the organized efforts of the government to create a national cult centering on the emperor and Japan's imperialist mission. The transformation is visible in the pages of the Aizawa diary. As a younger man, Aizawa was relatively unconscious of "Shintō" as a religion in any organized sense. The shrine was an integral part of village life, for which the young men of the village in particular were responsible, maintaining the village *mikoshi* (portable shrine) and leading the annual shrine festivities, held in August or September. But after the beginning of the twentieth century, Aizawa begins going to the shrine with a much more self-conscious agenda: to pray on the occasion of national festivals or national crises, and to pay his respects to the imperial family.

This increasing emphasis on Shintō worship was in keeping with the policies of the Meiji state, which were aimed at creating a nation of citizens united through emperor-centered Shintō practice. This policy had its ups and downs—after an ambitious start, the government was forced to scale back its financial commitments to Shintō shrines due to budgetary exigencies. However, the Sino-Japanese War (1894–95) spurred renewed interest by the government in the uses of Shintō as an ideology of national unity and patriotism. By 1902, shrine priests all the way down to the village level were categorized as government officials *(hannin-kan),* and the state was once again providing financial subsidies to major shrines, and offering government support for certain village shrine ceremonies.[1]

In 1906, the government launched an ambitious program to consolidate the more than fifty thousand shrines in Japan's villages and hamlets into a much smaller number, under the slogan of "one village, one shrine." The official justification for this policy was the large number of dilapidated shrines in hamlets around the country—shrines with "broken sanctuary roofs and caved-in walls, compounds rank with weeds and piled high with leaves," and that had become "playgrounds for children . . . or . . . storerooms or repositories for night soil." Such run-down shrines were seen as antithetical to the feelings of reverence and respect that the government wanted to encourage in Shintō worship: feelings that would make villagers "spontaneously feel like bowing their heads in gratitude."[2] The merger movement also was a logical outcome of the village mergers of 1889: since hamlets were being encouraged to merge their identity into that of a larger village entity, the same could logically be proposed for shrines. The "one village, one shrine" movement was launched with considerable fanfare, but turned out to be one of the hardest of the government's village policies to implement. The idea was that in each village, a single shrine would be selected and the other village shrines would be merged into it. Their deities would be transferred to the main shrine through the physical relocation of their sacred repositories *(shintai)* in which the spirit of the deity was supposed to reside. The shrine buildings would be deconsecrated and were subject to destruction or sale, while the merged shrines' land and assets would become the property of the main shrine. The idea was that this transfer of assets (in addition to one-time gains from the sale of buildings or lumber on the merged shrines' land) would make the surviving shrines economically viable and able to maintain their facilities in perpetuity and without government assistance.

And indeed, in the general atmosphere of financial stringency following the Russo-Japanese War, reducing the overall expenses of shrine facilities and festivals was seen as a desirable end in itself. As one circular issued by officials in Mie prefecture urged, "any surplus funds [resulting from the mergers should] be put to practical use as resources for the advancement of local town and village self-government."[3] The proliferation of local festivals, in particular, was seen as inimical to the policy of savings and thrift being promoted by the government. As a Home Ministry official put it: "[as a result of hamlet festivals] over a period of one year, the number of days taken off from work amounts to quite a few. Considerable money, moreover, is expended on food and drink. . . . These expenses are not such as can easily be calculated, but their effect even on the national economy must surely be great beyond expectation."[4]

A further goal of the "one village, one shrine" movement was to increase village solidarity. In spite of the amalgamation of most Japanese villages in 1889 into larger administrative units, many Japanese villagers continued to feel loyal to their hamlets above their administrative village homes. The continuing tension between hamlet and village loyalties was described by Shibusawa Keizō as "one of the most serious problems of the age."[5] Shrine mergers were a measure to help reduce "the evil custom of independent hamlet authority."[6] As Bureau of Shrines chief Tsukamoto Seiji put it, "It is generally true that parishioners who hold the same *ujigami* [local shrine deity] in common are singularly bound by a strong sense of unity. As an abuse of this feeling, people are sometimes inclined to clash with each other simply because they have a different *ujigami* and belong to a different shrine parish. Indeed, there are many instances where a difference in parish districts has even exercised an exceedingly harmful influence on city, town, and village administration." If the hamlet shrines are merged into a single village shrine, "all of the people in that village are thereby parishioners of the same shrine. This, indeed, is the most favorable of all situations."[7]

For Kōza county, the successful implementation of the "one village, one shrine" policy was a matter of pride, and it was in the name of

Figure 13. Inari Shrine in Aizawa's garden

county pride that Aizawa, as mayor of Aihara, was asked to implement
the policy for his village. There were four major shrines in the village, one in each hamlet. This was in addition to several other, smaller
"informal" shrines, such as the Inari (fox god) Shrine that Aizawa himself had recently built in his garden.

Oyama and Shinden hamlets were readily persuaded to decommis-
sion and amalgamate their shrines (Tenpaku Shrine and Jinmei Shrine
respectively) with Hashimoto's Jinmei Shrine. Perhaps they were motivated by the saving of expense and effort, as they would no longer be
responsible for upkeep. Certainly in the case of Shinden, the small size
of the community must have made it burdensome to maintain a shrine,
and the shrine was anyway relatively new, so the hamlet would not be
giving up a centuries-old tradition. But the villagers of Aihara hamlet
were strongly opposed to giving up the independence of their shrine.
Both the county chief and the local police chief (based in Kamimizo
village) came to Aihara to try to persuade the recalcitrant villagers to
give up their shrine. But on the contrary, the villagers of Aihara began
raising money to defend their shrine's independence, and on July 3,
1910, Aizawa had to write to the county chief that a resolution of the

issue appeared impossible. The next day, the representatives of each hamlet's *uji* or deity met to discuss the issue. They issued a statement saying: "Since last year, we have had many discussions aimed at merging the shrines so that our one village has one shrine. But Aihara has continued to press for its independence, and so we are forced to merge only three shrines. Certainly from the point of view of village governance, one village and two shrines is undesirable. It is truly a shame that we were unable to achieve the goal of one village one shrine and now find ourselves in this position. But in the interest of village peace, we will settle the matter according to [Aihara's] wishes."

Aizawa found himself in the embarrassing position of having to officially inform the county leadership of his failure to implement their policy. He went to Kamimizo on July 5 and apologized personally to the police chief there, after thanking him for his efforts on behalf of the merger plan. Then, on July 10, he made a speech to twenty-two leading figures (he had invited fifty) of the three hamlets:

> The idea of shrine merger is based on imperial rescript. The Home Ministry also issued an edict to this effect, and the prefecture and counties followed. According to the guideline, the four shrines in our four hamlets should be merged into one. Since last year we have held endless negotiations, but Aihara insisted on its independence, and so we have no choice but to go ahead with merger of the three hamlet shrines. Needless to say, having one village and two shrines will have consequences for the peace of the village. Also this outcome is harmful to the intent of the policy. But in spite of all our efforts to impress this on Aihara, they are intransigent. And so we must go forward with a merger of three shrines. I ask you not to think of this as Aihara and then the rest, which is a strange way to think, but rather think that for now the three hamlets will merge, and then hopefully Aihara will enter in future.

The shrines to be merged donated all of their land, trees, and assets to the new shrine. In the case of Shinden's Hikawa Shrine, these amounted to virtually nothing. The hamlet was specifically allowed to retain ownership of its stone basin used for purification rites. Since the shrine was otherwise so lacking in assets, the villagers of Shinden agreed to contribute ¥100 in cash to the new central shrine in Hashimoto.

The new shrine would in fact be identical with the existing Jinmei Shrine in Hashimoto. But nominally, the Jinmei would be dissolved and recreated as the Jinmei Daijingū Shrine. The new shrine would be recapitalized through the sale of the timber it inherited from the other two hamlets, added to the cash donation from Shinden. Following prefectural rules, the shrine's festivals would be paid for out of interest on capital, with any deficit to come from donations from wealthy villagers. The shrine would also follow prefectural policy in keeping its buildings simple and not lavishing money on them.

The failure to merge all the village's shrines was a festering issue in Aihara politics for the next ten years. The county and prefectural authorities repeatedly urged the village to try again to convince Aihara to accede to the policy. At one tense set of negotiations in March 1912, the mayors of three neighboring villages, as well as a representative from the prefecture, and several other local notables acted as mediators between Aihara and the other hamlets, but to no avail—in spite of one marathon session that lasted all day and continued into the night until dawn. It was not until September 1918—after endless painful rounds of negotiations, mediated by everyone from friendly locals to the county chief—that Aihara finally agreed to be brought into the fold. Even then, a vocal minority consisting mainly of the young men who were custodians of the Aihara Shrine Festival remained bitterly opposed to the merger. On September 19, two days after the merger agreement was signed, six youths from Aihara cornered Aizawa in his office and pressed him with demands. In exchange for giving up its independence, they demanded that the village should build a new subsidiary shrine for Aihara, that would be "established forever as the hamlet shrine." The costs of the shrine should be borne by the other hamlets in the village. Aizawa commented in despair: "The young men of Aihara are strong-headed, and opposed to the other three hamlets. All they want to do is have things Aihara's way. With this kind of selfishness they just ask for whatever they want. As the mayor of Aihara, I can not allow that sort of thinking. And of course the other three hamlets are opposed, so things will certainly not go smoothly. Really, it is a heavy burden to have the job of being in the middle of this."

Overall, the national shrine merger policy could hardly be considered a success. In many cases, regional authorities pursued the directive with far less vigor than was shown by the Kōza county government. The number of village shrines declined by only 13 percent between 1903 and 1920 to around forty-five thousand (this compares with approximately twelve thousand villages in Japan, so close to four shrines remained per village). This was in addition to the sixty-six thousand remaining "ungraded" shrines—which might be anything from a small consecrated site in a villager's garden to an ancient untended sacred tree in the village or a small hamlet shrine.[8]

The delicate negotiations over the shrine issue highlight the tension that continued to exist between the administrative structure of the village and the hamlets that were its constituent parts. Village administrators took it for granted that influential political figures would represent the interest of their own hamlet above all, and Aizawa was constantly reminding them to act on behalf of the village as a whole, and not just to think of narrow hamlet interests. Nevertheless, the political structure was clearly a delicate balancing act, squaring off local interests with equity in hamlet representation. And Aizawa himself was not above playing the game—as when he commented on some of his fellow villagers from Hashimoto who had voted for a non-Hashimoto candidate that "all this is doing is helping other hamlets and giving demerit to our own."[9]

In 1907 the chief of Kōza county—acting apparently on his own initiative—brought up the subject of a further reorganization of village structure. He was concerned about the precarious finances of the villages of Kōza county, and he reasoned that further amalgamation might strengthen the villages' balance sheets. The county chief proposed to further amalgamate villages so that each village had at least one thousand households—which he considered the minimum level for self-sustainable village finances. The proposal opened up an extensive debate within Aihara village; but rather than promote further amalgamation, once the topic was opened up it seemed to encourage further fragmentation. Influential members of both Aihara and Hashimoto hamlets, frustrated at the political trade-offs they were making for the sake of "village unity," went on to discuss possible independence from the rest of the village (in the end the talks came to nothing, and Aihara village retained its existing boundaries until it was amalgamated into the city of Sagamihara in 1941).

. . .

Aizawa served as mayor of Aihara village during a period of sustained strengthening of the influence of national bureaucrats over the everyday lives of villagers. The government had a variety of objectives. On one hand, enlightened bureaucrats wanted to relieve some of the problems in the Japanese rural economy by spreading more efficient methods of cultivation and farm management. They reasoned that while the problems of landlord and tenant would not be solved in the near future, and while the government could not commit sufficient financial resources to rural development, farmers could without much expense be taught to use rational and scientific management techniques such as improved crop cycles, budgeting and bookkeeping, and home improvement projects such as "rationalized" kitchens.[10] On the other hand, the government needed the active cooperation of villagers to achieve its national and imperial goals of security and expansion. Villagers could contribute through feeding their savings into the national economy—hence the constant emphasis on thrift and the repeated "savings drives" aimed at small communities throughout Japan—and through enthusiastic support of national undertakings, including the many military campaigns undertaken by Japan in the first two decades of the twentieth century.[11]

To these ends, bureaucrats from the Home Ministry, the Education Ministry, the army, and the Ministry of Agriculture and Commerce launched a variety of initiatives aimed at strengthening government influence over the daily lives of villagers. Their approaches were various, and to some extent conflicting.[12] It is not surprising that the contradiction inherent in these approaches at times contributed to tension and conflict in village communities.

On one hand, the government launched a number of measures to create direct ties between hamlet organizations and the national community, sometimes bypassing the village administration in the process. For example, the government began to assert increasing control over the neighborhood groups, hamlet women's and youth groups, and the industrial associations created under the auspices of the village Agricultural Associations (see chapter 3). Hamlet youth groups were corralled under the umbrella of the Japan Federation of Youth Associations (Dainippon Rengō Seinendan), while women's activities were increasingly channeled into the orbit of national organizations like the Japan Patriotic Women's Association. This was founded in 1901 as a purely private organization, with the goal of offering support to wounded soldiers and to the families of the dead; however, its central organization soon came under heavy government influence. It received a powerful impetus from the Russo-Japanese War, and by the end of the war had spread to almost every town and village in Japan.[13] At first, it was primarily a middle- and upper-class organization—indeed, it was criticized by some as "a society to which you can not attend meetings if you do not possess a white-sleeved crested kimono."[14] But within the four hamlets of Aihara village it had nevertheless gained a membership of thirty-eight women by the time of the Russo-Japanese War. Each paid annual membership dues of ¥0.50, and during the war the women raised ¥70 to buy stomach-warmers *(haramaki)* for soldiers serving on the continent.

On the other hand, the government adopted a variety of measures to undermine hamlet autonomy and promote a sense of belonging to the administrative village. These included the shrine merger program, as well as some sporadic and relatively ineffective efforts to transfer hamlet common land to village ownership (these are never mentioned in the Aizawa diary, so may not have affected Aihara village). Bureaucrats also promoted village-level organizations such as the Agricultural Associations (discussed in chapter 3), Military Reserve Associations, and the Broadcast of Virtue Societies (Hōtokukai). The Military Reserve Associations (Zaikyō Gunjinkai) aimed to foster an *esprit de corps* among former servicemen once their military service was completed (the associations should not be confused with the army reserves, in which all ex-soldiers were obliged to serve for eight years). Their activities included a great deal of sake drinking under the auspices of honoring the war dead, army and navy day ceremonies, readings of the Imperial Rescript to Soldiers and Sailors, and farewell and welcome-back parties for those called to active service. They also offered a substantial volunteer contribution to the village, taking on leadership roles in the youth associations, and helping out with village labor projects, and in local emergencies such as fire and flood. Although the associations were usually led by prominent villagers (in the case of Hashimoto it was the school principal), soldiers with a meritorious service history played a leading role—regardless of their social status in the village.[15] The Broadcast of Virtue societies were originally village-level groups, dedicated to the teachings of the farmer-philosopher Ninomiya Sontoku. By the second decade of the twentieth century, they had coalesced into a national movement under heavy government influence. Aihara does not seem to have had an active Broadcast of Virtue society, though Aizawa and his friends were certainly sympathetic to its goals and activities.[16]

Several of these programs were promoted under the umbrella of the local improvement movement, a national initiative launched at the turn of the century to reform various aspects of the village economy and everyday life.[17] Its principle was to offer a structured approach, based on well-worn principles of "self-help" combined with a few modern management techniques, to help villages to solve their own financial and social problems. The movement encouraged villages to carry out detailed self-studies ("statements of village affairs," or *sonze*). The reports included overviews of the national significance of the improvement movement, often specifically linking it with Japan's imperialist mission; detailed surveys of the geography, population, agricultural and business activities, income and expenditures, and local customs of the village; analysis of particular village problems; and sometimes proposals for alleviating them.[18] Since improvement initiatives were ultimately at the discretion of the villages, the specific activities carried out under the explicit banner of "local improvement" varied considerably. In Aihara (which unfortunately did not carry out a *sonze*), the activities included relatively trivial ones, like the submission of local produce to shows and competitions arranged by the county Improvement Association, and one significant measure: the creation of a compulsory "five-family group" system, created under Aizawa's direction in late 1912. Most villages had had some system of neighborhood groups *(kumi)* in operation for decades, if not centuries. These were the basic cooperative units for collaborative activities such as irrigation, rice-transplanting, roof-thatching, and hamlet maintenance. At times over the years they had also been subject to close government control—the twentieth century initiative was actually nothing new. Under the initiative, five-family groups were closely regulated by the village, and they took on important new responsibilities such as volunteer labor, imperial observances, and the collective submission of village and national taxes. This last was particularly useful for Aizawa, who as tax day approached had the unenviable job of dunning nonpayers and threatening them with anything from public shame to the forcible appropriation of their property.

For the central government, the five-family groups, youth groups, women's groups, and hamlet "industrial associations" were a direct channel into the administration of daily life at the neighborhood level. In subsequent decades, they became an essential tool in the system of government controls over food production, rationing, savings drives, "volunteer" labor, and other aspects of daily life in time of war. It is not surprising, then, that this movement originally billed as a technocratic initiative to improve economic problems in the villages, has come to be seen as a first step in the creation of a system of "Japanese-style fascism" in the countryside.[19]

. . .

To be a Japanese villager was to be called on to support Japan's military. Such support came in various forms—contributions of money or materials, requisitions of food or horses, financial assistance to soldiers called up for military service (or their families), military service through conscription, participation in rallies, or mailing letters of support and "comfort bags" to serving soldiers.

Aihara was perhaps called on more than most. Not only was its major food crop, wheat, in demand by the military; it was also located near the northern edge of the Kantō Plain, where military maneuvers were frequently conducted. As a result, soldiers often passed through Aihara, and quite often had to be billeted with Aihara families for the night.

The village also devoted substantial time and resources to the erection of a memorial stone honoring those villagers of Aihara who had served in the Russo-Japanese War. The village leaders decided to ask Prince Yamagata Aritomo—one of the leaders of the Meiji restoration and known as the "father of the Japanese army"—to write an inscription for the stone. To this end, Aizawa traveled to Tokyo to see if he could meet the great elder statesman. Although Aizawa was unable to meet the prince in person, an aide gave him a tour of the prince's magnificent gardens, originally one of the famous daimyō residences of Edo. In addition to the traditional perquisites of a Japanese aristocratic garden, the estate also boasted a museum devoted to memorabilia of Yamagata's life, including military artifacts and some of the clothes he wore in his youth, and a large bronze statue of the prince in his field marshal's uniform. Aizawa was also shown a horse which Yamagata had been given by the emperor: obligingly, the groom took the horse out and trotted it around the grounds.

Back in Hashimoto, Aizawa set to work drafting the design of the stone, and writing out the text. On the front were to be the names of the eight villagers who were killed in the Russo-Japanese War, above the names of the forty-three others who served. On the back were to be the names of the thirteen villagers who served in the Sino-Japanese War and the seven who took part in the Korean campaigns of 1907 and 1908. And on the side was to be the date that the stone was erected: December 1909. The whole job involved writing over one thousand *kanji* characters, and Aizawa noted that it took him all day.

The memorial stone was not complete until March of the next year, at a cost of ¥307. It was installed on the grounds of the village elementary school, at a ceremony in which the county chief exhorted villagers to adopt the same spirit of sacrifice that had been shown by the men who served in the wars.

In spite of all this patriotic and promilitary sentiment, Aizawa's family had a remarkably different attitude when it came to their own family members offering service to the country. In 1910 Aizawa's eldest son Shigeharu reached the age of twenty and thus became eligible for conscription. Shigeharu had graduated from middle school two years earlier, and was now a teacher in the Aihara Elementary School. Both Asako (who had just turned twelve) and Yoshihisa (now six) were students at the school. Shigeharu's physical exam was to take place in June. On May 8 Aizawa's eighty-year-old mother, his aunt, mother-in-law, and four other women all traveled to Saijōji Temple between Odawara and Hakone to pray for Shigeharu's draft exemption. This was no small journey—though it was made much easier by the arrival of the railway line. There were many shrines and temples closer by, but Saijōji was renowned for its power in answering prayers for exemption.

When the time came for Shigeharu's physical, Aizawa in his capacity as mayor accompanied his son together with twenty-four other youths to the grounds of the temple at Kamimizo. They were required to report for the inspection at 4:30 A.M., so they left Aihara at two in the morning, walking on the pitch-dark road the eight kilometers to Kamimizo. Youths from all seven of the northern Kōza county villages were being inspected, so once there the Aihara villagers had to wait for those from Ōsawa and Tana to be inspected first. Finally, Shigeharu's turn came. First, his vital statistics were taken: height (167 centimeters), weight (44.25 kilograms), and chest (81 centimeters) Then his eyes, ears, heart, and other key organs were examined. The result was a rank of *otsu* second level—several grades below the *kō* ranking that would have meant virtually certain conscription. As a result, Shigeharu was declared eligible to serve in the transport division, but not in the front-line divisions. Since the supply of transport recruits exceeded demand, Shigeharu had a good chance of complete exemption. No doubt the common saying was true, that the better educated you were, the more likely you were to have damaged your eyesight or some other part of your body. The poor farmers made for the healthiest recruits. After the examinations were over, the army doctor gave the young men a lecture on the importance of hygiene, and then the villagers went home.

Shigeharu would not know for sure if he was exempted from military service until the lottery. This took place the following week in Yokohama. Quotas were assigned to each county for front-line troops, artillery, transport, and so on. The quota for front-line troops for Kōza county was 145 men, only a few below the number of eligible conscripts—so a ranking of *kō* virtually assured conscription. In the artillery section, Shigeharu drew the number eighteen. The lower the number, the lower was the recruit's priority for conscription, so this low draw virtually guaranteed Shigeharu exemption. Instead of doing military service, he would be placed in the reserves, to be called on only in the event of a major emergency.

Aihara village continued to make financial contributions to the military, even after the end of the Russo-Japanese War. In the final months of the war, the county chief had called on Aihara to contribute over ¥600 to the purchase of a ship for a "volunteer fleet" *(giyūkantai)*. In spite of the peace treaty, Aizawa continued working to raise money into the following year and beyond. In April 1908, after his election as mayor, Aizawa received a letter from the governor appointing him to the committee of the Kōza county branch of the Kanagawa prefecture Volunteer Fleet Building Corporation. The ship purchased with the village's money, the *Sakura-maru,* was finally launched in October 1908. Aizawa received a detailed description of the ship, but did not attend its formal launch. On March 9, 1909, he received a photograph of the ship, and a scroll of appreciation presented in a wooden box.

.   .   .

In the early years of the twentieth century, the emperor and his family came to play an increasingly formal role in everyday life in the village—a role that was explicitly both political and spiritual. Aizawa was to meet several members of the imperial family, whom he encountered either through their involvement with prefectural activities or because they stopped in Aihara on their official duties. These were most commonly connected with military maneuvers, which were frequently carried out in the foothills around Hachiōji. Several times, members of the imperial family stopped to rest or to take a light meal in Hashimoto. Sometimes they even stayed overnight. Whenever this happened, it was an occasion for intense preparation on Aizawa's part.

For example, on November 12, 1908, Prince Kan'in, the younger brother of the emperor, an army general, and a well-known veteran of the Sino- and Russo-Japanese wars, stayed overnight in Hashimoto. The forty-two-year-old prince was presiding over large-scale military maneuvers that were taking place in the area. As mayor, Aizawa traveled on the eleventh to Hachiōji to offer humble greetings to the prince, and to report to him on the arrangements for his stay the following day. On the morning of the twelfth, two officials arrived from the prefectural office to make a final check of the arrangements. Then the officials, together with Aizawa, his brother, the county secretary, the local chief of police, and the village policeman all went to the Ryōgoku Bridge at the edge of Hashimoto to await their distinguished guest's arrival on horseback. They accompanied the prince back to Aizawa's brother's house, where he was to stay the night. The prince was accompanied by a large retinue of aides and guards, who bivouacked and set up guard posts all over the village, making the villagers work hard to meet their guests' needs. Aizawa was responsible for all of the arrangements, and he "returned to the village office and was up all night without sleep taking care of the arrangements."

On this particular occasion, the prince's stay was a part of a complex series of large-scale maneuvers lasting more than two weeks that required intense preparation and cooperation between army planners and village officials. After seeing the prince off on the morning of the thirteenth, Aizawa continued to follow the progress of the maneuvers as their center moved on to Atsugi and then Ōsawa village. On the twentieth Prince Kan'in again passed through Hashimoto on his way to Hachiōji. This time, all the mayors of the villages he had passed through were invited to accompany him on the train to Hachiōji before attending a luncheon to celebrate the end of the maneuvers. Together, the mayors and prefectural officials watched the final morning of the maneuvers. This was very much for public consumption. Indeed, the officer in charge took time out to greet the assembled mayors, and explained to them with the aid of maps what was taking place. The banquet that followed started at two o'clock and served six hundred people, including military officers, mayors, and other officials from Yokohama and the capital. The prince gave a speech and toasted the officers, who reciprocated by calling for *banzai*s for the emperor and then for the prince himself. One can imagine how impressive—as well as exhausting—this occasion must have been to a patriotic villager like Aizawa.

On another occasion, in September 1909, Prince Takeda, a young nephew of the emperor, stopped in Hashimoto together with fifty young officers, engaged in the student maneuvers of the Army College. The prince had lunch at Aizawa's brother's house, with Aizawa and other members of the village elite in attendance. After lunch the prince went on to Hachiōji where he was to spend the night. Aizawa, too, went to Hachiōji on village business (he did not travel in the company of the prince, though he did chat with some of the other officers). He returned

at about four in the afternoon. Unfortunately, after the prince's departure, it was found that he had left his pocket watch at Yasuemon's
house. In spite of his numerous other duties, Aizawa had to drop everything and take the train back to Hachiōji, where he hastened to the
house of Takura Sanzō, where the prince was staying. The prince was
unavailable for personal interview, but Aizawa met with Baron Mibu,
his aide, and gave the baron the watch. The baron asked Aizawa to
wait while he returned the watch to the prince, and he came back to
report that "the prince and all those under him are overjoyed." The
prince insisted on reimbursing Aizawa's travel expenses and on giving
him a reward. This was rather embarrassing, as the amount offered,
¥1.25, was a trivial sum for the comfortably off Aizawa. Nevertheless,
Aizawa felt he must accept the gift, as "Baron Mibu insisted that it
would be impolite not to accept. So even though I felt uncomfortable
about it, I reverently received the gift." Incidentally, Aizawa states the
amount of the gift not in yen but as "five hundred *hiki*." A *hiki* is a
roll of cloth, traditionally used as gifts by and among members of the
imperial household; by this time, it had come to be a euphemism for a
nominal sum of money equivalent to twenty-five *rin* (¥0.0025).

Shortly after this incident, Aizawa was called on to prepare for an
even more important imperial visitor. On November 4 Aizawa learned
that the crown prince (the future Emperor Taishō) was to visit Aihara
to attend the annual maneuvers of the Konoe guards regiment, of which
he was commander in chief. The preparations required were perhaps
similar to those involved in a modern-day presidential visit, though
the concerns were less with security than with showing appropriate
reverence and celebration in the royal presence. However, given that
only a week earlier the former prime minister, Prince Itō Hirobumi,
had been assassinated in Manchuria by a Korean nationalist, security
was certainly a concern too.

On November 5 four officials arrived from the imperial household
agency, together with six senior prefectural officials, the local police
chief, and the county secretary. This level of official attention was
unprecedented in Aihara. The entire group met with Aizawa and del-
egates from the village council to discuss in detail the preparations
for the prince's visit. The crown prince was to arrive in Hashimoto
station on November 18 by train, and proceed through the village on
horseback on his way to attend the maneuvers nearby.

The meeting on the fifth launched a week of intensive preparation.
The village council decided to build a celebratory arch in front of the

station in honor of the prince. They also decided to improve the roads around the station and along the route the prince would take. Aizawa even decided to move the toilet of a rental house that he owned, "in order to improve the sanitary appearance of the main street." In addition, the prince's horse was to be stabled in Hashimoto on the night of the seventeenth. The village had to build stables in the schoolyard for a total of fifteen horses, including special quarters for the prince's horse.

The village council budgeted ¥11 for materials for the arch and decided to use existing supplies for the stables, including a supply of zinc roofing material left over from a recent expansion of the school building. Villagers donated their own labor under the leadership of the hamlet's young men's associations. Work got underway on the fourteenth for the stables, and it was to begin on the fifteenth for the welcome arch. But early on the morning of the fifteenth, a confidential letter arrived from the police chief: an official announcement would be made later that day that the prince had changed his plans. He would no longer stop in Hashimoto.

This must certainly have been a disappointment to Aizawa and the villagers, especially as they had already spent a substantial amount of time, money, and labor in preparing for the visit. But early on the sixteenth, a messenger came to say that the prince's horse would still need stabling in Hashimoto, so the villagers had to go ahead and finish the stable building in the school yard. On November 17 the prince's horse, Tap, duly arrived, together with two other horses and accompanied by a team of grooms and its personal vet, all of whom slept that night in the stable with the horses. The prefectural secretary also arrived, and after examining the village's accounts for the preparations, he announced that the prefecture would reimburse ¥48 for the stable construction expenses. "The prefectural secretary said he was extremely grateful to us for doing this work so inexpensively. The quality was better than those in Nagatsuda or Isehara villages, but the cost lower."

The following week, Aizawa received a telegram from the county office in Fujisawa: "Come tomorrow in formal clothes." On arriving at the county office, he was informed that Prince Higashi, the uncle of the crown prince, was making a gift of ¥25 to Aihara village. Ten yen of this was in personal gifts to the officials who had worked so hard on the crown prince's putative visit and the other ¥15 was a donation to the school.

Even then, the incident of the crown prince's visit was not quite over.

There remained the question of what to do with the gifts of Prince Higashi—as imperial gifts, they must be treated with extraordinary deference. The six village leaders who had received the ¥10 gift voted unanimously to donate their share to the village general fund (this was an easy decision—the sum of money was derisory to these relatively wealthy men). On December 3 Aizawa traveled to Yokohama to give a pair of pheasants to the governor as a gift of thanks for the imperial gifts with which the village had been honored. "After talking for an hour about various matters, I retired from His Excellency the Governor's presence with deep feelings of affection." The next day, there was an article in the *Yokohama Bōeki* newspaper. The article related the story of the canceled imperial visit, commenting that the villagers had worked hard to make preparations for the visit and completed almost everything before he canceled the visit. "Both officials and people were deeply disappointed." Then the article told of the gift from Prince Higashi to the village, and of the village leaders' decision "do something to commemorate this extraordinary honor. . . . After consulting, they all offered to donate the money to the village basic fund. . . . In this way, the honor will remain with the village forever."

If the village was accumulating honor, it seems to have been purchased at a high price in terms of Aizawa's time and energy. It is striking how much time Aizawa devoted to matters connected to imperial ritual during his term as mayor. What is less clear is how personally committed Aizawa was to this cult of the emperor. There is clearly an evolution in the pages of the diary from a villager who, while patriotic and supportive of Japanese imperialism, saw these matters as of limited relevance to his personal affairs, to a mayor immersed in imperial ceremony.

In some cases, the initiatives taken in the name of the emperor seem to have fit well with Aizawa's own philosophy. For example, the emperor promulgated the Boshin rescript in October 1908, in response in part to the deteriorating state of village finances throughout Japan. Couched in Confucian language, the rescript exhorts Japanese subjects to observe thrift and diligence, and eschew extravagant consumption. By following these "ancestral" teachings, Japanese subjects would be able to "keep pace with the rapid progress of the world and share in the blessings of civilization."[20]

During and after the Russo-Japanese War, the village's budget had expanded dramatically, as it struggled to cope with the increasing demands placed on it. As the village leaders contemplated a growing deficit, the Boshin rescript seemed to point to a patriotic way out of their troubles. They made a formal resolution: "Recently, the Japanese Empire has held its own against the great powers of the world, and the time has come for it to enhance its national glory. However, the people must obey loyally, they must work industriously, they must be faithful, courteous, and avoid laziness, they must strive in each basic area, and they must perform service for their country. In this village, based on the imperial proclamation of October 13, 1908, we will make these principles our basis. As a result, we are issuing the Basic Rules Governing Assets and Saving for Aihara village, with the aim of ensuring the future tranquility of the village by creating a long-term surplus." The rules called for a long-term savings plan on the part of the village, with any surplus achieved after careful husbanding of funds to be placed in a post office savings account, eventually to provide ongoing income to the village in the form of interest.[21]

Early in 1909, the administrators of Kōza county asked each village to select a date for a formal annual reading of the Boshin rescript. Aihara chose March 31, which was the date on which Aihara had been launched as an administrative village. They decided to declare a holiday on that day and call it "Aihara Commemoration Day." This last day of the fiscal year was a sound choice for many reasons, not least of which was that schoolchildren and many others already took the day off. On the first celebration of this day, in 1910, the village unveiled its Russo-Japanese war memorial, so the ceremony was very well attended. But in future years Aizawa had to struggle to keep up the patriotic momentum. Each year, he dutifully called an assembly of villagers to listen to his reading of the rescript. In 1913, he reports that "there were few attendees." In subsequent years, the entire ceremony seems to have been quietly dropped.

The same can not be said of the education rescript, which became an increasingly important part of the school ritual. The rescript—said to have been composed by the emperor's Confucian tutor Motoda Eifu—was first issued in 1890. The rescript exhorted students to "be filial to your parents, affectionate to your brothers and sisters; as husbands and wives be harmonious, as friends true; bear yourselves in modesty and moderation; extend your benevolence to all: pursue learning and cultivate arts, and thereby develop intellectual faculties and perfect moral powers; furthermore advance public good and promote common interests: always respect the Constitution and observe the laws; should emergency arise, offer yourselves courageously to the State; and thus guard and maintain the prosperity of Our Imperial Throne coeval with heaven and earth."[22] On National Founding Day (*kigensetsu*, February 11), and on the school's Commemoration Day (April 15), the school principal would solemnly read the rescript to the entire school, as well as to an invited audience of guests. On April 15, 1911, for example, the principal invited fifty special guests to the school's commemoration day. The guests included Aizawa, the county school inspector, the school principal and mayor of nearby Kamimizo village, the local policeman, present and former village councilors, members of the village education committee (its chair was Aizawa's brother Yasuemon), the head and district chiefs of the village Young Men's Association, the heads of the district hygiene and military committees, the schoolteachers, and the employees of the village office. The assembly twice sang the national anthem ("Kimi ga yō"—may your reign last for a thousand generations . . .) before Principal Zama's reading of the education rescript. Then the mayor unrolled a scroll sent from the governor of Kanagawa prefecture, announcing his bestowal of a "flag of encouragement" on the school in the name of the nation. The principal hoisted the flag up on the school's new flagpole, while Aizawa made another speech to the assembled guests, before giving ¥10 in village funds to the teachers as "a mark of thanks."

The accessions and deaths of emperors also required special ceremonies in the village. When Aizawa heard the news of the Meiji Emperor's death on July 30, 1912, his first reactions were personal. "This morning I went to the village office and saw the special newspaper edition. This morning, at 0:43, His Sacred Majesty passed away. The entire nation is plunged into extreme grief. He was sixty-one years old. It is said to be same day as the death of his predecessor. During His Majesty's illness, all of his 60 million subjects, old and young, prayed for his recovery, but his illness was strong and now this undesired news has come. The whole nation is deeply saddened. With a penitent sincerity, I humbly conveyed this news to my colleagues."

The emperor's funeral was delayed until September, to allow time for dignitaries to arrive from all over the world. On September 13, the day of the funeral in Tokyo, the village observed its own ceremonies at the Jinmei Shrine. The ceremony began at 8:00 P.M., with the mayor leading all those gathered in Shintō prayers. Then Aizawa made an offering to the gods before reading a statement of grief in a loud voice. Then he clapped his hands three times to the gods and performed a purification ceremony. The head of the military affairs committee read

an imperial rescript, and all saluted. The solemn gathering ended at
11:00 at night. As the villagers departed, Aizawa noted that "there was
a glow in the sky from the direction of Tokyo, from the electric lights
at Aoyama" where the state funeral was taking place.

On October 24, 1915, Aizawa received word that the village would
be given a portrait of the new emperor, to be displayed in the village
school with appropriate reverence. On the morning of the twenty-ninth,
"I woke up at 3 A.M., washed my body and my hands and prayed for
His Majesty's health. The moon in the west illuminated the clouds in
the east. The sky was as clear as though it had been wiped clean, and
all of the stars were visible. Then I had breakfast and put on my formal
clothes." Aizawa and Principal Zama traveled to Yokohama in Western morning suits, catching the 5:32 A.M. train. Several other mayors
and school heads were traveling with them on the same mission. The
mayors commandeered ten rickshaws to carry them to the prefectural
headquarters, where representatives from 143 schools were to gather to
receive the imperial likenesses. They were divided up into groups, and
ceremonies were held for each, the governor of the prefecture personally handing them the portraits.

Following the established protocol, Zama and Aizawa received the
portrait and bowed deeply to the governor. Then they retired to the next
room where a specially purified wooden box was waiting. Reverently,
they wrapped the portrait with white gauze, then placed it in the box.
On the way home, a special first-class carriage had been arranged by
the railway company, in order to show due respect to the sacred charge
of the mayors and school principals. After being served lunch by the
Higashi Kanagawa stationmaster, the mayors boarded the train for the
journey home. On their arrival, the village notables, school staff, pupils,
and other designated villagers were waiting at the station to greet them,
and the entire assembly processed to the school. They held a ceremony in
the school yard, then all bowed deeply, while Zama placed the portrait
in its temporary home. For the time being, the portrait was to reside in
the principal's office, until the school had erected a proper repository.
Aizawa finished off the occasion by personally paying for sake for thirty
leading notables—"in order to show my joy at being bathed in this
unlimited radiance." After drinking the sake, the notables joined the
entire assembly in cheering *banzai*s for emperor, village, and school.

In October 1916 a portrait of the empress was distributed. Once
again Aizawa and Zama went to Yokohama for a similar ceremony to
that of the previous year. For Aizawa, the timing could not have been

worse. For the past several weeks he had been suffering from debilitating pain in his legs, which the village doctor suspected was caused by beriberi. "Today, although it is only three blocks from my house to the village office, I had to rest twice on the way or I wouldn't have made it. But I must go on working until I drop. Now on top of the pain in my legs I must catch the first train tomorrow morning . . ." And indeed, the next morning Aizawa rose at 2:30 in the morning, changed into a Western-style morning suit, and set off (by rickshaw, as his legs were too painful to walk) to the school to meet Principal Zama, before going on to the station to catch the 5:30 train. He arrived back in Hashimoto that evening after a long and exhausting day.

By this time, the school had followed the general practice of building a special repository for the portrait within the school premises. In many cases, this was a completely separate building, built in the style of a Shintō shrine. In the case of the Aihara Elementary School, the school converted one room inside the main school building into the *hōanshitsu*, or "treasure repository." It was here that the next day, Aizawa and Zama conducted the solemn ceremonies associated with the new portrait.

Another observance that clearly gave pleasure to Aizawa was the annual submission of poems to the imperial household agency. Poetry writing had for centuries been one of the main activities of the imperial court, and with the encouragement of the household agency and the newspapers, ordinary citizens began submitting patriotic poems at the end of the year. Aizawa began the practice in 1916, and thereafter he sent one every year. For the most part the content is patriotic and unoriginal.

There was undoubtedly an element of snobbery in these imperial activities—an element that was shrewdly encouraged by the bureaucrats of the imperial household and by the members of the aristocracy. A generation earlier, it would have been unthinkable for a villager to aspire to such courtly pursuits (although poetry composition was a common activity among the village elite, and even between villagers and commoner townsmen). When Aizawa received an invitation in July 1916 to a party to be given by Baron Hatano, head of the imperial household agency, he commented lovingly on the details of the invitation card—the chrysanthemum imperial seal, and the thick pasteboard (Aizawa noted the exact thickness, as well as the other measurements). Aizawa wrote of the invitation card that "this will be kept as a treasure in my family forever."

While Aizawa felt due reverence for the imperial institution, the same can not be said of his attitude to domestic politics. In January 1913 Aizawa commented on Prime Minister Katsura's sudden dissolution of a recalcitrant Diet: "As I see it, Japan's top politicians say pretty things with their mouths, but I see no sign of them carrying out their promises. Even though this should be a time for carefully supporting the new Emperor, Katsura has caused damage to His Majesty's very first Diet. Although I am just a petty subject, I can not help disagreeing with that. We must shun impurity, and strive to preserve and improve our true natures, and we must not forget the benevolence of our ruler."

Aizawa was also called on to serve both community and nation through volunteer activities in the county Agricultural Association and the prefectural chapter of the Japanese Red Cross. Sato was active in both the Red Cross and the Patriotic Women's Association. The Red Cross actually combined elements of imperial prestige, snobbery, patriotism, and imperialism. Members of the imperial family acted as patrons, and this was clearly a pull to Aizawa. In October 1906 he had the job of increasing membership in Aihara. On October 10 Aizawa visited the wealthy Ogawa family to persuade them to enroll. He wanted Mr. Ogawa to become a "special member," a status that required a donation of at least ¥200. The draw was that special members received recognition at ceremonies in Yokohama, with the possibility of receiving a citation directly from the hand of the empress. Ogawa agreed to make the donation, as did Hara Seibei, the village's wealthiest citizen, and Aizawa himself. They joined less than a dozen other "special members" in Kōza county. When he received a commendation from the emperor's brother for his services to the Red Cross, Aizawa commented: "All of us were moved to tears by this exceptional honor. I too was bathed in this radiance. This will be marked as a great event in our family."[23]

On New Year's Day the following year, Aizawa held a party at the village office for the village's most influential citizens. Proudly, Aizawa passed around a photograph he had had taken shortly after receiving his Red Cross awards. He is in formal Japanese clothes, sporting both the Red Cross medal and his Order of the Rising Sun, eighth class, received for his services during the Russo-Japanese War. The medals tie Aizawa to the national community. He is not just a wealthy villager, he is a patriotic citizen whose importance is recognized by the nation.

Although Aizawa gained satisfaction from his "special" membership, the majority of ordinary members of the Red Cross were women. Sato was a member, as was Aizawa's mother, Riu. The Red Cross was primarily aimed at middle-class women, who had the time and resources to devote to this volunteer cause. Sato was also an active member of the Patriotic Women's Association during the war, and when her husband became mayor she was a natural candidate for the leadership position. Because of ill health, though, she passed the baton on to Inoue Uta, wife of another elite villager and an exceptionally active woman. The activities of the association included support for Japanese troops serving abroad, such as the "comfort bags" Sato and others made for soldiers in Korea in September 1908. Each bag contained three handkerchiefs, one toothbrush set, and a letter. Sato made three bags that day, at a cost of ¥0.20 each. On November 2, 1913, Sato received her reward for her service to the Patriotic Women's Association. The Kanagawa chapter held its third annual general meeting in the park at Yokohama. Sato was unwell, so her daughter Asako (age fifteen) went in her place, accompanied by Aizawa. The event was a mirror of Aizawa's reception for the Red Cross, with the genders reversed. The patroness was the Princess Kan'in, and she presented Asako with Sato's medal. After the reception, Asako attended a banquet in honor of the princess, while Aizawa ate a boxed lunch sitting with his son Yasuo in the park. Yasuo, now age eighteen, had graduated from teacher training school (which he had attended instead of middle school), and was now a second year student at the Yokohama Industrial School, where he was studying engineering. Asako was a student at the girls' high school in Hachiōji, to which she commuted from Hashimoto.

. . .

Aizawa's position as mayor sometimes exposed him to interesting new experiences. On April 22, 1915, Aizawa received a telegram from an Englishman named Marshall Martin, announcing that he wanted to rent a tract of woodland for hunting. A week later, Martin showed up in person—unannounced, and arriving by car. After some bargaining, a group of landowning villagers—including Aizawa—agreed to rent Martin two hundred hectares of woodland for the sum of ¥150 per year. For the next two months, visits by Martin became quite frequent. There remained something disconcerting to Aizawa about this unusual presence—as, for example, when Martin arrived in his automobile at 6:30 in the evening while Aizawa was lounging in the bath. He had to jump out and rush to get dressed while his visitor waited in the reception room.

On July 19 Aizawa traveled to Yokohama to execute the contract

with Martin. Aizawa was accompanied by his son Yasuo, who was
studying in Yokohama at the time, as well as two middlemen. After
the formalities were completed, Martin invited Aizawa and his companions to lunch at the Grand Hotel. Aizawa was clearly somewhat
intimidated by this experience, even though Martin himself did not
accompany them. Martin instructed his clerk to make the arrangements for the Japanese visitors' lunch, then left them alone to enjoy it as
best they could. Aizawa records: "For all of us, it was the first time to
eat Western food in a famous hotel." Afterward, Aizawa made a little
holiday out of his visit. He and his companions paid a call on Marshall
Martin to thank him for the lunch, then Aizawa and Yasuo strolled
along the beach, even dipping into the water for a brief swim. Aizawa
spent the night at Yasuo's lodging.

Once the contract was signed, Martin and his friends began visiting Hashimoto to hunt. From Aizawa's point of view, these visits
were sometimes more successful than others. In June 1916 Martin
arrived in his car with an English friend and their wives, and Aizawa
went with them to do some fishing on the Sagami River. Aizawa, who
enjoyed fishing, records that "we caught a great number of *ayu* [sweet-
fish]." But on April 6, 1918, Marshall once again arrived with his
English friend Bent. This time they appear to have come by train, and
Aizawa met them at Fuchinobe station and introduced them to two
villagers who would act as their hunting assistants. Once again, the
men invited Aizawa to accompany them, and he spent a long day on
the hillsides vainly beating the bushes for game. That evening, Aizawa
took to his bed with a fever, which he did not shake off for the next
several days.

On another occasion in March 1916, Aizawa traveled out of the
Kantō region for the first time in his life, on a mayor's study trip. He
visited Aichi, Shiga, and Hyōgo prefectures, visiting county and village
administrations and seeing how others managed their affairs. He was
particularly impressed by the village of Tomotani in Shiga prefecture.
This village had a policy of encouraging landless villagers to leave the
village to make their fortunes; and "if they are not successful, they
are not allowed back in the village." The villagers' "lifestyle appears
to be excellent, as all are required to live up to a minimum standard."
The group went on to Kyoto, where they visited the mausoleums of the
Meiji Emperor and of the seventh-century Prince Shōtoku. These tombs
(the latter of very dubious authenticity) were located in Momoyama, an
evocative spot in the mountains outside Kyoto. Unfortunately, only the

three mayors who had thought to bring their Western-style morning coats were allowed inside for the VIP tour; the others had to mix with the crowds in the general viewing area. In Kyoto as in each of the other major stopping places, Aizawa went to the post office, and, after telegraphing home, he opened a "commemorative savings account" and received a souvenir pass-book. For all its excitement, the trip was not comfortable. The group took the night train down from Yokohama, which was so packed that they had to stand up most of the night. In spite of the closed windows, the railway car was freezing cold, and smoke from the engine kept wafting in, choking the passengers.

TECHNOLOGY AND CHANGE

The arrival of the railway in 1908 heralded enormous changes in the village. Some of these were the consequence of the railway itself, as Hashimoto and Aihara became increasingly integrated into the Tokyo-Yokohama metropolitan area. Hashimoto remained a rural community, but its residents now had easy access to the economic and cultural opportunities of the capital. Other changes resulted from successive new technologies introduced into the village, including telegraph and telephone services, electricity, and bicycles.

Starting in late 1910, the Dentō Kaisha began building telephone lines through the village. Their main goal was not to bring phone service to Aihara, but to link Yokohama and Hachiōji by telephone. Indeed, from the point of view of Aihara, the arrival of the telephone poles was mostly an inconvenience. They cut across the villagers' land, and the company had to arrange to pay compensation to each affected villager. The total compensation amounted to almost one thousand yen. Even if the company had offered immediate telephone service to the residents of Aihara, it is doubtful if many would have taken it on. The cost of telephoning was extremely high: it was still used mainly by businesses and by government officers. Aizawa, though, was well aware of the benefits of the telephone. On several occasions while the telephone lines were under construction, he went to the construction office of the Dentō Kaisha to borrow their telephone. He also occasionally borrowed the station-master's telephone: the railways used the phone for their internal communications. Aizawa had to wait until August of 1917 before the village office was able to get its own telephone line.

The telegraph, on the other hand, came relatively quickly. Once the telephone lines were in the village, it was a relatively simple matter to arrange for them to stop at the post office and convey telegraph traffic. In July 1911 Aizawa's brother (who was the village postmaster) negotiated with the telephone company for telegraph service to be brought to the post office. The cost was to be ¥300. Because the telegraph was considered a public amenity, the village (under Aizawa's direction) agreed to contribute ¥180 toward the total cost. The rest had to be raised through the time-honored way: donations, starting with the most prominent villagers. The money was raised, and on November 19 the village post office officially launched telegraph service. Yasuemon held a party to celebrate the event, inviting sixty people, including those from Hashimoto and neighboring hamlets, who donated money.

The telegraph, though, could hardly be called life changing. Telegram deliveries had been possible in Aihara since the previous century—the messages were sent by runner from Kamimizo village, where the nearest telegraph office was located. But in order to send a telegraph, it had been necessary to dispatch one's own runner to Kamimizo—or go oneself. Now all that was needed was a walk to the local post office. For the Aihara village office, which sent and received telegrams on a daily basis, this was certainly a convenience. And the profits from the telegraph service—for it was profitable to the post office proprietor—would stay in the village and indeed in the Aizawa family.

Another form of technology to enter the village was the bicycle. Bicycles were becoming increasingly popular in Europe and America in the last decades of the nineteenth century, and it was only a matter of time before Japanese manufacturers began imitating them. The Miyata Rifle Company began making bicycles in 1890, and many local makers produced their own versions. However, the price of bicycles remained far beyond the reach of most Japanese until the 1920s, when bicycle ownership began rapidly spreading. Prices dropped from as high as ¥200 in the Meiji era to around ¥50 to ¥70 in the 1920s—still a large sum for an indebted farmer, but manageable for landlords and wealthier farmers. In the Hashimoto area, the owner of a rice shop on the road between Hashimoto and Hachiōji began making bicycles according to a crude design from around 1907. He started the Ochiai Bicycle Shop and employed three assistants to manufacture the machines out of steel pipe. They had no mudguards, brakes, or free-wheeling capability, and they were hard to ride on the dirt road (and impossible after a rain), but Ochiai nevertheless did a good business renting out his machines (which he dubbed the "Tiger" model) for ¥0.20 per hour. Soon after, two other Hashimoto artisans began making bicycles: the blacksmith in Sakanoshita, who made a tire-less bicycle known locally as the "rat-tler" *(gatakuri-jitensha)* that rented for a mere ¥0.10 an hour; and the Katō Bicycle Shop, which opened in 1919 offering the home-made "Inari" model, available for sale or rent. In 1923, right after the Kantō earthquake, a new bicycle shop, the Takeuchi Bicycle Shop, opened beside the station. Takeuchi advertised his bicycles to passing travelers with a giant-size bicycle perched on his tile roof.[24]

For those who could afford them, these were a revolutionary inven-tion. Distances that had previously seemed daunting could now be covered in a matter of hours or less. Loads that had previously been hauled on the farmer's back could now be pulled on a cart behind the bicycle. Nevertheless, it took a long time for the potential of the bicycle to be realized in this and other villages. One village figure who did understand its importance was the policeman. The image of the village constable on his bicycle is a widespread symbol of the twenti-eth century in many countries. We first learn of the Aihara policeman using a bicycle on May 16, 1912, when Constable Kuroki accompa-nied Aizawa and a colleague as they carried the ballot boxes to Ebina village after a national Diet election (Aizawa and his colleague rode in rickshaws). Other than policemen, though, the bicycle was at first a plaything for the wealthy. Aizawa bought bicycles for his sons some time in 1914. He records on August 10 that Shigeharu and Yasuo rode their bicycles over to Ōshima to visit a friend there during their summer holiday. When the Meiji Shrine opened in November 1920, Sekiguchi Gentarō of Oyama hamlet traveled the forty kilometers to Tokyo by bicycle to see the new shrine. And the post office began using bicycles to deliver mail in 1924.[25] It was not until the mid-1920s that the potential of the bicycle began to be realized. One of the first changes that came to Hashimoto as a result of this development was fresh fish: from the mid-1920s, fish sellers began roaming the north-ern Kantō villages carrying iced fish on the back of their bicycles. The villagers of Hashimoto had formerly been dependent on salted fish, so this development heralded a significant improvement in their standard of living.

Electricity came relatively late to Aihara—it wasn't until September 19, 1917, that the first lights were switched on. As early as November 1912, Aizawa went to Hachiōji to enquire at the local power station how it might be possible to get electricity for Aihara. But nothing seems to have come of those talks. Negotiations truly got underway when Mr. Yamazaki, the president of the Sagami and Kōzu Electric Company, came to visit Aihara on March 29, 1917. Yamazaki and his subordinates made a tour of inspection of the village and agreed there and then to bring electric power to the villagers.

The work began at the beginning of June. Mr. Yamaguchi, who was in charge of the project, rented a house in Hashimoto and set up his headquarters. The company began by building more electrical poles—this time running along the sides of the village roads. The work was done quickly, and in early August the technicians came to Aizawa's house to set up the wiring for his new electrical service. They installed ten-candlepower bulbs in the three main living rooms downstairs and five-candlepower bulbs in the corridor. The kitchen does not seem to have merited any electric light. The switch was actually thrown on September 19. Company president Yamazaki came to the village for the occasion. One would think that Aizawa, like other villagers, would view the arrival of electricity as a momentous event, suddenly bringing light into the village darkness. But Aizawa makes no comment at all on what it was like to go back to a home lit up by electric lights. Indeed, the subject of electricity is never mentioned in the diary again. We may assume that it was something of an anticlimax: the electricity could only be used for lighting (there were no wall sockets, and subscribers paid not by usage but according to the number of light fixtures they had in their house). And the relatively weak power of the light bulbs installed may not even have matched the power of the paraffin lamps that the family was already using. Indeed, a year earlier (on February 3, 1916) Aizawa had purchased an improved "carbide lamp" running on battery power from a traveling salesman (at a fairly steep cost of ¥3.15). Light had already arrived in Aizawa's home, and by comparison electricity was perhaps not that impressive.

In spite of all the improvements in the village, Aizawa's outlook on economic affairs remained mostly pessimistic. World War I brought an extraordinary economic boom to Japan. Gross national product grew by 30 percent and more per year from 1916 to 1919 (though price increases were also steep). Aizawa records the amazing economic growth, but he focuses even more on the steep rises in the cost of living that made it harder for working families to get by. On December 31, 1916, for example, he acknowledges that the big increase in silk prices has been a great boon to silk-rearing farmers. Indeed, in 1916 there was not a single tenant who had been unable to make his rent payments. But still, Aizawa worried that a big drop in prices might follow. And he felt sympathetic to those who for whatever reason had no silk to sell that year—they still had to pay the higher prices for other commodities. In July 1918 Aizawa comments:

> The war in Europe has been continuing for five years. No one knows when peace will come. Japan is providing the needs of the belligerents and exports are at an extreme level, with income to Japan of ¥1.2 billion . . . . Now, farmers are running to work in the factories of the cities, and this economy has brought an extravagance by farmers that has never been seen before. And only three or four years ago they were mired in depression. On the tenth of this month I submitted a plan for diligence and economizing to the village council. We decided to implement it from October 1: it will help us if there us a depression after this boom. We also have to worry about defense—we are a belligerent in this war, and sending troops to Siberia [he is referring to Japan's ill-fated expedition to defend Siberia from the Bolshevik takeover of Russia]. One point two billion yen seems like a dream, but we are still a small country and the most important thing is national unity.

The price of rice rose faster than any other commodity, tripling in price between 1914 and 1918, with a particularly sharp spike in early 1918, and Aizawa—who like all the villagers of Hashimoto had to buy the majority of his rice—records anxiously the successive price spikes. By the summer of 1918, the soaring price of rice had turned into a national emergency that overshadowed the economic gains of the war. Showing considerable resourcefulness, Aizawa organized an expedition to Yokohama, where he made a bulk purchase of less expensive imported rice. He arranged for it all to be shipped back to Hashimoto, and he began selling it at cost through the auspices of the Agricultural Association. He continued releasing the cheaper rice onto the village market over the next several months, alleviating the pain of high prices in a village that had to buy almost all of its rice for cash.

In mid-August riots erupted around Japan in protest against rice prices. Aizawa comments:

> The rioters have been burning rice shops, and attacking the wealthy and prominent members of the community. Even in this prefecture things are looking more and more dangerous. In Tokyo there was a big disturbance on the evening of the thirteenth. Now the government is planning ways to help people throughout the country. In the Kansai area, the government has even had to send troops to keep the peace. Today the emperor announced a gift of ¥3 million to be distributed among the people. Kanagawa will get ¥75,000. Moreover, the nation's powerful are giving sums from ¥10,000 to ¥1 million. . . . The government is also donating ¥10 million in aid, so the disturbance should subside. But what with the departure of troops for Siberia and the high prices, people are really

in trouble. The European war has been going on for five years now. Japan has benefited, but much of the prosperity has gone into the hands of the nouveaux riches.

A GREAT SADNESS

Aizawa Kikutarō's duties as mayor of Aihara were extraordinarily heavy—so much so that Aizawa himself wondered at times if he could physically go on. They left him little time for his growing family, which by 1914 consisted of his wife Sato and six children—the last, Mieko, was born in 1911, when Aizawa was forty-five and Sato was thirty-nine. Aizawa depended on Sato—as well as their one or two maids and the women in their extended family network—to take care of his house and family. It must have been hard for his frail wife, although she could take comfort in her husband's undoubted devotion to his family.

But in August 1914—just days after the great war had erupted in Europe—disaster once again struck the Aizawa family. When Sato fell sick on August 20, there was nothing especially ominous in her condition. Still, Aizawa took the day off on the twenty-fourth to care for her—his first day off work the whole year. He asked one of their neighbors, Mrs. Matsuura, to come and look after Sato the next day. When Sato was still sick a week later, her mother moved in to take care of her. Still, there was no sense of impending disaster. But during the long month of September, Sato's condition continued to worsen, and it took on more and more of the colors of a final illness. She reached her first crisis on September 15. Aizawa once again took the day off to care for her, and in the evening he sent a telegram to Shigeharu in Yokohama. Shigeharu had quit his teaching job in Aihara the previous year, and entered the law department of Meiji University in Tokyo for a one-year certificate. He had graduated three months earlier and had just started a new job as a clerk in the Yokohama city hall. He obtained compassionate leave and came home to help care for his mother. Aizawa went back to work—he could not ignore his pressing duties. On September 16 he was in Fujisawa for a meeting of Kōza county mayors. The following day, he took that year's consignment of twenty-year-olds for their physical examination to determine eligibility for conscription. On the twenty-third, he records a little plaintively: "Worked all day at the village office, no lunch box." That night he sent Shigeharu to hire a professional nurse from Hachiōji. The next day, Shigeharu had to return to Yokohama. His compassionate leave was up.

But Sato's condition continued to deteriorate. By the end of September, a final crisis was on hand. On the twenty-eighth Aizawa stopped going to work. His job now was to spend her final days at his wife's side. On October 1 both Shigeharu and Aizawa's second son, Yasuo, were summoned from Yokohama (Yasuo was in his second year at the Yokohama Industrial School). Aizawa asked both of his sons to stop on the way to Hashimoto, to pray at the Kawasaki Daishi temple.

On October 4 Sato's mother—who had been at her bedside throughout—went to Hachiōji to consult with her pharmacist grandson, Chōichi. Yasuo's school leave expired, and he had to go back to Yokohama. It was on this day, with two important family members absent, that Sato passed through her final crisis. Dr. Yajima stayed by her bedside late into the night. As Aizawa describes it in his diary, which was his faithful companion during this ordeal: "Soon after midnight she became extremely ill. Her agony was not so great, but she slowly sank into a deep sleep as her spirit left her body—even though she could still understand us until about three o'clock. She died at 4 A.M." Aizawa went on: "I sent a telegram to her mother in Hachiōji, and Yasuo in Yokohama, but they did not arrive in time. It's just too sad. Asako is seventeen, Yoshihisa eleven, Hanako eight, Mieko only three, all of them cried at her pillow. Shigeharu and I, too, seized each other's hands and comforted each other. We could only cry at this terrible event."

Sato's mother and Yasuo came hurrying back. Mrs. Ushikubo arrived at dawn after taking the first train to Hashimoto. Yasuo arrived on his bicycle with a lantern borrowed from his school. He arrived at 6:30 in the morning, bathed in sweat from his thirty-five-kilometer ride. He had not wanted to wait for the first train, which would have arrived in Hashimoto at seven in the morning. He had hoped against hope that the extra few minutes might buy him one last meeting with his mother.

During the day, dozens of villagers stopped by the Aizawa house to convey their condolences. The family had accumulated more than sixty gifts during Sato's illness. Each would have to be acknowledged in due course. But first there was the funeral to think about. The Aizawa branch family did not yet have its own plot in the Kōfukuji graveyard. After consulting with his brother, Aizawa decided to carve out a section of the main family burial area, and set it up as his own family's plot. The funeral took place on October 7. All Sato's family was there with the exception of her sister Uta, who was far away in Yamaguchi prefecture where her husband was working, and Dr. Kawano, Uta's father-in-law, who was busy with his medical practice. The temple was crowded with the 180 attendees from the village and the surrounding area. There can be no doubt that the sympathy of his entire community was a powerful support for Aizawa. He records that the family received funeral gifts totaling ¥67, which would be applied to the total funeral expenses of ¥170. In the evening, Kobayashi Tensho, the priest of Kōfukuji, led sutra chants to pray for the repose of Sato's soul.

Aizawa went back to work on October 10. He had been away for two weeks—long enough for a world of cares to descend on him with his return. When he returned home, he had to deal with the needs of a family trying to adjust to its sad new situation. On the night of October 13, Mieko woke up crying for her mother. "I carried her out into the cold misty garden and walked back and forth, then I tried putting her back to bed. Finally after midnight she calmed down and went to sleep. Really, it is too hard to bear." A few days later, Shigeharu quit his job at the Yokohama city hall (the clerical work seems never to have suited him) and returned to Hashimoto. He was to stay there for the rest of his life. At the end of October, Shigeharu, Asako, Yoshihisa, and Hanako went to the annual *jūban* fair in Hachiōji, and then on to the Daizenji Temple to pray for their mother. When Mieko asked what they were going to do, they told her that they were going to help Sato to ascend Mount Fuji.

Life had to go on. Perhaps, indeed, Sato's death prompted Aizawa to pay more attention to his family's pressing needs. Within three months, Aizawa had begun arranging a marriage for his eldest son. Shigeharu married Adachihara Eiko, a girl from the village of Nakatsu. Aizawa enlisted his cousin Jungorō as go-between to arrange the endless details of gift-exchange and ceremonies. Aizawa also had to do a lot of consulting in order to ensure the full approval of his community. This is indeed a striking feature of village life in Hashimoto: the most personal matters are also subject to the general involvement of the community. Aizawa consulted with Ushikubo Isakichi, his brother-in-law; with the head of his five-man group, Namikichi; and with the head of the Yajima family. The marriage took place on April 4, 1915. The ceremonies took place over a period of three days, in both Hashimoto and Nakatsu. On the second day, the bridal party exchanged sake cups: first the bride and groom; then the parents and children; then the brothers and sisters; and then the family representatives. Then the whole party of twenty-one people sat down for a wedding feast. The bridal party stayed until nine in the evening, at which point they left to stay at Aizawa's cousin's house. However, the women in the party stayed behind for a women-only celebration. The next morning, a similar event was held for the men. In the afternoon, the family received callers come to congratu-late them. First at the door were the members of the Aihara village council.

Aizawa was rewarded for his efforts in arranging a bride for Shigeharu with a grandchild, born exactly a year later. Her name was Sumiyo. Sumiyo was only four years younger than her youngest aunt, Mieko. Shigeharu, meanwhile, had gone to work for his uncle as manager of the village post office. Aizawa must have been happy to see his family growing once again.

CHAPTER 5

A World Transformed

1918–1926

AN UNPRECEDENTED ECONOMY

As it was for much of Japan, World War I was a catalyst for change in Hashimoto. Year after year, Aizawa had recorded the hardships suffered by his tenant farmers and the depredations of the emerging industrial economy. Now, it seemed, at last everything was going the farmers' way. Although the war was now over, the price of silk continued to soar. On May 13, 1919, silk was being quoted at ¥1,700 to ¥2,000 per picul on the Yokohama market. On June 19 the price reached ¥2,350. Mulberry also fetched unprecedented prices, as high as ¥13 per horseload. A farmer who grew either mulberry or silkworms could make at least ¥2 per day—far higher than the customary wage of ¥1 or less for farm workers. As Aizawa commented on September 13, 1919, "with regard to mulberry, this year tenants who have been renting fields for eight or nine yen per *tan* have been able to sell their crop for more than ¥100 and so they have become 'nouveau riche tenant farmers' *(kosaku narikin)*."

The price of rice was on the increase, too. After declining by some 20 percent since the peak at the time of the rice riots the previous August, the price began rising again, reaching the August 1918 level in June, and rising another 20 percent by September. By that time, ¥1 would buy only 1.6 *shō* (about 2 kilograms) of rice—enough to feed a family of six for one day. On December 2 Aizawa comments that "a room in Tokyo now rents for ¥25 a month; a barrel of soy sauce that sold for ¥3 or ¥4 in June is now selling for ¥7 or ¥8; sake sells for ¥1.60 a *shō*, a piglet for more than ¥10, a good-quality calf sells for ¥300-¥400, and a builder's labor costs ¥2 per day." Land, too, was booming—surely good news for a major landowner like Aizawa: "Probably rents will go up next year. There are many people looking to buy fields but nobody wants to sell them, and even if they do sell the price for a lowland field is from ¥500 to as much as ¥800 per *tan*, while the price for a newly developed field is ¥300 to ¥400. The price has more than doubled since last year."[1] On December 2 he commented further that "even though buyers are willing to pay ¥300 per *tan* for newly developed land, there are no sellers." Aizawa's business investments were also sharing in the general prosperity. On June 21, 1919, Aizawa sold his shares in the Yokohama Warehouse Company for ¥77 per share—he had bought them the previous year for ¥25 per share. On January 26, 1920, he collected a 13 percent dividend on his shares in the Naigai Bussan Company.

As a landowner and shareholder, Aizawa must have congratulated himself at this increase in his wealth, but he seems to have resented the appropriation by his tenants of much of the windfall. Moreover, as a public official, he was very well aware of the difficulties faced by those on fixed salaries. His monthly salary of ¥23 plus ¥7 in expenses was rapidly being eroded by the relentless increase in prices. In July 1919 the village council voted him an additional ¥6 per month, most of which he used to offset higher travel expenses. But it was hardly enough to compensate. On February 26, 1920, Aizawa commented: "These days a hired farm hand earns ¥250 to ¥300 per year, and if you add the value of the food and clothes he receives, that comes to ¥500 a year. Although mine is supposed to be an honorable job, I make the same as a peasant laborer. Well, it is certainly a changeable world." Aizawa added: "These days a normal factory worker's monthly wage is ¥100—their standard of living is higher than ours! There is no point in writing any more about this, but . . . "

As prices continued to soar, Aizawa worried about the possibility of a collapse. In fact, his pessimism was to prove well founded. On April 27, 1920, Aizawa reported that the Hachiōji silk cloth market had suddenly plummeted. Silk thread was declining steeply in price, too, and fertilizer and grain prices were also falling. "There are many bankruptcies among the merchants." On May 24 Aizawa commented more extensively on the collapse.

Due to the financial tightening, the economy has moved into recession. First textiles, and then all sorts of other products have begun a big sell-off. Until April we were in an unprecedented economic boom, but over the past month it has changed dramatically. There are really no words for the intensity of the price decline. Up till last year we saw the emergence of textile millionaires, stock-investor millionaires, steel millionaires, sugar millionaires, property millionaires, and so on and so on. But the fair wind that blew on all these people has vanished like a dream in the night, leaving many worse off than when they started, some completely ruined, and some with broken bones—indeed, they have been subject to an infinite variety of difficulties. On the other hand, there are those who never wanted to be millionaires, who went about their business as normal. During the boom, they might have seemed abnormal or incompetent, but they continued progressing day by day, without wasting a single day, and now they are suffering no losses, they have no difficulties. Such people are commonly called "ten-year averagers," and there's truth in that.

Nevertheless, Aizawa cannot have been happy when he saw the decline in prices of his basic crops. During the 1920 mulberry-selling season, leaves that the previous year had sold for ¥15 to ¥20 a horseload were back down to ¥4 to ¥5. As Aizawa commented on June 19, silk cocoons that producers had been expecting to sell for ¥20 per *kan* were now selling for ¥4—and on top of that there was a very poor harvest due to inclement weather conditions: "Economic boom or bust, good or bad harvests, all are the natural workings of providence—there is no other way to look at it." Aizawa was to feel the pain of these workings throughout the year. On August 15 he reported that not a single tenant had come forward to make his semiannual rent payment.

And on October 16 Aizawa commented at length on the difficult conditions in his own village:

> The spring silkworm crop was unfortunately a disaster. Earlier, the winter crop of mulberry leaves was selling for ¥15 a horseload, but by the May silkworm season, the price had fallen to ¥4 to ¥5. Both silkworm producers and mulberry sellers were stunned by these unexpected blows. Then in July and August, on top of the poor silkworm crop, there was an unprecedented failure of the wheat crop. Even the old folks were saying they had never seen anything as bad. One *tan* of land yielded only one and a half bales. . . . Then prices collapsed, too. In July and August silk thread fell . . . and those who were holding four *kan* of silk thread in the spring, valued at ¥1,000, had to take a huge loss, selling it for around ¥250. The victims were everywhere: the people who up till last year were making the most profits were now the biggest losers, and indeed they felt themselves lucky if they could return to their original state, for there were many who suffered devastating losses.

Aizawa went on:

> Last year houses were being rebuilt all over the village; villagers were
> building storehouses and greatly improving the quality of their food and
> clothing. All of this showed the prosperity of the farmers. The typical
> farmer felt that even if he spent more on food, clothing, and housing, he
> would get all the money back with the next crop. So everyone exchanged
> their money for goods. But now the recession has come, goods have fallen
> in price, and can only be sold at a loss. So there is no money. Our farmers
> are in the habit of promising to pay their debts at the close of the silkworm
> season; so now they must pay for last year-end's sake, and for the orna-
> mental trees that they purchased this spring—not to mention their fertil-
> izer bills. But now the buyers are only offering ¥1 for eighteen or nineteen
> *momme* of silk thread . . .

Aizawa adds, though, that the worst seemed to be over. Silk thread
and woven silk prices were recovering, and the autumn crops were excellent. Even that, though, was a mixed blessing. On December 31 Aizawa
commented:

> In the fall, all of the crops were successful. The rice crop was one of the
> best ever (indeed, all over the world, there was an excellent crop). As a
> result, the price of rice fell, and now you can buy a bale for around ¥10.
> Last year, at the peak it was ¥23 or ¥24, so when you compare that, you
> can certainly see the ups and downs of this world. Thus, the flourish-
> ing farmer has suddenly become a fallen creature, his wallet empty and
> without the money to meet his obligations. Tenant rent in particular has
> suffered. This spring, we gave a reduction of from 10 percent to 30 per-
> cent on the newly adjusted rent, but even among those who received
> 30 percent, there were many who didn't pay a thing. Such is the poor
> state of feelings at present. It is extremely troublesome to negotiate rent
> reductions with each and every tenant, and there are many who pay only
> a down payment, leaving me with an unpaid debt of some 60 percent of
> the total.

Prices continued to fall into 1921: on June 2 Aizawa sold a large consignment of mulberry for a mere ¥2.50 a horseload.

A MODERN VILLAGE

In spite of the ups and downs of the economy, the village that Aizawa
had grown up in was changing beyond recognition. Life was becoming
more comfortable, entertainment more varied, work more urban—in
short, the village was becoming "modern." There was much to celebrate in these changes, and indeed, many of them were the result of

vigorous policies pursued by Aizawa and other elite villagers. But there was also much to lament. A way of life was passing, and Aizawa at times recognized the loss.

The landscape of the village was changing, too, as increasingly farm land was swallowed up by housing development. On May 9, 1923, Aizawa commented: "Recently there has been a huge growth in construction around the area of the Agriculture and Sericulture School. Bunkichi has built a house to the west of the school, and there's a house to the south, and one more under construction to the south of that. Then [heading south] there's Naruse's house, followed by the company housing for the Electric Light Company, and then there's the Keihin Electric Power Company. To the east there's still only the one house, belonging to Hiruma, and one more at the site of the boundary stone."

The school Aizawa refers to, which had opened just a month earlier, was located just to the south of the railway station. It was a large middle-school facility funded by the prefectural government, at a cost of ¥300,000—a huge sum by village standards. As with the railway, the Aizawa family had been deeply involved in bringing the school to Hashimoto. Aizawa had traveled to Yokohama several times to lobby key prefectural assemblymen when the decision to build a school was debated. Once the decision was made, he lobbied to locate it in Hashimoto—buttressing his campaign with offers of land and money from Hashimoto villagers. The Aizawa family donated most of the land—1.6 hectares—on which the school was built. It was a handsome Western-style set of buildings, with slate roofs instead of the customary tile. Aizawa had attended the opening ceremony on April 16, watching as a student representative addressed the three hundred entering students and family members, as well as the twelve teachers and other staff members. One of the teachers was Aizawa's second son, Yasuo. After graduating from Yokohama Industrial School, Yasuo had worked for a while in a manufacturing company in Yokohama, but like his elder brother, he found that the life of a salaried worker did not suit him. Yasuo had artistic inclinations and a deep love of the countryside around his birthplace. No doubt Aizawa's patronage of the school had helped his application to be one of the entering faculty.

In 1922, a sizeable power facility was built in Hashimoto. The Keihin Electric Power Company had been founded in November 1919, with the goal of harnessing water power in the mountains of Nagano prefecture and bringing the electricity generated from the mountain rivers down to the Kantō Plain. Its major shareholder was the Yokohama

Electric Company.[2] Yokohama Electric depended on coal-fired generating stations, and it had been badly hit by the steep increase in the price of coal during the war years. Keihin Electric was one of its initiatives to increase its access to water-powered generation. The line ran from Nagano through Yamanashi prefecture, with substations at Kōfu and, from 1922, in Hashimoto.

The Hashimoto substation, built on land sold to the company by the Aizawa family, permanently changed the landscape of Hashimoto. Rather than the wooden poles used by the telephone and electric companies to date, Keihin Electric's facilities were made of concrete and steel. The 0.8 hectare complex of sophisticated electrical equipment must have seemed an embodiment of the industrial age to the villagers of Hashimoto. For Aizawa, it seems to have been just another business deal. He made sure that the company paid not only for the land, but also for the mulberry growing on the land, which would be ripped out to make way for the new substation. During the construction process, the company set up a temporary headquarters in the offices of the Bussan Company. On July 21, 1922, Aizawa walked out to the construction site to watch the first steel pillars going up: "Today they were building steel pillars in Zenbei's field. This is the first such construction in this village." On September 29 Aizawa drew a picture of the poles in his diary, recording their exact dimensions. The electrical lines went right through the village, and Aizawa was involved in lengthy negotiations about compensation to villagers whose land was being disturbed by the construction.

Meanwhile, Aizawa lamented that good farming land was being neglected, and even allowed to grow wild. On April 10, 1922, he writes:

> At two o'clock I went to the main family house, then I went to look at several fields that are being returned by tenants. Many tenants in the Hashimoto and Aihara areas are giving up on farming in this time of low prices, and returning their land. Due to these conditions there are no new renters, and so it's not hard to imagine that in future there will be many overgrown fields. If a laborer goes to work in a factory or on the railroads, he can earn ¥70 or ¥80 a month, or he can earn ¥250 to ¥300 a year as a hired laborer on a farm. And so the number of self-employed farmers is declining and agricultural business is shrinking and the farmers present a miserable sight. This distress will not easily be dispelled in the next year or two.

On May 18, 1923, Aizawa went with two helpers to a field in the Ōnishi district. There they began pulling up the mulberry bushes and planting cypress saplings. Altogether they planted more than one thousand saplings. Aizawa explained his reasoning in tearing up a perfectly good field and replacing it with woodland: "This field has been allowed to grow wild. Recently, the trend has only been away from farming, and I can't find anyone to work the field. This particular field has woodland to the south, and to the east. Mr. Sasano has planted pine trees in the midst of his wheat field and will eventually turn it into pine woods, so there's really no choice but to turn it into woods." And again, on June 17, 1924, Aizawa comments: "A male farm laborer gets paid ¥1.50 per day. Adding in the value of meals brings his wage to around ¥2 per day. If he goes to work in Tokyo or Yokohama he can earn ¥5 or ¥6 per day for temporary work; and even for permanent employment he can get around ¥2 per day and have his daily train fare paid for. That work does not require such heavy physical labor so of course everyone is heading off to the cities, and happily moving away from agricultural labor." Aizawa adds: "Nobody is having a harder time than the landlords. This spring, many fields were returned to me. All of them are just going to turn into woodland. Next spring, it looks as though it's going to get even worse."

The landlord system had reached its peak at the turn of the twentieth century, when the lack of land and of alternative employments forced tenants to accept almost any terms. Now the wave had passed, and the system was heading into a slow decline. Hashimoto was in the vanguard of this decline, because its proximity to Tokyo and Yokohama opened up dramatic new opportunities for farmers who had formerly been tied to the village. But the trend was evident throughout Japan. Even in areas with less direct access to alternative employment, tenants used their growing experience with the market economy to push landlords to give them a greater share of the increasingly commercialized output of their rented land. Through the 1920s, tenants organized into unions and extracted substantial concessions from often defensive landlords. Although landlords were able to reassert some of their authority in the recession of the 1930s, their glory days were over. When landlords were stripped of all their surplus land in the great land reform of the American-led postwar occupation, the measure brought closure to a process that had been underway for more than two decades.

. . .

Gradually, as railway traffic increased, hire cars and buses began congregating around the station, pushing out the rickshaws that had been a fixture there before. On June 22, 1921, Aizawa commented: "These days there are many automobiles going in and out of Hashimoto station, and heading off in all directions. Thus, the passengers are happy, but the food stalls and rickshaw pullers are crying." The automobile could be very convenient. Aizawa records on July 6, 1921, that his brother, who had a meeting in the town of Atusgi, traveled there by automobile. "On the way back he drove through Hanbara, Tsukui, and Nakano, so that he could look at the geographical features." On October 10, 1922, Aizawa went to Hachiōji by bus, leaving Hashimoto station at 11 A.M. and getting off at the bus stop right in front of his destination, Nozaki Yasugoemon's house. After visiting with Nozaki, Aizawa did some shopping (he had his brother's gold watch repaired at a cost of ¥2.50), and then returned at 4:00 by steam train. On July 16, 1922, Aizawa commented on the large numbers of day trippers now visiting the area on Sundays—many of them to go fishing in the Sagami River: "From the direction of Yokohama and Hachiōji, the main road is full of people traveling by automobile. And the roads towards Tana and Tsukui county are also crowded with people who got off the train at Hashimoto station and hired automobiles, horse-drawn carts, or rickshaws to take them to the river banks." Inevitably, the arrival of so many automobiles and buses brought its share of traffic accidents. On June 5, 1923, Aizawa comments: "At four o'clock, the little child of the Ikedaya family was hit by a car in front of the Yoshidaya and injured. He was admitted to the Kaishundō, and I went to visit. Luckily he appears to have avoided major injury."

Automobile accidents paled in comparison with the excitement of June 15, 1923, when an airplane crashed in the grounds of the new Agriculture and Sericulture School. The citizens of Aihara had by this time got used to aircraft flying overhead, as both the Tokorozawa airbase and the new airbase at Tachikawa were rapidly expanding. On February 26, 1923, while visiting Tachikawa on business, Aizawa had asked for a tour of the base, and he was taken around by a conscript. There was a group of over fifty schoolchildren visiting from Yamanashi prefecture, and Aizawa listened in as an officer explained to them the finer points of an "L-style" reconnaissance plane. The diary includes many mentions of planes flying overhead, and even occasionally making planned landings in or near the village. On one occasion (May 31, 1920), Aizawa mentions the successful conclusion of a marathon thirty-day flight by two Italian planes from Italy to Japan—the planes landed in Osaka on the thirtieth and then flew on to a hero's welcome in Tokyo's Yoyogi Army Base on the thirty-first (Aizawa must have learned of these events from the evening newspaper). But this time, nothing was planned. As Aizawa records: "At noon, a plane crashed in the west grounds of the Agriculture and Sericulture School. Luckily, Lieutenant Ōshiba escaped unharmed. But the plane was wrecked. After telegraphing to Tokorozawa, a party of soldiers together with an engineer and some civilians arrived by truck. Ōshiba and the officers celebrated his escape, then they disassembled the aircraft, and by nightfall, they had loaded it all up and departed for Tokorozawa." Aizawa added slightly wistfully: "My whole family went to see it—only I stayed to look after the house."

Entertainment was modernized, too. On September 26, 1919, a new theater opened in Hashimoto: the six-hundred-seat Asahikan (Rising Sun Theater). The theater was the brainchild of a group of younger members of the village elite, including Aizawa's son, Shigeharu, who was its managing director. Aizawa himself bought two shares in the company, but otherwise seems to have been uninvolved in its creation. The theater was in a newly constructed building to the west of the railway station. Aizawa attended the opening celebration, which was followed by a revue put on by a troupe of actresses.

The Asahikan was an instant success and immediately became an essential part of the village's cultural life. The theater put on entertainments at least once or twice a week, and Aizawa or his family members usually attended at least one event, even if only to stand and watch for a while *(tachimi)*. The types of entertainment were quite varied. On some occasions, they included Western-style revues. On others, there were *gidayū* ballad dramas, *naniwabushi* storytelling performances, movies, and modern dramas *(shinpageki)*. The Asahikan also staged educational shows with considerably less entertainment value—such as a lecture on making sacks for baling wheat, a play about fire prevention, or a movie on chemical fertilizers (although on this occasion the projector broke, so Aizawa was unable to learn about the new technologies).[3] On September 15, 1920, Aizawa commented rather wryly: "Since it opened on the twelfth, the modern drama at the Asahikan has been sold out. It's as though there were no recession. Even though the three-day run is over, they say they are going to do another performance tonight. This August, not a single tenant paid their rent to me, and every other landlord I've spoken to said the situation was the same for them. When it suits [the tenants] not to, they don't pay. There's something wrong with that kind of thinking." Still, as a shareholder of Asahikan, Aizawa was able to benefit from its success. In 1923 it declared a 10 percent dividend, and it continued to be profitable in the following years. The Asahikan remained in business until 1981, when it was finally closed down and demolished.

A little later, in 1925, another theater opened in the neighboring village of Sakai—the Yūrakkan. On October 29, 1925, Aizawa's children and grandchildren went to the Yūrakkan to hear a female ballad singer. They took with them ¥3 worth of flowers to present to the performer.

Another modern enterprise in which Shigeharu was closely involved was the opening of a seasonal racecourse in Hashimoto. Horse racing became increasingly popular in Japan after the Russo-Japanese War, under the (perhaps self-serving) rationale of improving the nation's stock of horses in the event of another major war. Behind this patriotic façade, of course, was the rapid spread of urban mass culture and popular entertainment. The first races were held on May 5 and 6, 1923, on land rented to the organizers by Aizawa. The weather was good, businesses were closed (May 5 was Boys' Day, now renamed Children's Day, and May 6 was a Sunday), so the event was very well-attended— more than ten thousand visitors came to see the races over the two-day event. The racecourse was surrounded by cloth and straw fencing, to prevent those who did not buy a ticket from seeing inside. In addition to entrance tickets, betting slips were on sale at ¥0.50 per bet. In spite of the public holidays, areas shopkeepers set up stalls on the grounds to sell drinks and food.

Aizawa's entire family went to see the races, although Aizawa himself stayed home to mind the house. In 1923, the races were a once-only event; but the following year the races began on a regular schedule, with more extensive infrastructure and financing. This time, Shigeharu was involved as one of the leaders of the enterprise. Now that the race course was to be a properly constituted business, a permit was required from the county authorities. This Shigeharu secured on March 30, 1925. The races began just two days later, on April 2. The takings were good from the start: ¥2,200 on the first day and ¥6,700 on the second, with total profits for the two days of ¥2,600. On April 5 Shigeharu and several of his business partners set off by automobile to distribute flyers throughout the surrounding towns and villages. The next day, they sold 10,900 entrance tickets. The county chief and several other officials were there. The fall race was even more successful—presumably, by this time word had spread of the new local attraction. The race meet took in ¥62,000 over the three-day event, with a profit of ¥13,000.

For the most part, the competitors seem to have been local workhorses. Farmers from nearby villages arrived in horse-drawn carts

and put up overnight at the Sakaiya Restaurant near the railway station. At least one of the racehorse owners was from Hashimoto. Yugi
Tetsunosuke was the owner of the "Long Life" public bath house,
opened in October 1925. Tetsunosuke was one of the racy young men
of Hashimoto—in addition to horses, he had a collection of motorcycles
that he liked to ride loudly around the formerly placid village streets.[4]

By 1926 the racecourse seems to have run afoul of changes in the law
regulating the gambling business. The Hashimoto Horse-Racing Club,
as it was now called, was forcibly merged into the Fujisawa Racing
Organization, and the Hashimoto track was permanently closed. The
fields reverted to wheat and mulberry, and within a few years they had
been overrun by the rampant spread of suburban housing.

. . .

The village also continued to become modernized in its infrastructure—and in many cases this also profited Aizawa's family. In 1921
Hashimoto became connected to the outside world by telephone. In
the first instance, this was only by way of a public phone located in the
Hashimoto post office (where Shigeharu was the assistant postmaster
and which was also attached to the Aizawa main family residence).
The service formally opened on November 1, with a celebration at the
post office to which the project's key contributors were invited. An arch
was constructed in front of the post office and festooned with the flags
of the world, symbolizing Hashimoto's connection to the rest of the
world through communications technology. One hundred and twenty
commemorative trays were ordered, to be distributed to the guests and
other concerned parties. As in the case of the railway, the villagers of
Hashimoto had to put up a substantial sum of money in the form of a
"contribution" to the national telephone company. Shigeharu raised a
total of ¥2,700, of which ¥2,500 was donated to the telephone company, and the remaining ¥200 used to defray start-up expenses. Aizawa
Yasuemon was the largest contributor, donating ¥500. Kikutarō commented on the occasion of the opening: "Probably next year we will
also get private telephone lines. Kamimizo got permission for private
lines last year, and the service is currently under construction. They
recently held a lottery to assign the first fifty-three numbers."

And indeed, the village received approval to install private lines in
1922. As Aizawa recorded on November 9, the village of Aihara received
permission to install forty-five phone lines, and held a lottery to assign
the numbers. Aizawa's number was to be Hashimoto 20. The Aizawa

main house got the number two, and both Shigeharu and Yasuemon's wife were also awarded lines in their names, although (since both lived in a house that already had a line approved) they sublet their lines, Shigeharu to the grain inspection substation, and Yasuemon's wife to the Ikedaya store. According to Aizawa, no one wanted the number forty-two, which was considered unlucky (forty-two can be pronounced *shi-ni* which sounds like "unto death"). After some consultation, the villagers agreed that if an assignee by lottery should refuse the number, the village office should take it in exchange for its own assigned number. By chance, however, the village office in fact drew the number forty-two. Phone service actually began on December 26, connecting Aihara with Yokohama, Hachiōji, and Tokyo. On January 13, 1923, the Hashimoto post office held a celebration of the new service, with electric illuminations in front of the post office, a *taiko* drum performance by the hamlet's youth association, and a show of "hand-dancing" by a local troupe. The new service was convenient—particularly for Yoshihisa, Aizawa's fun-loving son, who often used it to invite his friends over or to call home from his frequent travels—but it was by no means inexpensive. In January 1924 Aizawa records paying a phone bill of ¥9.30 for the month.

Hashimoto also became increasingly bright at night, as houses were lit up by electric light and the streets of the hamlet gradually acquired street lights. The station area was the first to be lit up, but by February 1924 even Aizawa's street had lights. As in other cases, though, this involved a very specific effort by Aizawa and his neighbors: they formed an association to handle the administration, and they were required to pay for the electricity used by the lights.

Then, in August 1925, Aizawa's area of Hashimoto was connected to a water main. This was a private commercial venture, pioneered by Shigeharu and his frequent business partner Wada Hidetarō. They built a water tank on the property of Wada Kōkichi and connected a total of eighty houses to the supply. Their total investment came to over ¥10,000, but they could look forward to a steady income from the users, who were charged (based on the number of members in the family) anything from ¥0.70 to ¥1 per month. In February, Aizawa commented: "These days they are laying water mains every day on the main street, and with money loaned by [the Seya] bank and others, houses are springing up everywhere, so that everyone says they are surprised by this sudden growth." Aizawa commented on the new inn that was under construction in the village: an entrepreneur was moving a house from Tokyo to a site rented to him by Aizawa's brother. Until the inn opened, the only place to stay in Hashimoto was at the Sakaiya Restaurant, which accepted paying guests.

The finishing touches to the family's modernization came when Yasuemon bought, in succession, an automobile and a radio. He seems to have bought his car at least as early as 1921—on March 15, Aizawa records that his brother, after visiting their cousin Jungorō in hospital, "drove back by automobile on his own." The radio came soon after the introduction of public broadcasting in 1925: Aizawa records its installation on October 31, without further comment.

THE WORLD TURNED UPSIDE DOWN

On September 1, 1923, the hamlet of Hashimoto was preparing for its annual shrine festival to be held later that day. It was an official village half-holiday, and after working in the fields in the morning, the farming families of Hashimoto were preparing baths while their women made *soba* noodles and bean-filled rice cakes to celebrate the festival.[5] Aizawa was at home, when, shortly before noon, a massive earthquake struck.

He describes it in his diary:

> At noon there was a huge earthquake. We were right in the middle of lunch. I, Eiko, Matsuyo, Yoshihisa, and the maid Haru immediately ran out into the back garden. While we watched the tremors rapidly increase in intensity, the wall of the storehouse collapsed, while the main house bucked like a ship as the earth opened up here and there. The tremors kept on coming, and did not moderate until three o'clock. Although the movements of the earth had calmed down, we still feared a further disaster, so we made preparations to stay the night in the bamboo grove. Apart from the collapse of the storehouse wall, a wall fell down in the *tokonoma,* and the stone monument in the northeast part of the property was broken. Also the bathhouse and the storage room were thrown out of kilter. Shigeharu was at the main house, taking care of the post office during the emergency. At three o'clock he came home, and we talked about the condition of the house. The main family house was damaged considerably more than ours. But we, the main family, and the other branch family can all consider ourselves lucky that we suffered no worse loss. Yasuo went off in the morning to the Agriculture and Sericulture School, and when the earthquake struck he happened to be outside. He came home afterward.

Meanwhile, Aizawa's daughter Hanako had gone to the girls' high school in Hachiōji on the first train in the morning, and she was on her way home when the earthquake struck at noon. Everyone got off the train and began walking. Hanako—no doubt in shock from the disaster—suddenly felt unable to go on, and she rested for a while at a house by the roadside. Word of her distress eventually got back to her family, and Yoshihisa was getting ready to go rescue her, when she suddenly felt better and returned home alone.

Aizawa goes on: "Tonight our whole family is sleeping out in the bamboo grove. Kaneko Shimajirō's family, too, have come to stay in our bamboo grove, while the south neighbor, Inoue Asajirō, and his family slept in the neighboring grove. Kanda Inekichi and the cooper, Sakuma Asajirō, all took shelter at the entrance to our bamboo stand by the river."

Aizawa goes on to assess the extent of the damage in the village. Although many had suffered damage to their outbuildings—particularly their earth-walled storehouses—only four reports of collapsed residences had come in. "One notable example is the Marutsū [Naigai Bussan] warehouse near the station, which was built of stone and measured five *ken* by fifteen *ken* [9 meters by 27 meters], and which completely collapsed." The sake manufacturer Kannōya had almost fifty 150-*koku* (27,000-liter) barrels of freshly brewed sake in its cellars. The shock of the quake broached the massive barrels in which the liquor was kept, and suddenly the shop was knee-deep in rice wine. The owners tried pumping the sake into smaller barrels using a hand-pump, but they were only able to save a tiny fraction of their stores.[6]

In the evening Aizawa went for a walk around the village in the moonlight. He commented on the extensive damage to the village roads, with water seeping into the fissures in many places. He also saw landslides in the hillier parts of the village. The main road into the neighboring village of Sakai was impassable. He saw collapsed buildings in many places—though usually outbuildings, not residences. From the west, he heard reports of severe damage, with "deaths to both people and livestock."

The next day, the family continued to feel aftershocks: "I can't express the anxiety and fear that everyone is feeling." Their anxiety was deepened as reports began trickling in from returning villagers on the great disaster that had befallen Yokohama.

> Other than the Shōkin Bank, the entire center of the city has been destroyed by earthquake-induced collapse or by fire. The deaths are without number. Tokyo has met a similar fate. As a result of the disaster, electricity is disconnected, and travel and transport are impossible. . . . On the evening

of the first, from four to six o'clock, we all first saw that there was a white cloud in the sky, as though there were a thunderstorm approaching. It gave us a feeling of sadness to see it. Some people said it was like the smoke that comes from the crater of a volcano. Everyone thought it was very strange.

What they were witnessing was the aftermath of the greatest disaster ever to befall the metropolitan area around Japan's capital city. In the final accounting, the authorities estimated 106,000 dead, 52,000 injured, and 694,000 homes destroyed, with a total economic cost of around ¥10 billion. The city of Odawara, closest to the epicenter, was hit almost simultaneously by the earthquake, the tsunami that it spawned, and by the fires that followed. Some 80 to 90 percent of all houses were destroyed, and eleven thousand out of a population of twenty-four thousand were killed or injured. Many villages in the mountainous areas around Odawara were completely wiped out from the shock of the quake, the fires that followed, or from the devastating landslides that pitched entire hamlets into the abyss. Kamakura, the beautiful capital of the medieval shogunate, was hit by a tsunami nine meters high that wiped out virtually every house in the town, as well as many of its precious Buddhist and Shinto monuments. The oil terminals at the naval base of Yokosuka caught fire and burned fiercely for almost two weeks. The great city of Yokohama was pulverized: most of the brick and tile buildings in the center of the city collapsed, crushing those inside and nearby. The fires that followed, raging over an area of 1,300 hectares (80 percent of the entire city) caused death to thousands more. Some 410,000 out of a total population of 440,000 were rendered homeless—if they escaped with their lives.[7] Throughout the rest of Kanagawa prefecture, 230,000 families suffered losses in the quake, with a total death toll of 32,000.

Although squarely in the earthquake zone, Aihara suffered much less than the coastal cities. There were no deaths in the village, and only one reported serious injury. The final toll was 101 houses damaged, of which thirteen were destroyed; 245 outbuildings damaged, with fifty-eight destroyed; thirteen bridges damaged or collapsed; and 120 meters of damaged or collapsed road. The total cost was estimated at ¥174,000. The surrounding villages were not all so lucky. Ōsawa village suffered one fatality; forty-two houses collapsed in Ōno village (though only two injuries were reported).

The terror that the people of Hashimoto felt was not caused only by nature. The day after the earthquake, rumors began spreading throughout the Kantō region that gangs of Koreans were roaming the countryside attacking Japanese villagers. The rumors were completely unfounded, but for some time they were fostered by prefectural officials. Katō Shigeo, who was six years old at the time, recalls that "on the morning of September 2, there was a sudden commotion from the direction of the police office on the main road. When I went out to see what was happening, my father said 'go to the back of the house— there's a gang of insurgents *(bōto)* coming.' Constable Gotō from the police station was giving some sort of directions in a high voice, and a messenger was racing off on his bicycle in the direction of Aihara hamlet." The policeman had received a report of several gangs converging on the village from the direction of Machida. He ordered the village families to hide their children in the hills or in bushes closer to the village, and make sure that they stayed silent. When Shigeo was being hustled to his hiding place, he saw a pack of village men near the police station, armed with bamboo staves and wooden swords, with the occasional flash of steel amongst them Ōtsuka Kōji recalls his mother whispering to him in their hiding place: "The insurgents are going to come back, so you mustn't make a sound."[8]

Oshida Kumesaburō was one of the guards who took up a weapon to defend the village. A farm hand in the household of Aizawa's cousin, he was sent with several others to man the entrance to the village at the Ryōgoku Bridge. For the next ten days, he and his fellow vigilantes stopped and questioned anyone trying to enter the village. Those in need of help they directed to the aid station outside the Ushikubo home, or pointed on their way to their destination. To anyone considered suspicious, they denied entry to the village.[9]

Several days later, Ōtsuka's father set off with a group of villagers to look for metal jacks to prop up houses in their neighborhood that had come off their foundations. They went by bicycle in the direction of Tachikawa, hoping to find a blacksmith along the way or a hardware shop in Tachikawa willing to sell them the materials. In a village on the far bank of the Tama River, the group from Hashimoto was suddenly surrounded by a militia of hostile villagers. The most common method of investigation by the vigilante gangs formed in the aftermath of the quake was to question suspicious people, and listen if they spoke Japanese with a Korean accent. The members of the Hashimoto group were dressed in white shirts and white leggings. To the suspicious villagers, these looked like the white clothes usually worn by Koreans. To make matters worse, one of the Hashimoto group had a severe stutter, which made it appear as though he could not speak Japanese.

Fearful for their lives, a braver member of the group began explaining slowly and clearly why they appeared like they did, and what mission they were on. After being detained for an hour, they were allowed to carry on. But, intimidated by the vigilantes, they abandoned their mission and slunk back to Hashimoto. They had reason to be chastened. Vigilante groups killed as many as five thousand innocent Koreans, as well as fellow Japanese citizens, in the aftermath of the earthquake, in many cases choosing their victims by accent or clothing alone.[10]

Aizawa commented on the events:

> There is a report that several hundred Korean insurgents are running wild in the direction of Machida. It seems they are gradually spreading out in all directions. I informed the entire village of this, and the firefighting volunteers are standing ready. They have mounted a night watch, and infants have been evacuated from the bamboo groves to the fields. Our hearts are all the more filled with sadness. This evening, several people came to the village, but we chased them out and sent them on the way to Hachiōji. It is really like adding wind to rain. It is particularly hard for the women and children.

The aftershocks continued through the third day, and Aizawa, still sleeping out in the bamboo grove, commented that "there isn't a moment of peace of mind." He went on: "Thankfully, our village did not suffer any fires. By contrast, in Tokyo and Yokohama men have lost their wives and children to the fires, they have seen all their assets go up in smoke; I have heard that countless people are looking up at the sky and weeping." Shigeharu, although feeling ill, went to Hachiōji by rickshaw to look for supplies, Yasuo accompanying him on his bicycle. At night, the three brothers continued to mount guard with their unit of the firefighting volunteers (Shigeharu was the unit's chief), against a possible attack by marauding Koreans. It was only on the fourth day that the tremors finally subsided and the Aizawa family moved back to sleep in their house, although they slept in a room by the garden and left the shutters open so they could leave at a moment's notice. They were joined by a refugee family, acquaintances of Shigeharu who had lost their home in Yokohama and were now on their way on foot back to their home village. "People like this are passing to and fro on the main road all day and all night. The trains are out of service, so they are all traveling on foot. Many of them are trudging without umbrellas in the rain." Although these refugees were being allowed free passage, Aizawa went on: "We are continuing to keep a lookout against the arrival of lawless Koreans." Aihara village admitted two hundred refugees in the days after the earthquake. The villages that now comprise Sagamihara city took in a total of almost twelve hundred refugees.[11]

Meanwhile, the city of Tokyo had been placed under martial law and an imperial edict authorized the requisition of food, water, firewood, charcoal, paraffin, building materials, medicines, handcarts, and other supplies from the surrounding countryside. On September 3 martial law was extended to the entire metropolitan area including Kanagawa prefecture, and a Kantō Martial Law Headquarters was established under the direction of General Fukuda Masatarō. Instructions for the implementation of the martial law and requisitions were passed down from the headquarters to the county seats (Fujisawa was still operating in spite of catastrophic damage to the administrative buildings), which in turn commanded each village to establish a martial law headquarters within the village office. From the seventh, the army units stationed in the Sagami River area were mobilized to guard the water supplies for Yokohama, and units were dispatched to patrol the villages. Locally recruited brigades were allowed a night's leave to check on their families, so the villages around Aihara were busy with the coming and going of soldiers. On September 6 the Kamimizo police headquarters (the local headquarters for the surrounding villages, including Aihara) issued a series of instructions to villagers: "The possession of dangerous weapons is forbidden." "The relatives of earthquake victims should wherever possible shelter and assist them." "Those who are setting off to help earthquake victims should collect safe conduct passes from the police headquarters or the village office." "It is a good idea to remember to take a paraffin lamp with you if you need to evacuate your house." In addition, the police chief issued the following warnings:

> It is unavoidable that prices should increase at a time like this, but you must avoid any unfair or excessive price increases on the occasion of the disaster.

> It is urgently necessary for young men's associations and volunteer security forces to repair roads and prevent obstructions to transport and communication.

> It is desirable to offer assistance to earthquake victims who are traveling along local roads.

Indeed, by September 5 villages along the main roads (including Hashimoto) set up stations to offer help to the constant flow of fleeing victims, including serving tea and rice balls (donated by the wealthier villagers). The villages also set up sleeping facilities in temples and shrines, and offered medical services to the sick and injured. For example, Asamizo village accommodated twenty-four victims in the school and temple on the night of the fifth, and on the following day, the village doctor, Dr. Kobayashi, treated many of the victims—the main complaint was sore feet.[12] The Kamimizo police office (which set up its own relief outpost outside the police building) estimated that the villagers in its jurisdiction offered help to a total of 1,350 refugees between September 2 and September 7.

On the fifth day the village began pulling itself back together. Aizawa spent the morning tidying up his house from the mess caused by the earthquake, and in the afternoon he attended a meeting of the village council, which deliberated on defense and relief measures. Yasuo traveled to the Hachiōji suburbs to check up on his Suzuki cousins (they had come through unharmed). Aizawa commented: "Toward Atsugi, and to the south, there were few homes that survived the earthquake. Mr. Oshio lost his life, and the Ōshima family lost several members." On day six Aizawa received his first newspaper since the disaster—a single sheet published by the *Tokyo Nichinichi*. "I will keep this newssheet as a memento," he wrote.

On Friday November 7—the seventh day after the disaster—Aizawa's son Yasuo traveled to Tokyo. His purpose was to collect his fiancée, Itoko, and her father, who was sick in a private hospital there. He hired a car in the morning and drove straight to the city. Once he arrived at the hospital, he picked up Itoko and her father, and the three of them drove back to Hashimoto, arriving at two in the afternoon. The father's family in Nakatsu sent a palanquin to carry him home, and Aizawa helped settle him in and saw him on his way. Aizawa does not expand on Yasuo's visit or on the conditions in Tokyo, but the fact that he could drive into the center of the city and back out in a morning indicates that road conditions must have been passable. Meanwhile Yoshihisa went to stay with his cousin Chōichi in Hachiōji—presumably to resume his life of pleasure.

By this time villages in the region were mobilizing to send relief supplies to the worst-hit areas. The village of Asamizo, close to Hashimoto, asked each village family to use one *shō* (about one kilogram) of flour to make dumplings, which each hamlet then collected and bagged. A contingent from the village left on bicycles and took the consignment to the devastated center of Yokohama. Other villages in the area sent members of their youth associations to help the hard-hit southern part of the county with reconstruction efforts.[13]

Although much less frequent, the tremors continued for several more days. Almost daily, Aizawa commented on the anxiety that everyone continued to feel. Slowly, he and his family tidied up the house (although it had not sustained major damage, much of its contents had been displaced, and some of them smashed) and the family graveyard, where almost all the gravestones had suffered damage. Aizawa donated materials to those who faced major repairs—three pine trees for wooden planks to Bunshichi and some tin roofing materials for Wada Shōkichi (September 7 and 9). He helped his brother rebuild his storehouse roof. Yasuo and Shigeharu did night duty with the volunteer guard units.

On September 15 Yasuo once again traveled to "ground zero"—this time to the devastated center of Yokohama. Yasuo led a group of seventy students from the Agriculture and Sericulture School. The party went to the prefectural office, where they donated their produce to the prefecture.

On September 17 the Aihara village council voted to donate ¥192 from its disaster relief fund to the villagers who had suffered losses in the earthquake. This represented almost the entire fund, which was normally used for providing modest assistance to villagers who had suffered house fires or other such losses. Each of the thirteen villagers whose houses had collapsed received ¥13, as did the one injured villager. The village also sold rice at a subsidized price to those villagers who had been hit by the earthquake. By the end of its relief efforts, Aihara had dispensed a total of ¥416 in relief funds.[14]

The damage to the village was not only physical. The earthquake caused enormous disruption to the Japanese economy, with mixed effects in Aihara. The quake came just at the time of the sweet potato harvest, and the disruption to the region's transportation system made it virtually impossible to sell the crop, causing large losses to some farmers. The quake also came just as many families were rearing their fall crop of silkworms, and the mass evacuation of houses for a period of several days resulted in the loss of many families' silkworm colonies. Large consignments of silk thread were also lost in the fires in Yokohama, many of them belonging to local merchants. Kōza county's silk merchants and manufacturers lost a total of ¥300,000 worth of merchandise in this way (the Ekishinsha lost a large consignment in this way, and it was still reserving for the losses a decade later).[15]

On September 20 Aizawa went up into the hills to inspect his woodland property. "From Tsukui to the west, all along the Musashi highlands, you can see the red gashes of landslides. It is as though the

mountains were draped in red cloth. The valleys have been filled in
with fallen trees and rocks . . . there are fallen trees without number,
and the losses are incalculable." In the high ground overlooking the
Sagami River, a stretch of road four hundred meters long had collapsed
in a landslide; three houses on the road were swept almost a hundred
meters down the road into a ravine.

Toward the end of the month, the villagers of Aihara began traveling
on the reopened Hachiōji-Shinjuku railway line to see the wreckage of
Tokyo and Yokohama for themselves. Yoshihisa and his cousin Chōichi
went to Tokyo on the twenty-fifth. On September 28 Shigeharu and
Yoshihisa went into Yokohama. Because the Yokohama line was still
not operating, they drove by automobile to Hachiōji (giving Hanako a
ride to her school on the way), and took the train into Tokyo from there.
They went on to Yokohama, visited five different families with whom
the Aizawa had ties, and then returned to stay the night in Tokyo. One
of the families, the Mori, had lost their eldest son, who was crushed by
a falling building on his way home from school.

By early October the trains were running again, and even in the
destroyed cities life was resuming its patterns. On October 10 Yoshihisa
resumed his college career at Tōyō University in Tokyo. Rather than live
in the city, he opted to stay at home, and he purchased a monthly rail
pass from Hashimoto station to Tokyo's Sugamo, at a student's price of
¥12.50 a month. On October 14 Aizawa commented, "Although it has
been forty days since the great earthquake, we are still experiencing
aftershocks every day. Although each household is striving to repair the
earthquake damage, we are unable to calm our hearts."

On October 16 Aizawa himself made his first visit to Yokohama
since the earthquake. The purpose was to order fertilizer on behalf of
the village Agricultural Association. Aizawa proceeded straight to the
temporary quarters of the prefectural Agricultural Association, and
then returned home, but "this was the first time I had seen with my
own eyes the tragedy of the great earthquake and fire in Yokohama.
Really, there are no words to express the tragedy." A few days later, on
the twenty-eighth, Aizawa went to Fujisawa, the county seat, where
"the county office came close to collapsing, and is now operating out
of lean-tos in the grounds."

In spite of his sympathy for the victims of the tragedy, Aizawa was
not averse to profiting from it. The rebuilding effort sent the price of
building materials spiraling. Buyers began arriving in the village looking for bamboo and lumber. Aizawa noted that logs that were selling

for ¥0.50 in the village were being resold for as much as ¥3 in Tokyo. "Lumber is likely to continue to rise in future, so there's no hurry to sell," he noted. And on December 1, Aizawa attended a village meeting at which it was resolved to apply for a reduction in taxes for the year on account of earthquake damage—in spite of the relatively light losses suffered in Aihara.

Ironically, by the middle of September Aihara and other villages in the region began receiving supplies shipped to the earthquake zone from other parts of Japan and the rest of the world. Supplies of candles, rice, charcoal, cotton cloth, and clothes began arriving in the lightly-damaged villages around Aihara. The supplies were distributed to the families worst hit by the earthquake, but there were often considerable amounts left over, and many hamlets auctioned these off to the highest bidder. And in spite of the enormous damage to Yokohama and the coastal towns, several lightly affected inland villages applied to Kanagawa prefecture for reconstruction funds—Tana village, for example, asked the prefecture for ¥564 for road repairs, and Ōsawa asked for ¥217. Aihara assigned village funds of ¥4,019 to reconstruction over a period of three years, but it appears to have done so without asking for handouts more urgently needed elsewhere.[16]

On December 27, 1923, the prince regent, Hirohito, traveled by automobile to preside over the opening ceremony of the forty-eighth Diet session. As the prince passed near the Toranomon Gate of the imperial palace, Nanba Daisuke, the son of a Diet member and the scion of a distinguished family, drew a gun from inside a converted walking stick, pointed it at the prince's car, and fired. His bullet shattered the car window, but missed the prince. Coming as it did on the heels of the earthquake, the incident threw the nation into shock. The entire cabinet resigned. Daisuke's father immediately resigned from his seat in the Diet (soon after, he and his family changed their name to Kurokawa and emigrated to Java). Shōriki Matsutarō, the prefect of the Tokyo Metropolitan Police, also resigned (the next year he purchased the *Yomiuri* newspaper, which he turned into the world's largest-circulation daily). Nanba himself was arrested on the spot and hanged the following year. A shocked Aizawa commented: "This incident is unprecedented since the opening of the country. It is so deplorable that words fail me. Although people say that the recent degradation of political thought is a natural trend, there has been huge influx of ignorant know-it-alls who have no real understanding of foreign ideas, but who are destroying the beautiful customs of the Japanese Empire.

Because of this, those who represent pure Japanese values are being made to suffer by these villains. They are causing unendurable anxiety to both high and low without distinction. Really, what kind of person could cause this disgraceful incident!" Aizawa went on to blame the political world for the situation.

> The present cabinet of Yamamoto Gonnohyōe was sworn in on September 1, the day of the earthquake, and Gotō Shinpei became the home minister. Gotō introduced all sorts of high-handed measures without any good effects. Moreover, the Reconstruction Bureau that he formed in the wake of the earthquake has this month had the budget for its plan reduced by the special Diet, and so the bureau is barely able to survive. There is something suspicious about the way the home minister calmly shows his face to the world. Seeing this man's lack of virtue together with this disgraceful incident, I feel that it will be hard for our nation to recover.

THE FAMILY PATRIARCH

By the turn of the 1920s, Aizawa was in his mid-fifties—a relatively old man by the standards of the day. In fact he was to live another forty-plus years, but it is unlikely that he or anyone else in the village imagined he had such good fortune in store. In his last years as mayor of Aihara, Aizawa suffered increasingly from a variety of ailments, while his friends and relatives began dying all around him. In January 1919, for example, Aizawa's neighbor and relative Kutarō died at the age of forty-six. It was the start of a grim year for Kutarō's family—on November 6 his granddaughter died from unexplained causes; and just two months later, on January 9, the girl's mother, Asa, also died. On October 3, 1920, Aizawa's mother died (though at the advanced age of eighty-six). Then, on December 11, Aizawa's aunt (Jungorō's mother) died at the age of eighty-eight. They were the two oldest residents of Hashimoto. Just three months later, on March 22, her son Jungorō also died. Jungorō was from Aizawa's own generation—he was only fifty-seven years old—and his death was undoubtedly a shock to Aizawa, in spite of the many financial problems that Aizawa had had with his cousin. Just a few months later, on August 18, 1921, Aizawa's brother-in-law and friend Ushikubo Seigorō died. He was sixty years old. Aizawa commented that Seigorō had been in ill health for several years, but "he has only cleared up [the marriages of] his eldest son and daughter. He still has seven other children. This will only increase [his wife] Kiwa's troubles. But there is nothing to be done—one can not change the span of one's life, alas." And indeed, Kiwa's own turn was to follow very soon afterward. On a trip to Tokyo to deliver some mementoes of her husband to a relative in Tsukiji, she suddenly fell ill and died a few days later. During the course of the early 1920s, many other friends, relatives, and business partners died.

Meanwhile Aizawa himself was the victim of increasingly frequent bouts of illness. On June 22, 1922, he suddenly began to feel extreme stomach pains, and he took to his bed for the next four days. Dr. Yajima came to give him a shot (presumably an opiate), which relieved the pain temporarily. But it was not until he had a bowel movement on June 27 that he began to feel really better. That same year, on September 30, he wrote: "I felt cold and unwell from this morning, but I had to participate in the meeting with Nozaki. But on the way home I felt unbearably cold, my heart was palpitating and I felt that I could hardly make it home. I parted with my brother at the gate to his house, and went home and went to bed without having any dinner." Aizawa had problems with his teeth, too. Several times he took to his bed for a day or more, suffering from toothache. His nephew, Chōichi, was a pharmacist and dentist in Hachiōji, and after the turn of the 1920s, Aizawa turned to him for treatment (before that, he appears to have had no dental care whatever). In February 1920 Aizawa made a series of visits to Chōichi, to have himself fitted for some false teeth: "I have been five or six times, and finally I have the new teeth. It feels very unpleasant." On September 13, 1924, Chōichi pulled a tooth, and had a gold replacement made up. Seeing the condition of Aizawa's remaining teeth, Chōichi recommended not one but three gold teeth, to replace those lost or too worn to be serviceable (Aizawa paid ¥5 each for the teeth, and bought one for his youngest son into the bargain). On the way home from the dentist, Aizawa picked up a pair of reading glasses. A widower with deteriorating health and friends and relatives dying at an alarming rate—no doubt Aizawa felt his mortality.

However, Aizawa still had young children in the house—and his overwhelming responsibility was to get them married off securely. This was an enormously time-consuming affair, involving endless negotiations and consultation with family members as well as prospective spouses and their families.

On June 24, 1919, Aihara's leading citizen, Hara Seibei, came to Aizawa with a marriage proposal for Aizawa's daughter Asako, who was twenty years old. Asako had attended girls' high school in Hachiōji, and her education was now considered complete. Aizawa was receptive to—indeed, excited about—the proposal, and events moved quite rapidly thereafter. The wedding took place on November 5, at the bridegroom's home village of Oyamada. Asako's new husband was Wakabayashi Masanari, a teacher in the Oyamada elementary school. Although the family were village landlords on a similar level to Aizawa, he was clearly attracted by their family background, which appears to have included warrior ancestors. A little over a year later, on February 16, 1922, Asako presented her new family with a daughter, and Aizawa with another granddaughter. Her name was Hatsue. Aizawa sent gifts of white rice, fish, underwear, sugar, and red and white flannel cloth—all symbolizing purity (white) and celebration (red). Asako had another daughter, named Yoshiko, on October 31, 1925.

Soon after Asako's marriage, Aizawa got to work looking for a suitable bride for his second son, Yasuo. Aizawa was approached on May 2, 1920, by Yasumuro Hakushin, an acquaintance who lived in Yokohama. He suggested an alliance with the Ōsugi family of Yokohama. Evidently the result was acceptable, and Yasuo got married on November 27, 1920, to Ōsugi Setsuko. Yasuo and his bride remained in Yokohama after their marriage. Yasuo was working at the time for the Yokohama Lead Piping Company.

Unfortunately, for reasons that are not made clear in the diary, Yasuo's marriage did not work out. This was no doubt one of the reasons why he chose to quit his job in Yokohama and return to Hashimoto to work as a teacher. On April 27, 1924, Yasuo remarried, this time to Umezawa Itoko, twenty-four years old. Itoko came from the village of Nakatsu—the same village as Shigeharu's bride's family, who had clearly been instrumental in helping arrange the alliance. Subsequently, in late 1925, Aizawa built for his son a substantial house on a plot of land near the railway station. Yasuo and his wife moved in on December 13. This seems to have been the start of a happy and settled life for Yasuo. Once settled into his new job, Yasuo found the time to pursue his real passion: painting. Yasuo surprised his father by entering a Western-style painting of the source of the Sagami River in a competition in Yokohama—and winning a prize.

Aizawa was left with three unmarried children: Yoshihisa, Hanako, and Mieko. Mieko was still in elementary school, and was closer in age to Aizawa's grandchildren than to his older children (in 1925, she was accepted into the public high school in Hachiōji). Hanako attended the girls' high school in Hachiōji, and was not yet ready for marriage. Yoshihisa, the most carefree and easygoing of Aizawa's children, was enjoying life, staying with friends and inviting them to the Aizawa home; staying out late at night; and spending Aizawa's money with some abandon. Aizawa never complained in the diary about Yoshihisa's behavior, but we can detect a measure of disapproval in the thrifty Aizawa, in incidents such as that of May 4, 1923: "Today a boy came from the Yonedaya in Hachiōji, bringing a raincoat. After questioning him, I realized it must have been Yoshihisa who ordered it. Yoshihisa hadn't mentioned anything about it to me. However, I paid the boy ¥33, and took delivery of the coat."

By 1920 Aizawa had been mayor of Aihara for twelve years. He had suffered attacks of beriberi, arduous winter journeys to distant Fujisawa, war and the accompanying demands on the village, bitter disputes over shrines and hamlet mergers, as well as the stunning modernization of the village. He was in his mid-fifties, the age at which a man's career could respectably come to an end. On May 2, 1920, after serving two extended terms, Aizawa passed on the baton. The new mayor of Aihara was Shindō Yoshitarō—a long-serving member of the village administration. Although Shindō came from one of the leading families of Aihara hamlet, Aizawa was unhappy with his election as mayor—he did not have a high opinion of his colleague. But, as he commented on May 29, "I do not like to express my opinion, and so I just ignored the announcement." On August 11 the new mayor presented Aizawa with his farewell gift from the village: a gold watch. The new mayor had spent quite lavishly on the gift—it was an American Waltham pocket watch, of eighteen-carat gold. It came with a fifteen-jewel movement, an eighteen-carat gold chain, and a twenty-year warranty. The watch was inscribed: "A gift to Mr. Aizawa Kikutarō, from Aihara village." The cost of the watch, including accessories, was ¥198. In a meeting with the new mayor on July 2 before the presentation, Aizawa mildly protested that "as mayor, I always strove to reduce the village's expenses, and I did not consider it desirable to have a big outlay for this purpose." But his loving description of the watch's every detail clearly shows how happy he was with the gift.

Aizawa's life changed immediately. It was as though an enormous weight had been lifted from his shoulders. Although he continued to make occasional trips to Fujisawa in connection with his continuing duties as president of the village Agricultural Association, he was now free to take care of his own business, to stay home with his grandchildren, and to go for walks along the Sagami River. At times this newfound freedom seems to have left him feeling a little lost: he was now among the ranks of the elderly—no longer influential in public affairs, no longer essential to the running of the village. Sometimes he found himself left alone at home when all the other members of the family were out living their busy lives, as he commented on February 21, 1924: "Cold with a strong wind. Eiko went to the main family's house, Shigeharu went to the post office, Yasuo went to work at the Agriculture and Sericulture School, Yoshihisa did not return from Fuchū, Hanako is at the girls' high school. I stayed home alone to watch the house. I spent the time preparing the Taishō 13 [1924] budget for the Aihara Agricultural Association."

In retirement, Aizawa formed a friendship with the chief executive of neighboring Tsukui county. Ironically, the Tsukui county seat was much closer than Fujisawa, the capital of Kōza county in which Aihara was located. On June 22, 1924, the two men met for a long walk along the banks of the Tama River, stopping for a beer at a lovely lakeside restaurant before crossing the river by boat: "On all four sides we could enjoy the beauty of the water and the mountains; the coolness coming from the pure current was delightful." Aizawa added, though, that "recently the South Tama railway has been under construction, and the work is going on all over the place. There are many Korean laborers engaged in the construction. In Tama village a steel bridge is under construction, and you can see its twenty-one supports [in the river]. It must be at least one hundred *ken* [180 meters] long. . . . In future, there will undoubtedly be great development along the course of this railway line."

In the pages of his diary, Aizawa continued to write about the deteriorating economy: "[The landlords] are all going round to collect their rents, but they are getting hardly any income. It's due to the worsening business conditions and to the [national] recession."[17] He commented on the hardship of village life compared to that in the cities: "Government officials are feeling so pleased with themselves. Somebody who works in the government office gets a salary of ¥80 a month for doing next to nothing. Even the mayor of a village only gets ¥75 a month including expenses, and a deputy mayor gets only ¥60. Compared to that these people are getting too much money."[18] He wrote about the strange things that were happening to the world that he knew: "This evening we all went to the Asahi Elementary School's 'cool of the evening concert' [given by pupils and volunteers]. This is the first time I have been to an evening party organized by schoolchildren—and one where they perform dance and singing, and where they missed classes in order to rehearse it. The world is changing in strange ways." And he commented on the gloomy state of Japan's foreign policy:

> Today, twenty-two nautical miles to the southeast of Ōshima, according to the provisions of the Washington Conference, our battleships are being scrapped. The Prince Regent is aboard the battleship Kongō, which has departed from Yokosuka to the Bay of Tateyama, where he is staying aboard the ship. There, he will witness the sinking of the Satsuma and the Aki by the great forty-centimeter guns of the Nagato and the Mutsu. Although this is the result of an international agreement, I can't help feeling a sense of futility. These ships which took us twenty years and a huge outlay of money to build are now being relegated to the depths.[19]

Underlying these comments one can sense the subtle dissatisfaction and frustration of an able, energetic man who finds himself relegated to the sidelines in a rapidly changing world. Not that he wanted to go back to the stresses and thankless labors of being mayor. Indeed, when he was invited to become mayor of a neighboring village, he rejected the offer with a measure of vehemence.

But in mid-1924 Aizawa received an overture that he found more appealing. The Seya Bank, founded in the 1890s in nearby Seya village, had become a major source of finance for farmers and landlords in the district. The bank had expanded with branches in Machida, Kamimizo, and, from 1911, in Hashimoto itself. Now the management of the bank were looking for a manager for the Hashimoto branch. Aizawa evidently showed interest in the position, and on October 7, 1924, the bank's president, Kojima Kaname, called Aizawa by phone to confirm the appointment. Aizawa immediately went to the bank to take up his position.

The job of bank manager suited Aizawa perfectly. He enjoyed the prestige and sense of usefulness that went with the job, but he never felt the heavy stress and responsibility associated with the onerous job of mayor. On the contrary, Aizawa enjoyed the regular hours (eight to four-thirty, though Aizawa did not hesitate to take extra time off when he needed to for family or other business), the relatively undemanding work (the bank was mainly involved in financing the continuing construction boom in the Hashimoto area), and the modest monthly salary of ¥55. On January 22, 1925, Aizawa had his photograph taken to hang in the bank. He wore formal Japanese clothes, with his medals displayed. The photo did not turn out very well: "My face came out grainy. It was morning when the picture was taken, and cloudy and very cold. Thus, some parts of the picture did not develop well. . . .

Everyone who saw the picture laughed and said that I came out looking older than I really do."

Throughout his life, Aizawa had been an active participant in the creation of a world that was very different from that of his birth. At the opening of his diary he was a farmer, closely tied to the rhythm of the seasons, in a community that, while close to the major centers of political power and foreign trade, was still isolated by its rural location and limited economic activities. By his sixties, he was the manager of a joint stock company in a community that was connected to modern life by an increasingly dense network of railway, telegraph, telephone, improved roads, money, and consumption. But Aizawa the mature bank manager of the 1920s still had much in common with Aizawa the farm manager and younger son of the 1880s. Above all, he was a man of his place. Throughout his life, he closely identified his own interests with those of his village (later hamlet) community—so closely that he saw his stewardship of the family land as compatible with a lifetime of public service.

While deeply rooted in his past, Aizawa remained throughout his life both interested in and open to change and innovation. Much of this interest derived from the prospect of bettering himself and his family economically. He lived in a world of exciting new opportunities, and he was lucky enough to have the education and financial means to take advantage of many of those opportunities—indeed, he belonged to a social class whose wealth and status increased dramatically during his lifetime. But wealth and privilege were not the defining features of his life. Aizawa, a second son with no personal birthright, had to reach out to grasp the opportunities that the changing world presented to him. In doing so, he became one of the major actors for change within his community. By extension, Aizawa was also an important actor in the dramatic social and economic transformation of Japan in the decades following the Meiji restoration.

Conclusion

I came to this study through my fascination with social change in Japan in the nineteenth and twentieth centuries. Although Aizawa Kikutarō lived in a village, he was nevertheless at the center of the profound changes that swept over Japan in the late nineteenth and early twentieth centuries—for the village was where most Japanese lived and experienced such changes. But Aizawa was just one individual among twenty-seven million village residents (in 1920). His village was one among ten thousand. The ways in which Aizawa and Hashimoto experienced change were unique.

Hashimoto's path was influenced by its proximity to the capital, Tokyo, and to the emerging center of international trade in Yokohama. Hashimoto's location on one of the main highways leading into Yokohama ensured its active participation in domestic and international trade. Its location also placed it in a favored position for integration into Japan's new, modern transportation networks. And as Tokyo and Yokohama grew into vast industrial cities, Hashimoto was an ideal provider of industrial and clerical labor—even, by the end of the period covered in this book, on a daily commuting basis. Other villages were variously affected by their geography (Were they in the mountains, where agriculture was usually harder? On the coast, which would permit fishing, collection of seaweed, and salt manufacture? In the fertile plains, where they could feed the nearby cities?); by the development of regional industry (such as the silk reeling industry in

Suwa, which employed surplus labor from the region's poor mountain villages); by their natural resources (the coal mines of northern Kyushu, the briefly flourishing oilfields of Niigata); and by their access to the nation's developing communications networks.

How, then, can the life of one man illuminate the vast scope of change in a society of tens of millions? How can one community represent the immense diversity of Japan's rural villages? What, in fact, have I set out to achieve in writing this biography?

Ultimately, I believe that my intention has been somewhat spiritual. Intellectually, I wanted to study Japan's social transformation during six decades of dramatic change. Emotionally, though, I wanted to pay homage to those who have been forgotten by history—to the millions of individuals, most of them living in villages, who did not lead Japan's profound transformation during the Meiji (1868–1912) and Taishō periods (1912–26), but who *lived* it.

The fabric of history is woven of countless such stories, none of which is sufficient in itself to reveal the past. Since the beginning of recorded history, political leaders have commandeered selected narratives for their own narrow goals of power and contest, constructing seamless tales of progress and ethnicity, tales that are belied by their very effortlessness. Seen in this light, the tale of an individual may stand out precisely because of its uniqueness. It can, indeed, stand as a protest against the merciless and often deliberate leveling of history. It can make as important a statement as the conscientious objector who refuses to go nameless into the oblivion of a great battle fought in the name of abstract principles, such as nation or emperor (though Aizawa would surely have been horrified by this analogy). I want the reader to value the story of Aizawa Kikutarō not for its representativeness, but for its individuality. Aizawa was not a "type" of the Meiji or Taishō villager or landlord; he was a real human being, with his own special loves and losses, his own frailties, his own triumphs and tragedies. If I have brought even a dimension of this forgotten individual back to life, I feel I have accomplished an important component of the historian's task.

Perhaps this reconstruction of forgotten pasts is the allure of the genre of microhistory, to which this project probably belongs. I say *perhaps* and *probably,* because in spite of having attracted great interest over the past three decades, microhistory remains remarkably undertheorized. It seems that its practitioners have been more interested in telling their stories than in cluttering the field with yet more reflexive analysis. Since most writers of microhistory do not talk extensively about method, it remains up to the individual to interpret the opportunities and limitations of the genre.

One limitation is clear. A microhistory can not tell any story but its own. The story of an individual life, or even of the community in which that life was lived, is unlikely to provide the body of empirical evidence needed to shift a paradigm. It may not even enable a significant intervention in the great debates of Japanese rural history. Those few practitioners who have set out agendas for microhistory have tended to focus on the illustrative power of individual narratives. Jill Lepore, in a thoughtful essay on microhistory and biography, argues that "however singular a person's life may be, the value of examining it lies in how it serves as an allegory for the culture as a whole." Giovanni Levi makes a similar claim, drawing an analogy to the interpretive power of anthropology, whose practitioners might seek to understand an entire culture through a detailed study of ritual and kinship in a single village: "Historians [by extension] do not study villages . . . they study *in* villages." And Istvan Szijarto argues that the ideal work of microhistory "with all the lines branching out from the event, person or community in focus . . . points towards the general."[1]

Personally I find even these claims to be somewhat idealistic. What culture might the story of Aizawa's life be taken as allegory for? The culture of his village? Of his region? Of rural Japan? Of the Japanese nation? Surely the diverse village communities of Japan had many cultures, with much in common no doubt, but also with much to distinguish them. To interpret "the culture" from a single life seems as generalizing as to construct "the history" from a single case study, or "the nation" from a few heroic tales.

What microhistory can do, though, is open a window onto another world. I like to think of it as a window in a Dutch master painting. The room that the window reveals is an ordinary one. Nothing particularly dramatic is happening. But the floorboards, the items of clothing, the pieces of furniture, the papers on the desk, the quill pen sticking out of its glass holder, and of course the faces of the unremarkable people caught in the painting, are portrayed in revealing detail. And since the world revealed, on however small a scale, is a lost one—lost, indeed, precisely *because* of its ordinariness—the details captured in the painting become a precious historical artifact, imbued with a significance that needs no particular exegesis or justification. Aizawa Kikutarō was who he was. Regardless of his significance for a wider history of Japan, constructing this portrait of him has been an enormously rewarding endeavor.

Given that orientation, it may seem futile to try to draw any conclusions from my story. But I am reluctant to leave Aizawa and his community without attempting to relate their experiences back to my original interest: the enormous transformations of late nineteenth- and early twentieth-century Japanese society. So, albeit hesitantly, I will devote the rest of this chapter to "pointing the lines" that branch out from Aizawa's life "toward the general."

While unique, the experiences of Aizawa and his fellow villagers did not take place in isolation. The changes that took place in their lives reflect broader currents of change taking place throughout rural Japan. Through the window of Aizawa's life, we may glimpse not only the detail of his own experience, but also the landscape of these common experiences and an illustration of how they were lived in one community. Indeed, the contiguity of unique community and common experience offers its own possibilities for analysis. With a little probing, it may help reveal some of the gaps in the *macro*history of rural Japan; some of the ways in which narratives constructed at the national scale may elide the nuances and complexities of actual lived experience. For while the experiences of Aizawa and Hashimoto conformed in many ways to the textbook account of change in rural Japan, they also diverged. To some extent, these divergences are due to the specific circumstances of Hashimoto. But they also, I suggest, raise important questions about the nature of change itself.

In particular, they challenge a pair of broad assumptions that underlie and inform much of the scholarship on rural Japan in the Meiji and Taishō periods. The first is that the changes that villagers experienced in the late nineteenth and early twentieth century were the product of a transformative political regime—that of the emerging Meiji state. The emergence of the Meiji regime is deeply inscribed into the intellectual and even institutional structure of the historical profession as the starting point for modern Japanese history; however, my story of Aizawa and his fellow villagers of Hashimoto calls this model of a radical new departure into question. Second, and closely linked to the first, is the assumption that the state—with its allies, the landlord elites and capitalist business enterprise—was the principal instigator of change in the Japanese countryside. Certainly, the villagers of Hashimoto were deeply affected by government policies of taxation, education, village administration, and imperialism. But I also argue that the transfor-

mations initiated by government policy only go so far in explaining
the profound transformation that Hashimoto experienced in the six
decades covered by this book. What is missing is the active agency of
the villagers themselves.

DID HASHIMOTO EVER BECOME "MODERN"?

Let me start by summarizing the common experiences that Aizawa and
Hashimoto shared with villagers throughout Japan. These should be
familiar to the reader, as they have been frequently alluded to through
the chapters of this book.[2] First was an increasing homogeneity of educational culture. Villagers throughout Japan received at least four (in
1907, this was increased to six) years of schooling. Schoolteachers were
qualified based on national standards, and the educational curriculum was centrally mandated by the Ministry of Education. Education
included not only basic skills of literacy and numeracy, but also a
variety of materials likely to increase consciousness of the nation and
national identity: a program of national history that emphasized the
role of the imperial family in creating national unity; a program of
geography that fostered a sense of national integrity—including, as
time went on, the newly acquired imperial territories; an ethics curriculum that was grounded to some extent in a "Japanese" interpretation of Western and Confucian moral doctrines; and a strong sense
of the identity and role of the emperor in the national political and
spiritual essence. Aizawa as a student experienced this system only in
its early stage; but as mayor of Aihara village, he participated in many
of the rituals it had come to include, including solemn readings of the
Imperial Rescript on Education, and the enshrinement of portraits of
the emperor and empress.[3]

Second, and related, was the increasing role of the emperor and
imperial family in everyday life. At school, children were taught that the
emperor was the father of the nation and the central symbol of Japan's
national essence. In the newspapers, the activities of the emperor were
invested with enormous significance, wrapped in a package of reverent
terminology. The government, which derived its legitimacy from its
association with the emperor, went to great lengths to create or resur-
rect ceremonies around the imperial institution, in which it encouraged village citizens and village administrations to participate.[4] Shrine
ceremonies that had previously been centered on local cults were given
a new imperial slant. And those village men who experienced military

training received heavy indoctrination in a cult of loyalty and reverence for the emperor. As mayor of Aihara, Aizawa spent an enormous amount of time leading the village in activities and rites related to the imperial family. By the twentieth century, loyalty and reverence for the imperial institution and the person of the emperor were widespread throughout rural Japan, creating shared values that were frequently commented on by foreign visitors.[5]

Third was increasing participation in national affairs through the consumption of written materials. Although the circulation of newspapers, books and magazines was limited (especially in the Meiji period) by the low purchasing power and literacy levels of the majority of villagers, these materials were available in villages throughout Japan by the turn of the twentieth century. There was hardly a village where at least a few families did not subscribe to a daily newspaper, and undoubtedly these families passed on some of what they gleaned, either verbally or by distributing the printed material. Newspapers covered both local and national affairs, with a heavy slant in the latter to national politics, imperial and military affairs, and the activities of the emperor and his family. Newspapers also helped create and spread other elements of a national culture, such as celebrity actors and movie stars, popular music, and popular works of fiction and poetry. In addition to newspapers, villagers who could afford it consumed an array of magazines, from specialist agricultural journals to popular monthlies. By the mid-1920s, the magazine *Ie no Hikari* (Light of the Home) was being targeted specifically at village audiences. By the 1920s also, print culture was being augmented by movies, some of which traveled as far as the villages.[6]

Fourth was participation in a national program of imperialist expansion. Villagers were to some extent forced to participate in Japan's military adventures, as men were conscripted into the army and families were required to pay special taxes and to provide requisitions of grain and livestock. But villagers were also encouraged to participate through a variety of more subtle means. Newspapers fostered patriotic and martial sentiment through their sometimes provocative coverage of Asian affairs. Villages held ceremonies to commemorate fallen soldiers, to send off those departing for military service, and to welcome those who returned home. Shrines offered prayers for national success in military affairs. Returning conscripts inspired their fellow villagers with stirring tales of foreign adventure, and they retained their newfound status though participation in the military reserve associations.

Regional administrations set village quotas for "voluntary" contributions to war bond subscriptions, savings drives, and gifts to the nation. Women were encouraged to support military endeavors by participating in the Patriotic Women's Association and the Red Cross. While the extent of villagers' support for Japan's military campaigns must have varied—and was no doubt less than government publicists claimed—there can be no doubt of the wholehearted rejoicing in Japan's success, particularly when it brought increasing economic opportunity in the form of jobs, emigration, and investments.[7]

Fifth was increasing involvement in a national capitalist economy. During the Meiji and Taishō periods, villagers increasingly diversified into cash-producing enterprises such as the production and processing of silk and labor for wages in local enterprises or in nearby urban centers. Cash was then used to pay tax obligations or purchase manufactured products such as clothing, textiles, newspapers, household implements, clocks, and national flags.[8] They also experienced many of the perils of the capitalist economy—a reliance on distant markets, poor bargaining power, and exposure to national and international economic crises.[9]

Sixth was increasing integration of the nation through a network of transport and communications. This was not a sudden transformation, and it was by no means even in its impact on rural communities. Many remoter regions continued to rely on premodern transport systems until well into the twentieth century. And even when modern transportation such as the railway became available, many villagers continued to travel on foot due to the high cost of rail travel. Nevertheless, over time the gradual improvement of roads, the increased use of wheeled vehicles, the inauguration of public transport services, the development of a national postal system, the spread of telegraph lines to towns and then villages, and the spread of railway networks and (finally) of automobile and bus transportation brought villagers closer to their regional centers, and even to the major metropolitan centers. These improved communications allowed villagers to participate more actively in regional, national, and international markets; they increased the range over which goods traveled for sale or consumption; they brought consumer goods and print culture into the villages; they increased the exposure of villagers to urban culture; and increasingly, they facilitated the flow of villagers into jobs in the cities.[10]

Finally, seventh was the growing integration of villagers into the administrative systems of a modern bureaucratic government. The vil-

lage amalgamation program of 1889 allowed for limited village participation in regional and national administration, through the electoral
system established for regional assemblies and then the national Diet.
Over time, the government developed increasingly sophisticated vehicles for consolidating its influence in local administration, and even
over the daily lives of villagers. These included the propagation of military reserve associations, of patriotic women's associations, of village
agricultural associations, of "five-family groups," and of the activities
associated with the local improvement movement. Most of these initiatives placed apparently autonomous village or hamlet organizations
within a national framework: policies and activities were generated by
government-operated or semiautonomous national headquarters, and
sent down through the prefectural and county level to the villages.

The political implications of these transformations are, of course,
controversial. Interpretations range from those that point a starkly
accusing finger at the state (under the ideological mantle of the emperor
system, that "hideous miasma, enveloping and subsuming the popular
mind"), to those that take a more multifaceted view of the process of
"modernization," reflecting perhaps the work of Eugen Weber, who, in
his well-known study *Peasants into Frenchman,* pointed to the combined forces of capital, technology, and the state, as they "provided
[significant shared] experiences, swept away old commitments, instilled
a national view of things in regional minds, and confirmed the power
of that view by offering advancement to those who adopted it."[11]

What many approaches have in common, though, is a reinscription
of the importance of the Tokugawa-Meiji divide. Ever since the momentous political events of the 1860s, the Meiji restoration has been perceived as drawing a sharp line between feudal and modern—so sharp
that one observer commented at the turn of the twentieth century: "to
have lived through the transition stage of modern Japan makes a man
feel preternaturally old; for here he is in modern times, with the air
full of talk of bicycles and bacilli and 'spheres of influence,' and yet he
can himself distinctly remember the middle ages."[12] Academic institutions have tended to follow this bifurcation by organizing their studies
around "early modern" (Tokugawa) versus "modern" (Meiji and after)
Japanese history. Certainly, much scholarship has questioned the valid-
ity of this dividing line. The pioneering work of Thomas Smith in the
1950s pointed to the vital legacy of agricultural development in the
Tokugawa period (1603–1868) as an enabling factor for Meiji economic
growth and industrialization.[13] The *kōzaha* school of Marxist histori-

ography in the prewar and early postwar periods also emphasized the enduring nature of premodern social and political structures—"feudal remnants" in the terminology of the time—in Meiji rural society and beyond.[14] Nevertheless, much of the historiography continues to emphasize the revolutionary nature of the Meiji government as it introduced the transformative influences of modern technology, ideology, and political economy. Indeed, the cultural turn in historical studies has tended to further reinscribe this "instant of historical rupture."[15]

How was this "rupture" experienced by the villagers of Hashimoto? I would like to suggest that if we are looking for the causes of change in the Hashimoto region—and perhaps more widely in rural Japan—the changes wrought by the Meiji restoration and the modernizing policies of the Meiji government offer only part of the answer. To understand this, we must look both backward—to the ways in which Hashimoto was "modern" even before Meiji—and forward, to the ways in which systems of government and control created during the Tokugawa era continued to dominate the relationship between state and subject through Meiji and even into the Taishō era.

My story of Hashimoto opens in the 1860s. As such, it can not do justice to the complex history of the Kantō region in the two and a half centuries of the Tokugawa era, nor to the many transformations of the political and social fabric during that period. But at the very outset of this story, Hashimoto was, in many ways, already strikingly "modern." Economically, one of the most important features of the latter half of the Tokugawa era is the rapid growth of rural manufactures. This growth was evident in different regions throughout Japan, but it was particularly vibrant in the regions, like Hashimoto, that enjoyed ready communications with Japan's commercial centers. Although silk for the export market had by this time come to be the commercial product on which the majority of villagers depended, cash-based commercial agriculture, manufacturing, and services had already become deeply entrenched in the economy of the Kantō villages before Commodore Perry ever trained his threatening broadsides on Edo Bay. As early as the mid-eighteenth century the villagers of Hashimoto and its neighboring communities were selling firewood, lumber, wheat, and vegetables in local markets and even directly to Edo. They were offering food and lodging to travelers on the Kamakura highway. They were manufacturing silk thread, silk cloth, straw bags, and other products, working at times in factory-like operations owned by wealthy villagers. They were paying their rent and their taxes in cash, which they were lending and borrowing in transactions that transcended village boundaries. The growth of Hachioji as a regional center for the production and trading of silk thread and silk cloth brought opportunities for villages like Hashimoto that left few families unaffected.

By the 1860s, when this story opens, the countryside around Hashimoto was already in the throes of tumultuous change. A part of this had come from the opening of Japan to foreign trade—a development that was also a key factor in the collapse of the Tokugawa regime. But a part also came from dramatic new tensions within the village itself. Wide discrepancies in income between the entrepreneurial and landowning elites and the village underclass of tenants and wage workers led to violent protests targeting the wealthy. These protests were more pronounced in the poorer mountain villages north and east of Hachioji, but they also threatened more stable villages like Hashimoto. The protests were triggered by rising prices and by disruptions in the market on which poor villagers in the Kantō area had come to depend for their livelihood: the international market for raw silk thread. The dependency of villagers on this cash-based commodity, and on the global market that supported it, is evident in the available statistics for Hashimoto. More than half of the families in the village farmed less than a half hectare of land—clearly not enough to feed a family averaging six members. At the same time, villagers identified silk as their primary economic activity.

However, Hashimoto in the Meiji and Taishō periods also shows striking continuities with its "premodern" past. In spite of the many reforms introduced by the Meiji government, the most pertinent feature of the relationship between state and subject through most of the six decades covered by this book is its continued reliance on coercion, enforced by well-tried and not very technology-intensive institutions.

The introduction of the administrative village system starting in 1889 is often seen as a new departure in the relationship between villager and state. In this analysis, the "natural" village prior to amalgamation into the new administrative system is portrayed as a communitarian social unit that evolved during the Middle Ages due to the pragmatic need for cooperation between families to manage communal resources such as water and forest land. Over time, these natural village units came to represent a corporate identity for their constituent families, negotiating matters such as tax and tribute with the external authorities, and administering systems of welfare and justice internally. Under the new administrative system, though, the natural village unit lost its autonomy and legal status in favor of artificially constituted administrative villages. The administrative villages were closely supervised by regional authorities, and their mayors were co-opted as the lowest rung in a ladder of authority stretching up through county and prefectural administration to the central government. The activities of the new system "aimed at absorbing and reforming the 'autonomous community' that the hamlet had to this point been, and creating a modern community that represented the smallest administrative unit in a system of support for the modern state."[16] The administrative village undertook state-mandated public duties such as conscription, compulsory education, hygiene, religious practice and ceremony, mandating the observance of national holidays, and appropriate displays of reverence to the person of the emperor. By the time of the Sino-Japanese and Russo-Japanese wars, the administrative village was "accelerating the penetration of emperor-system nationalism through the domains of education, military affairs, and the police, and it was indeed the regional basis for the establishment of the modern emperor-system state."[17]

I find that the experience of Hashimoto departs from this model in surprising ways. The dichotomy of natural versus administrative village, for example, seems a gross oversimplification in the case of Hashimoto. One of the most striking features of Hashimoto is the contingent nature of its identity since the earliest recorded times. In the 1600s Hashimoto was not in fact an autonomous village unit, but rather it was a subunit in a larger community composed of Aihara, Oyama, and Hashimoto—most, in fact, of the units that were brought back together in 1889 to comprise Aihara village. Subsequently, Hashimoto was divided into four different administrative units, each with a different *hatamoto* lord. "Hashimoto" was therefore radically bisected by the dictates of power and patronage in nearby Edo. By the late Tokugawa period, "Hashimoto" included one hundred households that were physically located almost two kilometers away, amongst the households of Aihara. In the early Meiji years, these households were carved off from "Hashimoto," and returned to Aihara. In other words, the identity of Hashimoto was always subject to the administrative vagaries of governments that were primarily concerned with the most effective exploitation of village resources.

Certainly, Aizawa seems to have identified himself first and foremost with the community of Hashimoto, however that was constituted in his mind. In his youth, he served Hashimoto through his membership in the youth association and his support of the shrine festival. For Aizawa, Hashimoto undoubtedly had a meaningful identity: it was, after all, the community of which his family was the leading clan. But Aizawa's identity was not limited exclusively to Hashimoto. At times, his scope seems to have been both wider and narrower. On one hand, his extended family lived in communities dotted across the Kantō Plain, while his family's lending activities apparently encompassed not only the surrounding villages, but also the market town of Hachiōji. On the other, for every mention of Hashimoto in the diary, there is also a reference to one of the subunits of the hamlet—units that never had legal status in either the Tokugawa or the Meiji systems, but that clearly had meaningful identity for Aizawa. Aizawa himself lived in "Higashi," and there are certainly times when it is this neighborhood that represents his local identity.

If the story of Aizawa and Hashimoto causes us to question the dichotomy of "natural" or "communitarian" Tokugawa village unit versus artificial "administrative" Meiji village, it also—paradoxically perhaps—highlights the endurance of hamlet identity even in the face of government attempts to erase it. As mayor of Aihara, Aizawa's biggest challenge was to overcome hamlet rivalries to forge a unified village policy. The structure of village administration forced hamlets to fight against each other for the limited resources of the combined village community, and Aizawa's job was to maintain the precarious harmony that Aihara showed to the outside world. This required constant care and attention—to the particular needs and grievances of each hamlet, as well as to the political balance within the village.

This tension between hamlet and village interests—and the relative powerlessness of the central government to impose its will through the village system—is most evident in the campaign to amalgamate the various hamlet shrines within Aihara village. For more than a decade, Aizawa cajoled, begged, and castigated the villagers of Aihara to agree to give up their hamlet shrines in the cause of village unity and economic efficiency. But some of the villagers stubbornly refused to give up the shrines that were so integral to their hamlet culture. The struggle continued in a desultory way for upwards of fifteen years. Sometimes it just simmered in the background; other times it flared into major conflict. Aizawa was supported by visits from the county chief and other representatives of regional authority. But nothing they said could quell the resistance of villagers loyal to their hamlet traditions. Indeed, we see from Aizawa's own experience the importance to the young men of the hamlet of their shrine, its festivals, and the *mikoshi* float that they labored so hard to build.

In the case of the shrine merger, Aizawa clearly placed himself on the side of village authority and unity over hamlet interests. This was perhaps easier for him because Hashimoto's shrine was not one of those designated for amalgamation. But in another case, that of the opening of the Yokohama Line railway and the construction of a station in the village, Aizawa placed hamlet interests over those of the administrative village. Even though he served as deputy mayor and then as mayor of Aihara throughout the negotiations, it is clear that Aizawa represented the interests of Hashimoto as he negotiated with the railway company for a station to open in Hashimoto. And it was during these negotiations that the leading villagers of Hashimoto went so far as to threaten complete secession from Aihara village if their demands for burden-sharing were not acceded to.

At least through the watershed events of the Sino- and Russo-Japanese wars, the relations between Aihara village and the regional government seem to have continued patterns that were already well-established before the beginning of the "modern" era. For example, although in theory the modern state established a direct relationship between the family unit and the government to which it owed tax and service, in practice the village continued to mediate this relationship, taking responsibility for the communal submission of tax and produce, and allocating quotas to hamlets and villagers. In spite of Hashimoto's privileged position on a major road close to the capital, I found it striking that even as late as 1905, communication between Aihara and the regional authorities relied on foot transport and consisted mostly of the provision of various forms of tribute from village to state.

Indeed, coercion remained the dominant factor in the relationship between villager and state. Aizawa, as village official, acted as mediator in a variety of forms of state coercion. He was the collector of taxes on behalf of both village and state, and in cases where villagers failed to meet their tax obligations, he was the administrator of the dreaded *sashiosae*, or seizure of property in lieu of debts. He was the enforcer of government requisitions of village crops in time of war—setting quotas for each hamlet, and for each family within his hamlet, inspecting for quantity and quality, and directing shipment to the military collection point. He was the administrator of military call-ups, often served in the early hours of the morning, forcing eligible villagers to report for service in Japan's costly wars. In other words, villagers bore all of the obligations of *subjecthood*, sternly enforced by a combination of village authority and national power, but they enjoyed few of the rights or rewards associated with a modern concept of *citizenship*.

The "modern" state, then, presented itself to the majority of villagers as a harsh master, making inexorable demands on the village community. But if coercion—of a type little distinguishable from that practiced by the Tokugawa authorities—was the dominant feature of the relationship between village and nation through the Meiji era, what of the much-vaunted project of "emperor-system nationalism"? While the Meiji government undeniably relied on coercion to collect tribute and to supply its military with manpower and resources, it also recognized the need to create "active subjects" who participated willingly in the projects of the state—particularly its overseas adventures.[18] Postwar scholarship has tended to emphasize the power of the Meiji state, combining the tools and technologies of modern administration and the subtle arts of propaganda, to extend its reach "into the very souls of the people."[19]

Aizawa was certainly in the thick of government-inspired initiatives to increase the ideological commitment of villagers. He led prayers for victory at the village shrine during the Russo-Japanese War. He read imperial rescripts on state sanctioned holidays. He supervised the construction of a war memorial. He led the elaborate preparations for the planned visit of the crown prince. He encouraged villagers to join the Japan Red Cross and the Patriotic Women's Association, attending the annual gatherings of these organizations with his family members. He carried pictures of the emperor and empress back to the village with all due ceremony and supervised their installation in appropriately reverent settings. But did the villagers of Aihara share this experience of "active subjecthood"? Did they join in supporting, even promoting, Japan's overseas adventures? Did they feel their relationship with the emperor with the requisite intensity? Did the village mothers really, to quote a British journalist commenting on Japan's nationalist spirit at the time of the Russo-Japanese War, "instead of regretting that the call has included their sons, sigh because they have no more sons to give"?[20]

Aizawa's personal support for the status quo is evident throughout the pages of his diary. In spite of the heavy burden they sometimes placed on him as a village administrator, Aizawa uncomplainingly followed the government's directives in issues of conscription, education, and taxation. He supported the government's national initiatives—

including war—by paying a substantial sum in taxes, by subscribing to war bonds, by supporting national celebrations, by attending shrine ceremonies, and by honoring the emperor and his family in a host of different ways.

But Aizawa was a landlord. As the Meiji political system stabilized after the introduction of constitutional government in 1890, the landlord class emerged as key supporters of the political and economic status quo. They were motivated to offer this support because the system offered them important advantages. The privileges of landlords like Aizawa were not limited to their wealth. As substantial taxpayers, they also had a privileged political status through their special rights in the two-tier voting system. Since they were also better educated and better traveled, more likely to subscribe to newspapers and magazines, and less likely to have felt the oppression of the conscription system, it is not surprising that they would identify more with national policies and ideologies. Landowners were represented in regional assemblies and the national Diet, and regional officials themselves often came from the rural landlord class. They enjoyed the perquisites of status, such as contacts with the imperial family and medals for meritorious service. Neither they nor their children were likely to be summoned for military service or required to die in Japan's foreign wars. Both government and landowners shared the aim of preventing unrest or protest by the less privileged rural classes. They also shared a desire to promote capitalist enterprise and overseas empire, which offered investment opportunities to landlords and allowed them to diversify beyond their village-centered activities of collecting rent and money-lending.

By contrast, villagers in the lower social echelon remained essentially disenfranchised until near the end of the Taishō era. Even local elections for the village council were limited to male household heads over the age of twenty-five, who paid more than ¥2 in national taxes. In 1890, more than 40 percent of village households failed to meet this requirement.[21] Regional and national elections were much more restrictive still—excluding the great majority of villagers.[22] Moreover, although compulsory education gradually increased the levels of literacy in Japanese villages, villagers remained ill equipped to consume the newspapers and magazines that were the most obvious medium for state-centered ideology. Numerous surveys around the turn of the twentieth century reveal that only a small proportion of villagers—generally the landlord and independent farmer classes—subscribed to newspapers, or owned iconic consumer products such as national flags (to show patriotism) or clocks (to promote conformity to state-mandated timetables of school, work, and observance).[23]

It is not surprising, then, that Aizawa was often disappointed by the response of the villagers to his patriotic initiatives. There is a distinct sense in his diary that the village observances of state-mandated ceremonies such as national holidays, victory prayers, or the reading of imperial rescripts were half-hearted at best. Unlike the cities where crowds were mobilized to celebrate victories in raucous public ceremonies, Aihara appears to have had few public ceremonies to support foreign wars. Aizawa is forced to lament the poor turnout for his readings of imperial rescripts, except at official school ceremonies when all the schoolchildren were required to be present. And although villagers supported their friends and family members who fought in the wars with enthusiastic send-offs and a fine war memorial, there is a clear element of sympathy in their support, even at times of solidarity in the face of government coercion.

VILLAGERS IN CONTROL OF THEIR DESTINY?

In my analysis so far, I have tried to show how the transformation of Hashimoto works against a simplistic binary of premodern versus modern, Tokugawa versus Meiji. There was much about "modern" Hashimoto that resembled the early nineteenth-century village; just as there was much about Hashimoto in the Tokugawa period that was strikingly "modern." But I would not want this argument to be interpreted as a denial of change. On the contrary, it was the dramatic transformation of Hashimoto that first attracted me to this project. Rather, I would argue that interpretations of change that focus too much on modernizing policies and on villagers as passive recipients of the effects of modernity tell only a part of the story. If we look for the causes of change in the actions of the Meiji government, or in the policy shift accompanying the overthrow of the Tokugawa, we may be in danger of missing the most important actors in the drama of change: the village people themselves.

The single most transformative event in Hashimoto was the arrival of the railway, with a station in Hashimoto. The consequences of this, for work opportunities, urbanization, and the entire local economy, were immeasurable. Hashimoto had always been a part of the Kantō region's communications network. Its position on the Kōshū highway connected it to the trade centers and gave it some of the characteristics of a commercial community long before the arrival of the railway. This legacy no doubt made Hashimoto a convincing candidate for the construction of a railway station. But the station should not be seen as just a natural outcome of the modernization process. Nor should it be seen as something that just "happened" to the villagers of Hashimoto. Quite to the contrary, it was the culmination of an enormous effort by the hamlet's leading members. Over a period of several years, the overriding goal of the leaders of Hashimoto was to bring a station to the hamlet. For years, the hamlet leaders met regularly at the Zuikōji Temple to plan strategy, to allocate resources, to contribute money and land, and to negotiate with railway officials. The effort to bring a station to Hashimoto seems to have been much more prominent in the minds of villagers even than momentous national events such as the Russo-Japanese War. Ultimately, the village leaders were able to bring a station to Hashimoto—even though another station was already planned less than two kilometers up the line—through a series of bold and costly initiatives, starting with the provision of land by the Aizawa family and ending with the direct subsidy of the station, with funds that the villagers had to borrow at high rates of interest and without any early prospect of compensating revenue.

The railway was of course a leading example of the impact of modern technology on village life. Its effects were far reaching. In the pages of the Aizawa diary, we see it carrying goods from the Hashimoto region to the trading centers of Yokohama and Tokyo. We see it transforming Hashimoto's biggest trading enterprise from a local supplier of fertilizer and farm tools to a regional player in the movement of goods. We see it connecting Hashimoto's village officials to their distant masters in Fujisawa and Yokohama. We see it bringing symbols of the imperial regime into the village—the portraits of the emperor and empress, as well as the persons of visiting dignitaries, including members of the imperial family. We see it bringing urban development to the area surrounding the station—offices, shops, rickshaw and bus services, a bank, a technical school, a theater. We see it carrying weekend tourists into Hashimoto, and villagers into jobs in the towns and cities, relieving them of their dependence on the landlord economy.

As we watch these changes unfold, we can also, I think, understand *why* the village leaders of Hashimoto should have been so committed to the arrival of a station—even though from the railway company's point of view it was redundant. In the pages of the diary, we can clearly see the railway bringing wealth, comfort, and entertainment to the villagers, and rising property values to landowners. It was these material incentives that inspired Aizawa and his peers to strive not just to introduce new technology, but actively to influence the direction of technological change.

The same tendency can be seen in the engagement of Hashimoto's leading villagers with other important new institutions and technologies, including the introduction of electrical, telegraph, and telephone services; the opening of a post office and the subsequent addition of a savings account service; the creation of a municipal water system; the introduction of transportation technologies including bicycles, automobiles, and buses; and the construction of a theater. All of these transforming innovations were actively initiated and striven for, both for the comfort and ease they would bring to villagers, and in some cases for the profit that would accrue to the prime movers. That Aizawa, his elder brother, and (later) his sons were central to many of these initiatives is an indication not only of their family's pivotal status within the village, but also of the enduring power of self-interest as a motive force for social change.

By contrast, government-inspired policies aimed at transforming the village community—the new administrative system, the ceremony and cult surrounding the emperor, conscription, the nationalistic aspects of the educational system—seem to have had a much more ambiguous impact on the direction of change. Some encountered outright resistance—whether passive in the form of prayers for exemption from the draft, or active in the form of outright protest. Others, such as the observance of imperial rites on state-sanctioned national holidays, were the domain mostly of dutiful village leaders like Aizawa. In the pages of the Aizawa diary, we frequently see government policy bumping up against village and hamlet solidarity; while on the occasions when villagers were united in their desire for innovation and change, nothing seems to have stopped them from achieving their goals.

Arguably, this analysis merely strengthens the view that the Meiji and Taishō governments ruled the countryside by forging an alliance with key village elites from the landlord class. What was in Aizawa's interest was not necessarily good for the rest of the village, and the confluence of government and landlord interests enabled these elite groups to maintain and even strengthen their often oppressive hold over less privileged villagers. But there is evidence from the Aizawa diary that the village elites were not the only ones striving to influence the direction of change in their lives.

Of course, the study of resistance to the changes imposed on the countryside by government, landlords, and capitalists is a vital stream in the historical tradition.[24] It became particularly important to historians in the early postwar years, as they looked for a Japanese model of democracy that might serve as an alternative to the "top-down" democracy imposed on Japan by the American-led occupation. Numerous studies focused on peasant rebellions, and on tenant unions and the antilandlord activism that was rife in the 1920s. But we must also acknowledge the ways in which Japanese villagers participated in, even strove for, economic and technological changes not from political idealism, but simply to improve the comfort and ease of their lives. In the pages of the Aizawa diary, we glimpse how even the weakest members of the hamlet community showed their will to improve their economic well-being, to find ways out of the web of tenancy and debt in which they were caught, to seek entertainment and ease. To the extent that they saw the comfort of their lives being improved, villagers participated wholeheartedly in the transformation of the community, and at times they significantly influenced the path that modernity took in their community.

We glimpse this agency at work mostly in the complaints that Aizawa the landlord makes about the village lower classes. Frequently, he comments on the extravagance and thriftlessness of the tenant farmers, who rush out to buy silk clothes and modern conveniences when times are good, leaving them penniless and unable to pay their rent or debts when the economic winds change. Clearly from Aizawa's point of view this was an undesirable tendency. But looking at it from the villagers' point of view, it could also be interpreted as active and eager participation in the emerging consumer economy. The villagers were using the means available to them—including the development of commercial markets and the institutions of credit—to acquire material comforts that they had never been able to enjoy in the past. Once the railway was open and connected Hashimoto to the metropolitan center, Aizawa begins also to lament that the villagers were using it in ways that, if he might have foreseen, he surely never intended. Now that they were within commuting distance of factory jobs in the city, tenants lost interest in cultivating the land that had offered them such a precarious existence in previous decades. Rents were declining, and more and more land was being left untended.

Indeed, the very innovations that Aizawa pursued so passionately based on his own perception of interest ultimately worked to undermine the economic hegemony that he and the other leading families of Hashimoto had enjoyed—with government support—in previous decades. With the granting of universal male suffrage in 1925, and the increasing assertiveness of tenant farmers, army veterans, and other new contenders for influence, it was perhaps only a matter of time before the landlord elite's political influence also began to wane.

In this context, though, we should not feel too sorry for Aizawa and his ilk. The village elite were constantly responding to—and initiating— new opportunities emerging from the cauldron of modern economic development. Whether it in was a racetrack, a theater, or a new joint stock enterprise in the capital or the colonies, the era of Japan's first "economic miracle" offered unprecedented investment opportunities. What Aizawa lost in economic power as a landlord, he more than made up as a major landowner in an era of spiraling prices for development property. As the mulberry fields were plowed under to give way to new office buildings, shops, and restaurants, Aizawa the landowner and bank manager remained in the thick of profit-motivated change.

The technologies that transformed Hashimoto in the early decades of the twentieth century were not, for the most part, those implemented by the government to increase its control over the people. Rather, they were the technologies that worked as much to the economic advantage of the villagers as binding them to the coercion of the state. The railway, in particular, offered villagers the opportunity to escape from the very feudal and capitalistic landlord-tenant relations that are sometimes held to have been the principal evil of the prewar Japanese state system. Perhaps they commuted to equally oppressive positions as members of an industrial working class, but the villagers of Hashimoto seem to have reacted actively to opportunities to improve their own material well-being—an improvement that Aizawa often laments in the pages of his diary. And for those who stayed in the village, the pleasures of entertainment—movies, traveling shows, and horse racing—surely added to the brighter side of modern life.

THE MEANING OF A LIFE

To conclude, I return to my principal topic: the life of an individual. Who was Aizawa Kikutarō, and what was the significance of his life? I have stated at the beginning of this chapter that for me at least, rescuing a forgotten life from oblivion is goal enough in itself. But of course, Aizawa offers much more than that. As a member of the privileged landlord class during the period of its maximum influence, and as deputy mayor and then mayor of an administrative village during the formative years of Japanese imperialism, Aizawa offers a wealth of insight into the inner workings of Japan's rural politics and society. Perhaps during the course of this book I have been able to use his life story to illuminate some of the issues, the challenges, and the experiences of landlords, businessmen, and village leaders in the changing landscape of Meiji and Taishō Japan. But I also want to emphasize once again that Aizawa was in no way a type of the Meiji landlord, businessman, or local politician. He was a unique individual, and he brought his own particular personality and talents to his roles in his community, molding them to some extent to who he was, rather than the other way around.

Throughout his life, Aizawa was a diligent and generally successful landlord and businessman. He showed his interest in money and business from the very earliest pages of the diary. As a young man, he copied out passages from the newspaper on the importance of money. He trawled through public records looking for possible property acquisitions. He diligently managed his brother's farming operations, uncomplainingly devoting long days to outdoor labor. He carefully recorded his income and expenses, including those of his own wedding, and he concluded each year with a summary of his family's financial fortunes. Once he became an independent landowner, he negotiated firmly with his fifty or more tenants. He lent money where he found it profitable, and he dealt with the unpleasant task of cajoling debtors into making their payments, sometimes resorting to foreclosure and seizure of their property. Nor was he unwilling to spend generously when the occasion required it. He traveled to Tokyo to study and purchase the latest machinery. He built himself a solid house, which remains standing to this day. And he married off his children with a respectable level of ceremony.

Aizawa seems to have been comfortable in his role as one of Hashimoto's wealthiest landlords and business leaders—even though this role must surely have created hostility at times on the part of his many debtors, at whose expense Aizawa's wealth had been created. In the pages of his diary, Aizawa is surprisingly insensitive to this aspect of his financial affairs. Rather than dwell on his own role in the suffering and oppression of the village poor, he tends to comment on their profligacy and thriftlessness.

Still, Aizawa was by no means the stereotypical rapacious landlord.

Unlike many who moved to the city to live in comfort on their rents, Aizawa stayed in the village and remained actively involved, deeply committed even, to the management of his land. In his youth, he was a tireless student of new equipment, new seed varieties, and the improvement of sericulture. And in his maturity, he was not only a lender of last resort for poor villagers (however exploitative, this was surely an important function within the village economy), he was also a supporter of and investor in a variety of new business ventures in the district—ventures that might not otherwise have had access to capital. On balance, Aizawa seems to have accepted his privilege with little question, but he also recognized his responsibility to use it for the betterment of the community.

As a village leader, Aizawa was in a sense accepting his birthright. His ancestors had been leaders of Hashimoto village, and it was only natural that he should follow in their path. But there were significant differences in Aizawa's status compared to that of his headman forebears— differences that reveal much about Aizawa the man. Aizawa was the younger son. As such, he was not predestined for leadership, and had he so desired, he could have chosen a very different walk of life. As a child, Aizawa would have been forced to accept that his elder brother had everything, and he was guaranteed nothing. Even in wealthier families, younger brothers frequently left the village to pursue a professional calling in the towns or cities. Instead, Aizawa stayed in the village and served his brother as farm and business manager. This must have been a bitter task in some ways—the hard work fell to Aizawa, while the wealth and privilege accrued to his brother. But Aizawa carried it out uncomplainingly, apparently equating his own interests with those of his family. It was only after he had proven his ability that his brother agreed to set him up as head of an independent branch family. Even then, there was no natural path to a position of village leadership. But the same qualities that made Aizawa an effective farm manager and an appropriate candidate for his own family headship also made him a stronger candidate than his brother for villager leadership. Aizawa's elder brother seems to have been a philanthropist and dilettante, more interested in the pleasures of spending than in the burdens of day-to-day business. Aizawa was the born leader—hard working, methodical, able to work with others, and possessed of a vision of the betterment of his community. It was these qualities that enabled him to assume the mantle of authority in his brother's stead.

Moreover, Aizawa was leader not of Hashimoto, the village of his ancestors, but of Aihara, a "village" created by the national government. As mayor of Aihara, Aizawa represented interests that were not necessarily congruent with those of Hashimoto. Indeed, at times hamlet and village interests seriously clashed. When hamlet interests were directly threatened, Aizawa seems to have placed Hashimoto first. But in most of his activities, it was Aihara and not Hashimoto that was his focus. On its own, Aizawa's family privilege was not enough to secure him success in this undertaking. Once again, Aizawa's designation as mayor and subsequent successes in the role depended on qualities that belonged to him and not to his genealogy.

The third dimension of Aizawa Kikutarō is that of husband and father. It is clear that family was enormously important to Aizawa throughout his life. Unlike many Japanese diaries in which the women and children of the family are never mentioned, Aizawa's diary includes numerous entries on his wife and family, and on the significant milestones in the lives of his children. His marriage appears to have been an exceptionally loving one, and in the pages of the diary he never once complains of the difficulties the entire family suffered due to his wife's frequent illnesses. When Sato dies, he is clearly distraught. And among the most touching pages in the diary are those in which he describes his efforts to comfort his children, particularly his youngest who was just three years old, after the death of their mother. In spite of the demands of his busy job and his motherless children, Aizawa never remarried. Although he had help from family members and domestic servants, it must have been an enormous effort to bring up his younger children on his own. There is every indication that he was a loving and patient father. The diary contains almost no hints of friction with his children—even when his third son, Yoshihisa, adopted extravagant ways that Aizawa could never have condoned.

It is particularly striking how closely these three personae were related. Aizawa's had been the leading family in Hashimoto for generations. It was expected that a member of the family would play a leading role in hamlet affairs, and, once Hashimoto merged into Aihara, Aizawa was a leading candidate for village leadership by virtue of his family membership. The basis for the family's political power was its wealth, which in turn came from its ownership of land. The link between land, wealth, and hereditary political power extended back to the Tokugawa period, and it had undoubtedly opened up a gap between the village elite, whose privileges were sanctioned by government authority, and the poorer villagers, who were often dispossessed of their land and heavily dependent on the elite families for financial support. The Meiji transition might have disrupted this system of wealth and family based hereditary authority. It might have opened up opportunity to less privileged villagers to vie for political office. It might have put the village leadership more squarely on the side of villagers and in opposition to new and potentially harmful government policies. But instead, the unity of wealth, family status, and political authority survived and even in some areas strengthened during the Meiji and Taishō eras. The government helped ensure this by sanctioning a preferential voting system within the village. It also brought elites, but not ordinary villagers, into the national political process by including them in the limited vote for the national Diet. And the growth of the industrial and imperial economy opened up new opportunities for elites to increase their wealth even more. Psychologically, it seems clear that Aizawa accepted this unity of family, political status, and business activity as a matter of course. He clearly felt a deep sense of belonging to his village community. And he was willing to devote many years of arduous service to the community that he cherished. Certainly there was tension between his position as representative of Hashimoto and his position as mayor of Aihara. Perhaps there was sometimes tension between his heavy duties as mayor of Aihara and his need to spend time with his family, especially during his wife's illness and in the years that followed her death. But above all, both in Aizawa's public career and in his private diary, we see his lifelong devotion to his community—a devotion so profound that one feels it is inseparable from his humanity. Perhaps it is true that his job as mayor allowed him to protect and further his own interests. But his twenty years as deputy mayor and mayor also reflect his profound sense of obligation to serve the community that nurtured him.

Aizawa Kikutarō was very much a man of his time and place. An enlightened landlord, a canny beneficiary of the economic opportunities of the industrial age, a hard and often judgmental creditor, a worthy successor to his village headman ancestors—Aizawa was in many ways a fitting representative of the powerful village elites who made such a strong mark on the history of the Meiji period. But as with any life, Aizawa's is above all an individual—and a human—story. His diary affords us unique insights into his personal thoughts and feelings. The love he felt for his family, his grief at the loss of wife and child, the bonds that tied him to friends and kinfolk, his curiosity and love of learning, his hard work and dedication to his village community and to his job as mayor—these transcend the historical circumstances of time and place. Aizawa was fortunate enough to have been spared the want and hard labor of the huge underclass of dispossessed. But what he made of his life, he made himself. I hope that this portrait has reflected my respect for him as a man whose guiding principles were discipline, loyalty, and service to his community. Love of family, love of friends, love of and identification with the community of Hashimoto. For Aizawa, these were perhaps even greater realities than industrialization, empire, railways, or capitalist enterprise.

Notes

INTRODUCTION

1. F. G. Notehelfer, ed., *Japan through American Eyes: The Journal of Francis Hall, Kanagawa and Yokohama, 1859–1866* (Princeton: Princeton University Press, 1992), 412, 359–60.

2. Aizawa Kikutarō, *Aizawa nikki* (Sagamihara: Privately published by Aizawa Yoshihisa, 1965); *Aizawa nikki (zoku)* (Sagamihara: Privately published by Aizawa Yoshihisa, 1966); *Aizawa nikki (zokuzoku)* (Sagamihara: Privately published by Aizawa Yoshihisa, 1967); *Aizawa nikki (Taishōhen)* (Sagamihara: Privately published by Aizawa Yoshihisa, 1972); *Aizawa nikki (zōhoban)* (Sagamihara: Privately published by Aizawa Yoshihisa, 1977).

1. THE VILLAGE ENTERS THE MODERN ERA (1866–1885)

1. Strictly speaking, Hashimoto in 1866 had 155 resident families. However, one-third of these actually lived in Aihara village and were designated residents of Hashimoto only for administrative purposes. This anomaly was reversed in 1876 when the district was returned to Aihara.

2. F. G. Notehelfer, ed., *Japan through American Eyes: The Journal of Francis Hall, Kanagawa and Yokohama, 1859–1866* (Princeton: Princeton University Press, 1992), 594.

3. Sagamiharashi, *Sagamihara shishi dai-6-kan,* vol. 6, *Sagamihara shishi* (Sagamihara: Sagamiharashi, 1968), 65.

4. Edward E. Pratt, *Japan's Protoindustrial Elite: The Economic Foundations of the Gōnō* (Cambridge, MA: Harvard University Asia Center, 1999), 145.

5. Kawamura Zenjirō, ed., *Seiō bunmei no shōgeki,* vol. 7, *Shinpan Nihon seikatsu bunkashi* (Tokyo: Kawade Shobō Shinsha, 1986), 170.

6. http://www.city.kawasaki.jp/28/28kikaku/home/isan/la/lao070.htm. See also Pratt, *Japan's Protoindustrial Elite,* 55–56. Early *zaguri* could reel

only one strand at a time, but later improvements enabled the *zaguri* to reel several strands simultaneously.

7. Isabella Bird, *Unbeaten Tracks in Japan* (London: Virago, 1984), 257.

8. Ibid., 257–58.

9. Sagamiharashi, *Sagamihara shishi dai-6-kan*, 18. In 1876, revenue from silk production was ¥2,000 compared with ¥326 from wheat production.

10. Ibid., 94–96.

11. See Ogi Shinzō, *Aru Meijijin no seikatsushi: Aizawa Kikutarō no shichijūhachinenkan no kiroku* (Tokyo: Chūō Kōronsha, 1983). Since most estimates put output per hectare at five to ten *koku* even on poor land, there seems to be a big disparity between the family's declared income in *koku* and its actual land holdings. This is presumably because the Aizawa, like all families, tried to minimize its declared income so as to be taxed as little as possible.

12. Herbert P. Bix, *Peasant Protest in Japan, 1590–1884* (New Haven, CT: Yale University Press, 1986), 169.

13. Ibid., 169.

14. Patricia Sippel, "Popular Protest in Early Modern Japan: The Bushū Outburst," *Harvard Journal of Asiatic Studies* 37, no. 2 (1977): 291.

15. M. William Steele, *Alternative Narratives in Modern Japanese History* (London: RoutledgeCurzon, 2003), 38.

16. Bird, *Unbeaten Tracks,* 82–83.

17. See http://www.riyo.or.jp/library/etc_rekisi_01_02.html.

18. http://www2.gol.com/users/stever/calendar.htm; "Taiintaiyōreki": Japan Wikipedia, http://ja.wikipedia.org/wiki/%E5%A4%AA%E9%99%B0%E5%A4%AA%E9%99%BD%E6%9A%A6.

19. Herbert Plutschow, *Japan's Name Culture: The Significance of Names in a Religious, Political and Social Context* (Folkestone: Japan Library, 1995), 179.

20. For example, the *Shinpen Musashino fudoki kō* lists family names for almost all the peasants mentioned in its twelve volumes. Ibid., 180.

21. Takemitsu Makoto, *Myōji to Nihonjin: Senzo kara no messeji* (Tokyo: Bunshun Shinso, 1998), 166; Herbert Plutschow, *Japan's Name Culture: The Significance of Names in a Religious, Political and Social Context,* 194.

22. Takemitsu, *Myōji to Nihonjin,* 167.

23. Plutschow, *Japan's Name Culture,* 194.

24. Takemitsu, *Myōji to Nihonjin,* 169.

25. "Jinshinkoseki," Japan Wikipedia, http://ja.wikipedia.org/wiki/%E5%A3%AC%E7%94%B3%E6%88%B8%E7%B1%8D.

26. Sagamiharashi, *Sagamihara shishi dai-6-kan,* 168.

27. See M. A. McKean, "Common-Pool Resources in the Context of Japanese History," *World Wide Business Review* 5, no. 1 (2003).

28. Sagamiharashi, *Sagamihara shishi dai-6-kan,* 60, 68. Information on the 1867 tax is in Sagamiharashi, *Sagamihara shishi dai-3-kan,* vol. 3, *Sagamihara shishi* (Sagamihara: Sagamiharashi, 1968), 126.

29. The village of Chiarajima, to the northeast of Hashimoto, saw a comparable sharp increase in nominal taxation after the reform. William Chambliss suggests that this is accounted for by a combination of exchange rate anomalies and more complete registration of productive land. See William J.

Chambliss, *Chiaraijima Village: Land Tenure, Taxation, and Local Trade, 1818–1884* (Tucson: University of Arizona, 1965), 79–86.

30. Samuel Smiles, *Self-Help* (London: John Murray, 1858). The Japanese version was translated by Nakamura Masanao and published under the title *Saikoku Risshihen* (Tales of Success from Western Nations).

31. Kawamura, *Seiō bunmei no shōgeki,* 174.

32. Notehelfer, ed., *Japan through American Eyes,* 164.

33. Sagamiharashi, *Sagamihara shishi dai-3-kan,* 243.

34. Ibid., 238.

35. Ibid., 252.

36. Ibid., 262.

37. Kawamura, *Seiō bunmei no shōgeki,* 172–73.

38. Quoted in Ibid., 174.

39. Sagamiharashi, *Sagamihara shishi dai-3-kan,* 272.

40. Rokuhara Hiroko, "Local Officials and the Meiji Conscription Campaign," *Monumenta Nipponica* 60, no. 1 (2005): 84.

41. Ibid., 85–86.

42. Nihon Sonrakushi Kōza Henshu Iinkai, *Seikatsu 3: Kingendai,* vol. 8, *Nihon sonrakushi kōza* (Tokyo: Yuzankaku, 1990), 7–8.

43. Notehelfer, *Japan through American Eyes,* 594.

44. For a detailed account of a Kantō community's transition from the Tokugawa to the Meiji regimes, see Neil Waters, *Japan's Local Pragmatists: The Transition from Bakumatsu to Meiji in the Kawasaki Region* (Cambridge, MA: Harvard University Press, 1983). Waters emphasizes the relatively smooth transition in this and, presumably, many comparable communities.

45. Eiichi Shibusawa, *The Autobiography of Shibusawa Eiichi: From Peasant to Entrepreneur* (Tokyo: University of Tokyo Press, 1994), 21.

46. Irokawa Daikichi, *The Culture of the Meiji Period,* Princeton Library of Asian Translations (Princeton: Princeton University Press, 1988), 98.

47. Stephen Vlastos, "Opposition Movements in Early Meiji, 1868–1885," in *The Cambridge History of Japan,* ed. Marius Jansen (Cambridge: Cambridge University Press, 1989), 5:368. Using Aoki's data, White gives a total number of 7,331 protests from 1590 to 1877, most of them minor and nonviolent. See James White, *Ikki: Social Conflict and Political Protest in Early Modern Japan* (Ithaca, NY: Cornell University Press, 1993), 135.

48. White, *Ikki,* 136.

49. George Wilson, *Patriots and Redeemers: Motives in the Meiji Restoration* (Chicago: Chicago University Press, 1992), 98.

50. Ibid., 98.

51. See for example Sasaki Junnosuke, *Yonaoshi,* vol. 5, *Minshū Nihon no rekishi* (Tokyo: Sanseidō, 1974). For an English language discussion of Japanese interpretations of *yonaoshi,* see Katsunori Miyazaki, "Characteristics of Popular Movements in Nineteenth-Century Japan: Riots During the Second Chōshū War," *Japan Forum* 17, no. 1 (2005).

52. Stephen Vlastos, "Yonaoshi in Aizu," in *Conflict in Modern Japanese History: The Neglected Tradition,* ed. Tetsuo Najita and J. Victor Koschmann (Princeton: Princeton University Press, 1982), 174. Elsewhere, though, Vlastos

has pointed out that many of the protests had specific economic causes that had nothing to do with apocalypse or world renewal. Japan suffered from three consecutive years of poor harvests in 1867, 1868, and 1869. These crop failures coincided with the disruptive effects of the civil war: villages throughout Japan were affected by requisitions of crops, manpower and money by both sides, if not by actual fighting. Such protests were "indistinguishable from the Tokugawa peasant protest movements in most respects" and "did not indicate opposition to the Meiji Restoration" as such. See Vlastos, "Opposition Movements in Early Meiji," 369–70.

53. Ono Takeo, *Ishin nōson shakai shiron* (Tokyo: Tōkō Shoin, 1932), 384.

54. Quoted in Matsushita Shigeo, *Chōheirei seitei no zengo* (Tokyo: Kaikōsha, 1932), 137.

55. Tsuchiya Takao and Ono Michio, eds., *Meiji shonen nōmin sōjōroku* (Tokyo: Nanboku shoin, 1931), 339.

56. Ono, *Ishin nōson shakai shiron,* 384.

57. For a discussion of the economic consequences of the tax reform see notes 59, 60, and 61 and Nakamura Masanori, "The Japanese Landlord System and Tenancy Disputes: A Reply to Richard Smethurst's Criticisms," *Bulletin of Concerned Asian Scholars* 20, no. 1 (1988).

58. The best English-language source on the various forms of resistance to the new school system is Brian Platt, *Burning and Building: Schooling and State Formation in Japan, 1750–1890,* Harvard East Asian Monographs 237 (Cambridge, MA: Harvard University Asia Center, 2004).

59. Steven J. Ericson argues that the deflation began before Matsukata became minister of finance, and was only exacerbated, not caused, by Matsukata's policies ("'Poor Peasant, Poor Country!' The Matsukata Deflation and Rural Distress in Mid-Meiji Japan," in *New Directions in the Study of Meiji Japan,* ed. Helen Hardacre and Adam L. Kern [Leiden: Brill, 1997], 389–92.

60. The rate of tenantry has been a controversial topic in Japanese rural history, but this is one of the few statistics on which there is general agreement. See E. Herbert Norman, *Soldier and Peasant in Japan: The Origins of Conscription* (New York: Institute of Pacific Relations, 1943), 137; Richard J. Smethurst, *Agricultural Development and Tenancy Disputes in Japan, 1870–1940* (Princeton: Princeton University Press, 1996), 62; Yoshiaki Nishida, "Growth of the Meiji Landlord System and Tenancy Disputes after World War I: A Critique of Richard Smethurst, *Agricultural Development and Tenancy Disputes in Japan, 1870–1940,*" *Journal of Japanese Studies* 15, no. 2 (1989), 399–400.

61. See Nishida, "Growth of the Meiji Landlord System," 400. Smethurst argues that much of the increase in tenanted land was due to an increase in reclaimed land, much of which was worked by tenants, and thus does not reflect impoverishment of the tenant class. However, this argument (and indeed his whole book) was strongly disputed by several historians of rural Japan. See Smethurst, *Agricultural Development;* Nishida, "Growth of the Meiji Landlord System"; Nakamura Masanori, "The Japanese Landlord System and Tenancy Disputes: A Reply to Richard Smethurst's Criticisms."

62. Norman, *Soldier and Peasant in Japan,* 146, n. 20.

63. Sagamiharashi, *Sagamihara shishi dai-6-kan*, 65.

64. Quoted in Bannō Junji, *Kindai Nihon no shuppatsu*, vol. 13, *Taikei Nihon no rekishi* (Tokyo: Shōgakkan, 1993), 114–15. See also Thomas Smith, "Landlord's Sons in the Business Elite" *Economic Development and Cultural Change* 9, no. 1 (October 1960): 93–107, which quotes the contemporary journal *Kokumin no Tomo*: "In the twenty years since the Revolution, [the rural middle] class has been given so much political power, it can scarcely hold it in its two hands."

65. Sagamiharashi, *Sagamihara shishi dai-3-kan*, 59.

66. Ibid., 63–64.

67. There are a number of accounts in English of the Chichibu uprising. See, for example, Irokawa, *Culture of the Meiji Period*, chapter 5 and Mikiso Hane, *Peasants, Rebels, Women, and Outcastes: The Underside of Modern Japan* (Lanham: Rowman and Littlefield, 2003), 24–27.

2. FROM FARM MANAGER TO INDEPENDENT LANDOWNER (1885–1894)

1. Aizawa diary, August 13, 1890. Aizawa Kikutarō, *Aizawa nikki* (Sagamihara: Privately published by Aizawa Yoshihisa, 1965).

2. See Aizawa diary, March 20, 1895, for the free rent; February 10, 1895 for the ¥28 per hectare rent (pro rata based on rent of ¥4.20 for 0.15 hectares). Aizawa Kikutarō, *Aizawa nikki (zoku)* (Sagamihara: Privately published by Aizawa Yoshihisa, 1966).

3. Sagamiharashi, *Sagamihara shishi dai-6-kan*, vol. 6, *Sagamihara shishi* (Sagamihara: Sagamiharashi, 1968), 59.

4. Sagamiharashi, *Sagamihara shishi dai-3-kan*, vol. 3, *Sagamihara shishi* (Sagamihara: Sagamiharashi, 1968), 407. This quote is from a popular rights campaigner who visited Aihara village in 1884.

5. Ibid., 407.

6. http://www.tnm.jp/jp/history/07.html.

7. See http://memorialhall.mass.edu/collection/itempage.jsp?itemid=7248; http://blog.livedoor.jp/honda2043/archives/2006-01.html.

8. http://www4.ocn.ne.jp/~noukai/. On September 4, 1886, Aizawa also mentions reading the *Nōkōshō kōhō* (Report of the Ministry of Agriculture and Commerce).

9. George Bullen, *The Story of Count Bismarck's Life: For Popular Perusal* (London: John Camden Hotten, 1871), translated as *Gaisei no igyō: Doitsu saishō Bisumaruku Kō jitsuden*, trans. Yamaguchi Sōkichi (Tokyo: Shunyōdō, 1887).

10. Sagamiharashi, *Sagamihara shishi dai-3-kan*, 8.

11. Sagamiharashi, *Sagamihara shishi dai-6-kan*, 70–71.

12. Sagamiharashi, *Sagamihara shishi dai-3-kan*, 410.

13. http://www.nttcom.co.jp/comzine/no003/long_seller/index.html.

14. See, for example, Aizawa diary, August 16, 1896. Aizawa Kikutarō, *Aizawa nikki (zōhoban)* (Sagamihara: Privately published by Aizawa Yoshihisa, 1977).

15. Janine Tasca Sawada, *Practical Pursuits: Religion, Politics, and Personal Cultivation in Nineteenth-Century Japan* (Honolulu: University of Hawai'i Press, 2004), 39.

16. http://www.konan-wu.ac.jp/~kikuchi/kodan/bunkasi.htm.

17. http://www.tokyo-kurenaidan.com/touson-komoro.htm.

18. http://d.hatena.ne.jp/yskszk/searchdiary?word=%B4%AB%B9%A9%BE%EC+%B6%E5%C3%CA&.submit=%B8%A1%BA%F7.

3. FOR VILLAGE AND NATION (1894–1908)

1. "Kyonbusen," Japan Wikipedia, http://ja.wikipedia.org/wiki/%E4%BA%AC%E9%87%9C%E7%B7%9A. I am also grateful to Steven Ericson for additional information on the Keifu railway.

2. Sagamiharashi, *Sagamihara shishi dai-3-kan*, vol. 3, *Sagamihara shishi* (Sagamihara: Sagamiharashi, 1968), 348–49.

3. Ibid., 350–51.

4. Sagamiharashi, *Sagamihara shishi dai-6-kan*, vol. 6, *Sagamihara shishi* (Sagamihara: Sagamiharashi, 1968), 32–33.

5. Katō Shigeo, *Hashimoto no mukashibanashi* (Tokyo: Gyōsei, 1985), 59.

6. Ayase-shi, *Kanagawa-ken Kōza-gun Ayase-sonze chōsasho* (Ayase: Ayase-shi, 1993), 40.

7. Ōe Shinobu, *Chōheisei* (Tokyo: Iwanami Shoten, 1981), 108. Unfortunately there are no surviving records after 1897 until 1916, when evasion was much lower.

8. Ibid., 108–18.

9. During the course of the war, the Japanese government issued six separate bonds totaling ¥480 million in face value. The bond issues were notably successful: all of the issues were oversubscribed, some by as much as a factor of five. See Ōhama Tetsuya, *Meiji No bōhyō: Nisshin Nichiro uzumoreta shomin no kiroku* (Tokyo: Shūei Shuppan, 1970), 211.

10. Ayase village in Kanagawa reported in 1903 that the market price for average quality rice land was 494 percent of the assessed value. For dry fields, it was 444 percent. Ayase-shi, *Kanagawa-ken Kōza-gun Ayase-sonze chōsasho,* 47.

11. Ogi Shinzō, *Aru Meijijin no seikatsushi: Aizawa Kikutarō no shichijū-hachinenkan no kiroku* (Tokyo: Chūō Kōronsha, 1983), 30–31.

12. See, for example, the entries on March 23, 1904, and August 17, 1904.

13. Katō, *Hashimoto*, 45.

14. Ibid., 46.

15. Aizawa diary, March 19, 1906. Aizawa Kikutarō, *Aizawa nikki (zokuzoku)* (Sagamihara: Privately published by Aizawa Yoshihisa, 1967).

16. Katō, *Hashimoto*, 48.

4. THE MAYOR OF AIHARA (1908–1918)

1. Wilbur M. Fridell, *Japanese Shrine Mergers 1906–12: State Shinto Moves to the Grassroots* (Tokyo: Sophia University, 1973), 5–7.

2. The comments are by Bureau of Shrines official Tsukamoto Seiji, quoted in ibid., 17.

3. Ibid., 47.

4. Quoted in ibid., 48.

5. Keizo Shibusawa, *Japanese Life and Culture in the Meiji Era* (Tokyo: Ōbunsha, 1958), 351, quoted in Wilbur M. Fridell, *Japanese Shrine Mergers 1906–12: State Shinto Moves to the Grassroots* (Tokyo: Sophia University, 1973), 49.

6. Home Ministry statement, quoted in Fridell, *Japanese Shrine Mergers,* 50.

7. Quoted in ibid., 52–53.

8. Ibid., 19.

9. Aizawa diary, April 19, 1917. Aizawa Kikutarō, *Aizawa nikki (Taishō-hen)* (Sagamihara: Privately published by Aizawa Yoshihisa, 1972).

10. For a discussion of the "lifestyle improvement" aspects of the local improvement movement and the subsequent trajectory of these initiatives, see Simon Partner, "Taming the Wilderness: The Lifestyle Improvement Movement in Rural Japan, 1925–1965," *Monumenta Nipponica* 56, no. 4 (2001): 487–520.

11. See Sheldon Garon, *Molding Japanese Minds: The State in Everyday Life* (Princeton: Princeton University Press, 1997).

12. Japanese historians, too, have conflicting interpretations of government policies in this period, dividing between those who emphasize initiatives that strengthened hamlet solidarity and those who emphasize efforts to increase the centrality of administrative villages to rural life. For an example of the former, see Ōshima Mitsuko, "Chihō zaisei to chihō kairyō undō," in *Kyōdoshi kenkyū kōza,* ed. Furushima Toshio et al., 33–49 (Tokyo: Asakura Shoten, 1970). For the latter, Masato Miyachi, *Nichiro sengo seijishi no kenkyū* (Tokyo: Tokyo Daigaku Shuppankai, 1973).

13. For an overview of the movement, see Keiko Morita, "Activities of the Japanese Patriotic Ladies Association (Aikoku Fujinkai)," in *Women, Activism and Social Change,* ed. Maja Mikula, 49–70 (London: Routledge, 2005).

14. Tadatoshi Fujii, *Kokubō Fujinkai: Hinomaru to kappōgi* (Tokyo: Iwanami Shoten, 1985), 96.

15. For a full treatment of the military reserve associations, see Richard J. Smethurst, "The Creation of the Imperial Military Reserve Association in Japan," *Journal of Asian Studies* 30, no. 4 (1971): 815–28. For a wider discussion of the significance of the military reserve associations, agricultural associations, youth groups, and other state-sponsored organizations, see Ann Waswo, "The Transformation of Rural Society, 1920–1950," in *The Twentieth Century,* ed. Peter Duus, 541–605, vol. 6, *The Cambridge History of Japan* (Cambridge: Cambridge University Press, 1988).

16. For a fuller discussion of the Hōtokukai, see Kenneth B. Pyle, "The Technology of Japanese Nationalism: The Local Improvement Movement, 1900–1918," *Journal of Asian Studies* 33, no. 1 (1973): 51–65. See also Thomas R.H. Havens, "Religion and Agriculture in Nineteenth-Century Japan: Ninomiya

Sontoku and the Hotoku Movement," *Japan Christian Quarterly* 38, no. 2 (1972): 98–105.

17. For an overview of the local improvement movement, see Pyle, "Technology of Japanese Nationalism," 51–65. See also Masao Tsutsui, "The Impact of the Local Improvement Movement on Farmers and Rural Communities" in *Farmers and Village Life in Twentieth-Century Japan,* ed. Ann Waswo and Yoshiaki Nishida, 61–78 (London: RoutledgeCurzon, 2003).

18. "Unless we are victorious in this peacetime economic warfare, it will make no difference whether or not we have trained a million brave soldiers. . . . The fortunes of a nation depend on the prosperity of its villages" (Pyle, "Technology of Japanese Nationalism," 59).

19. See chapter 2, sections 3 and 4 of Ishida Takeshi, *Kindai Nihon seiji kōzō no kenkyū* (Tokyo: Miraisha, 1956). Pyle makes a similar argument but does not take it quite so far in terms of the links to fascism ("Technology of Japanese Nationalism," 51–65).

20. Quoted in Carol Gluck, *Japan's Modern Myths: Ideology in the Late Meiji Period* (Princeton: Princeton University Press, 1985), 92.

21. Sagamiharashi, *Sagamihara shishi dai-3-kan,* vol. 3, *Sagamihara shishi* (Sagamihara: Sagamiharashi, 1968), 355–56.

22. David John Lu, *Sources of Japanese History,* vol. 2 (New York: McGraw-Hill, 1974), 70.

23. Aizawa Diary, November 4, 1911. Aizawa Kikutarō, *Aizawa nikki (zokuzoku)* (Sagamihara: Privately published by Aizawa Yoshihisa, 1967).

24. Katō Shigeo, *Hashimoto no mukashibanashi* (Tokyo: Gyōsei, 1985), 94–97. The Katō Bicycle Shop was still in business as late as 1985.

25. Ibid.

5. A WORLD TRANSFORMED (1918–1926)

1. Aizawa diary, September 13, 1919. Aizawa Kikutarō, *Aizawa nikki (Taishōhen)* (Sagamihara: Privately published by Aizawa Yoshihisa, 1972).

2. Kusakabe Kinzaburō, *Keihin Denryoku Kabushikikaisha enkakushi* (Tokyo: Daiyamondosha, 1926), 1.

3. Representative dates for these events are: *gidayū* (January 6, 1920); *naniwabushi* (February 6, 1920); *shinpageki* (September 15, 1920); movie (December 1, 1920); sack-making lecture (February 10, 1922); fire prevention play (January 29, 1924); chemical fertilizer movie (January 28, 1920).

4. Katō Shigeo, *Hashimoto no mukashibanashi* (Tokyo: Gyōsei, 1985), 64, 52.

5. Ibid., 159.

6. Sagamiharashi, *Sagamihara shishi dai-4-kan,* vol. 4, Sagamihara shishi (Sagamihara: Sagamiharashi, 1971), 44.

7. Ibid., 40, 41, 43.

8. Katō Shigeo, *Hashimoto no mukashibanashi* (Tokyo: Gyōsei, 1985), 134–35, 159.

9. Ibid., 163.

10. Ibid., 160.

11. Sagamiharashi, *Sagamihara shishi dai-4-kan*, 41.
12. Ibid., 46–47.
13. Ibid., 48.
14. Ibid., 48.
15. Ibid., 49.
16. Ibid., 53.
17. Aizawa diary, July 31, 1924. *Aizawa nikki (Taishōhen)*.
18. Aizawa diary, June 17, 1924. *Aizawa nikki (Taishōhen)*.
19. Aizawa diary, September 4, 1924. *Aizawa nikki (Taishōhen)*.

CONCLUSION

1. Jill Lepore, "Historians Who Love Too Much," *The Journal of American History* 88, no. 1 (June 2001): 129–44; Giovanni Levi, "On Microhistory" in *New Perspectives on Historical Writing*, ed. Peter Burke, 97–119 (University Park: University of Pennsylvania Press, 2001)—Levi is paraphrasing a famous quote of Clifford Geertz; Istvan Szijarto, "Four Arguments for Microhistory," *Rethinking History*, 6, no. 2 (2002): 209–15.

2. For a useful summary of this argument that draws on a wide range of Japanese historiography and fills it out with fascinating detail, see Ōkado Masakatsu, *Meiji Taishō no nōson* (Tokyo: Iwanami Shoten, 1992).

3. See Takeda Kiyoko, *Tennōsei shisō to kyōiku* (Tokyo: Meiji Tosho Shuppan, 1964).

4. See Takashi Fujitani, *Splendid Monarchy: Power and Pageantry in Modern Japan* (Berkeley: University of California Press, 1996).

5. There is an enormous literature on the changing role of the emperor in Meiji and Taishō Japan. A useful review can be found in Nakamura Masanori, "Gendai rekishigaku to tennōsei" in *Gendai shigaku no seika to kadai, 1980–2000-nen II: Kokkazō, shakaizō no henyō*, ed. Rekishigaku Kenkyūkai, 120–35 (Tokyo: Aoki Shoten, 2003).

6. See James Huffman, *Creating a Public: People and Press in Meiji Japan* (Honolulu: University of Hawai'i Press, 1997).

7. A standard work on conscription is Ōe Shinobu, *Chōheisei* (Tokyo: Iwanami Shoten, 1981). On support on the home front, see Stewart Lone, "Remapping Japanese Militarism: Provincial Society at War, 1904–1905," *Japanese Studies* 25, no. 1 (May 2005): 53–63; and Hiroko Rokuhara, "Local Officials and the Meiji Conscription Campaign," *Monumenta Nipponica* 60, no. 1 (2005): 81–110.

8. Between 1890 and 1927, for example, cash expenditures increased from 42 percent of all expenditures to 52 percent for owner-farmers, and from 22 percent to 48 percent for tenant farmers. Ōkado, *Meiji Taishō no nōson*, 19.

9. An excellent general reference work on economic development in the Meiji and Taishō periods is Penelope Francks, *Rural Economic Development in Japan: From the Nineteenth Century to the Pacific War* (Abingdon, UK: Routledge, 2006).

10. See Steven Ericson, *The Sound of the Whistle: Railroads and the State in Meiji Japan* (Cambridge, MA: Harvard University Press, 1996). For a broader

treatment in Japanese, see Hirooka Haruya, *Kindai Nihon kotsushi: Meiji ishin kara dainiji taisen made* (Tokyo: Hosei Daigaku Shuppankyoku, 1987).

11. Irokawa Daikichi, *The Culture of the Meiji Period* (Princeton: Princeton University Press, 1988), 13; see also Masuda Tomoko, *Tennōsei to kokka* (Tokyo: Aoki Shoten, 1999). Weber, *Peasants into Frenchmen: The Modernization of Rural France, 1870–1914* (Palo Alto: Stanford University Press, 1976). Francks's *Rural Economic Development in Japan* offers a decidedly rosy view of the changes that took place in the Japanese countryside.

12. Quoted in the publisher's foreword to Basil Hall Chamberlain, *The Kojiki: Records of Ancient Matters* (Tokyo: Tuttle, 2005).

13. See Thomas Smith, *The Agrarian Origins of Modern Japan* (Palo Alto: Stanford University Press, 1959). The continuity approach was also adopted by the *Cambridge History of Japan* series, which devoted a volume to the nineteenth century in an explicit gesture to Tokugawa-Meiji continuity. See Marius Jansen, ed., *The Nineteenth Century*, vol. 5 of *The Cambridge History of Japan* (Cambridge: Cambridge University Press, 1989).

14. A good English-language summary of *kōzaha* thought can be found in Germaine Hoston, *Marxism and the Crisis of Development in Prewar Japan* (Princeton: Princeton University Press, 1986), especially chapters 5–8.

15. Takashi Fujitani, *Splendid Monarchy*, 4.

16. Ōkado, *Meiji Taishō no nōson*, 37.

17. Ibid. For a much fuller treatment of the administrative village system—with much the same take-home message—see Nishida Yoshiaki and Ōishi Kaiichirō, *Kindai Nihon no gyōseimura: Naganoken Hanishinagun Gokamura no kenkyū* (Tokyo: Nihon Keizai Hyōronsha, 1994).

18. See Suzuki Masayuki, *Kokumin kokka to tennosei* (Tokyo: Azekura Shobō, 2000), 26.

19. Takashi Fujitani, *Splendid Monarchy*, 20.

20. Quoted in W. Petrie Watson, *The Future of Japan* (London: Duckworth, 1907), 259.

21. Ōkado, *Meiji Taishō no nōson*, 37.

22. The voting restrictions were gradually lifted, but even after the passage of universal male suffrage in 1925, more than half the adults—women and those under 25—were excluded.

23. See Simon Partner, "Peasants into Citizens? The Meiji Village in the Russo-Japanese War," *Monumenta Nipponica* 62, no. 2 (Summer 2007): 179–209.

24. For an overview of protests movements in the earlier period, see Stephen Vlastos, "Opposition Movements in Early Meiji Japan," in *The Nineteenth Century*, ed. Marius Jansen, 367–431, vol. 5, *The Cambridge History of Japan* (Cambridge University Press, 1989). A good summary of later protests, centering on the tenant movement, is Nakamura Masanori, "The Japanese Landlord System and Tenancy Disputes: A Reply to Richard Smethurst's Criticisms," *Bulletin of Concerned Asian Scholars* 20, no. 1 (1988): 36–50. Nakamura, one of the great scholars of the tenant movement, called the tenant farmers who came together to resist the depredations of the landlord system "martyrs of the farmers' movement."

Bibliography

Aizawa Kikutarō. *Aizawa nikki* [1885–1892]. Sagamihara: Privately published by Aizawa Yoshihisa, 1965.

———. *Aizawa nikki (Taishōhen)* [1913–1926]. Sagamihara: Privately published by Aizawa Yoshihisa, 1972.

———. *Aizawa nikki (zōhoban)* [1896–1902]. Sagamihara: Privately published by Aizawa Yoshihisa, 1977.

———. *Aizawa nikki (zoku)* [1893–1895]. Sagamihara: Privately published by Aizawa Yoshihisa, 1966.

———. *Aizawa nikki (zokuzoku)* [1903–1912]. Sagamihara: Privately published by Aizawa Yoshihisa, 1967.

Ayase-shi. *Kanagawa-ken Kōza-gun Ayase-sonze chōsasho*. Ayase: Ayase-shi, 1993.

Bannō Junji. *Kindai Nihon no shuppatsu*. Vol. 13, *Taikei Nihon no rekishi*. Tokyo: Shōgakkan, 1993.

Bird, Isabella. *Unbeaten Tracks in Japan*. London: Virago, 1984.

Bix, Herbert P. *Peasant Protest in Japan, 1590–1884*. New Haven, CT: Yale University Press, 1986.

Bullen, George. *The Story of Count Bismarck's Life: For Popular Perusal*. London: John Camden Hotten, 1871. Translated by Yamaguchi Sōkichi as *Gaisei no igyō: Doitsu saishō Bisumaruku kō jitsuden*. Tokyo: Shunyōdō, 1887.

Chamberlain, Basil Hall. *The Kojiki: Records of Ancient Matters*. Tokyo: Tuttle, 2005.

Chambliss, William J. *Chiaraijima Village: Land Tenure, Taxation, and Local Trade, 1818–1884*. Tucson: University of Arizona, 1965.

Ericson, Steven J. "'Poor Peasant, Poor Country!' The Matsukata Deflation and Rural Distress in Mid-Meiji Japan." In *New Directions in the Study of Meiji Japan*, edited by Helen Hardacre and Adam L. Kern, 387–96. Leiden: Brill, 1997.

————. *The Sound of the Whistle: Railroads and the State in Meiji Japan*. Cambridge, MA: Harvard University Press, 1996.

Francks, Penelope. *Rural Economic Development in Japan: From the Nineteenth Century to the Pacific War*. Abingdon, UK: Routledge, 2006.

Fridell, Wilbur M. *Japanese Shrine Mergers, 1906–12: State Shinto Moves to the Grassroots*. Tokyo: Sophia University, 1973.

Fujii Tadatoshi. *Kokubō fujinkai: Hinomaru to kappōgi*. Tokyo: Iwanami Shoten, 1985.

Fujitani Takashi. *Splendid Monarchy: Power and Pageantry in Modern Japan*. Berkeley: University of California Press, 1996.

Garon, Sheldon. *Molding Japanese Minds: The State in Everyday Life*. Princeton: Princeton University Press, 1997.

Gluck, Carol. *Japan's Modern Myths: Ideology in the Late Meiji Period*. Princeton: Princeton University Press, 1985.

Havens, Thomas R. H. "Religion and Agriculture in Nineteenth-Century Japan: Ninomiya Sontoku and the Hotoku Movement." *Japan Christian Quarterly* 38, no. 2 (1972): 98–105.

Hirooka Haruya. *Kindai Nihon kōtsūshi: Meiji ishin kara dainiji taisen made*. Tokyo : Hōsei Daigaku Shuppankyoku, 1987.

Hoston, Germaine. *Marxism and the Crisis of Development in Prewar Japan*. Princeton: Princeton University Press, 1986.

Huffman, James. *Creating a Public: People and Press in Meiji Japan*. Honolulu: University of Hawai'i Press, 1997.

Irokawa, Daikichi. *The Culture of the Meiji Period*, Princeton Library of Asian Translations. Princeton: Princeton University Press, 1988.

Ishida Takeshi. *Kindai Nihon seiji kōzō no kenkyū*. Tokyo: Miraisha, 1956.

Jansen, Marius, ed. *The Nineteenth Century*. Vol. 5, *The Cambridge History of Japan*. Cambridge: Cambridge University Press, 1989.

Katō Shigeo. *Hashimoto no mukashibanashi*. Tokyo: Gyōsei, 1985.

Kawamura Zenjirō, ed. *Seiō bunmein no shōgeki*. Vol. 7, *Shinpan Nihon seikatsu bunkashi*. Tokyo: Kawade Shobō Shinsha, 1986.

Kondō Yasuo, and Ōtani Seizō. *Nōson mondai kōza*. 3 vols. Tōkyō: Kawade Shobō, 1954.

Kusakabe Kinzaburō. *Keihin Denryoku Kabushikikaisha enkakushi*. Tokyo: Daiyamondosha, 1926.

Kuwabara Sakuji. *Tennōsei kyōiku*. Tokyo: Sanseidō, 1977.

Lepore, Jill. "Historians Who Love Too Much." *The Journal of American History* 88, no.1 (June 2001): 129–44.

Levi, Giovanni. "On Microhistory." In *New Perspectives on Historical Writing*, edited by Peter Burke, 97–119. University Park: University of Pennsylvania Press, 2001.

Lone, Stewart. "Remapping Japanese Militarism: Provincial Society at War, 1904–1905." *Japanese Studies* 25, no. 1 (May 2005): 53–63.

Lu, David John. *Sources of Japanese History*. 2 vols. New York: McGraw-Hill, 1974.

Masuda Tomoko. *Tennōsei to kokka*. Tokyo: Aoki Shoten, 1999.

Matsushita Shigeo. *Chōheirei seitei no zengo*. Tokyo: Kaikōsha, 1932.

McKean, M. A. "Common-Pool Resources in the Context of Japanese History." *World Wide Business Review* 5, no. 1 (2003): 132–59.

Miyachi Masato. *Nichiro sengo seijishi no kenkyū*. Tokyo: Tokyo Daigaku Shuppankai, 1973.

Miyazaki, Katsunori. "Characteristics of Popular Movements in Nineteenth-Century Japan: Riots During the Second Chōshū War." *Japan Forum* 17, no. 1 (2005): 1–24.

Morita, Keiko. "Activities of the Japanese Patriotic Ladies Association (Aikoku Fujinkai)." In *Women, Activism and Social Change*, edited by Maja Mikula, 49–70. London: Routledge, 2005.

Nagahara Keiji, Nakamura Masanori, Nishida Yoshiaki, and Matsumoto Hiroshi. *Nihon jinushisei no kōsei to dankai*. Tokyo: Tokyo Daigaku Shuppankai, 1972.

Nakamura Masanori, "Gendai rekishigaku to tennōsei." In *Gendai shigaku no seika to kadai, 1980–2000-nen II: Kokkazō, shakaizō no henyō*, edited by Rekishigaku Kenkyūkai, 120–135. Tokyo: Aoki Shoten, 2003.

———. "The Japanese Landlord System and Tenancy Disputes: A Reply to Richard Smethurst's Criticisms." *Bulletin of Concerned Asian Scholars* 20, no. 1 (1988): 36–50.

———. *Kindai Nihon jinushisei shi kenkyū: Shihon shugi to jinushisei*. Tokyo: Tokyo Daigaku Shuppankai, 1979.

Nihon Sonrakushi Kōza Henshu Iinkai. *Seikatsu 3: Kingendai*. Vol. 8, *Nihon sonrakushi kōza*. Tokyo: Yuzankaku, 1990.

Nishida, Yoshiaki. "Growth of the Meiji Landlord System and Tenancy Disputes after World War 1: A Critique of Richard Smethurst, *Agricultural Development and Tenancy Disputes in Japan, 1870–1940*." *Journal of Japanese Studies* 15, no. 2 (1989): 389–415.

Nishida Yoshiaki, and Ōishi Kaiichirō. *Kindai Nihon no gyōseimura: Nagano-ken Hanishinagun Gokamura no kenkyū*. Tokyo: Nihon Keizai Hyōronsha, 1994.

Norman, E. Herbert. *Soldier and Peasant in Japan: The Origins of Conscription*. New York: Institute of Pacific Relations, 1943.

Notehelfer, F. G., ed. *Japan through American Eyes: The Journal of Francis Hall, Kanagawa and Yokohama, 1859–1866*. Princeton: Princeton University Press, 1992.

Ōe Shinobu. *Chōheisei*. Tōkyō: Iwanami Shoten, 1981.

Ogi Shinzō. *Aru Meijijin no seikatsushi: Aizawa Kikutarō no shichijūha-chinenkan no kiroku*. Tokyo: Chūō Kōronsha, 1983.

Ōhama Tetsuya. *Meiji no bōhyō: Nisshin Nichiro uzumoreta shomin no kiroku*. Tokyo: Shūei Shuppan, 1970.

Ohkawa, Kazushi, Bruce F. Johnson, and Hiromitsu Kaneda, eds. *Agriculture and Economic Growth: Japan's Experience*. Princeton: Princeton University Press, 1969.

Ōkado Masakatsu. *Meiji Taishō no nōson*. Tokyo: Iwanami Shoten, 1992.

———. "The Women of Rural Japan: An Overview of the Twentieth Century." In *Farmers and Village Life in Twentieth-Century Japan*, edited by Ann Waswo and Yoshiaki Nishida, 38–59. London: RoutledgeCurzon, 2003.

Okuma, Count Shigenobu. *Fifty Years of New Japan*. 2 vols. London: Smith, Elder, 1909.

Ono Takeo. *Ishin nōson shakai shiron*. Tokyo: Tōkō Shoin, 1932.

——. *Nōson shakaishi ronkō*. Tokyo: Ganshōdōshoten, 1927.

Ōshima, Mitsuko. "Chihō zaisei to chihō kairyō undō." In *Kyōdoshi kenkyū kōza*, edited by Furushima Toshio et al., 33–49. Tokyo: Asakura Shoten, 1970.

Partner, Simon. "Peasants into Citizens? The Meiji Village in the Russo-Japanese War." *Monumenta Nipponica* 62, no. 2 (2007): 179–209.

——. "Taming the Wilderness: The Lifestyle Improvement Movement in Rural Japan, 1925–1965." *Monumenta Nipponica* 56, no. 4 (2001): 487–520.

——. *Toshié: A Story of Village Life in Twentieth Century Japan*. Berkeley: University of California Press, 2001.

Platt, Brian. *Burning and Building: Schooling and State Formation in Japan, 1750–1890*. Harvard East Asian Monographs 237. Cambridge, MA: Harvard University Asia Center, 2004.

Plutschow, Herbert. *Japan's Name Culture: The Significance of Names in a Religious, Political and Social Context*. Folkestone, UK: Japan Library, 1995.

Pratt, Edward E. *Japan's Protoindustrial Elite: The Economic Foundations of the Gōnō*. Cambridge, MA: Harvard University Asia Center, 1999.

Pyle, Kenneth B. "The Technology of Japanese Nationalism: The Local Improvement Movement, 1900–1918." *Journal of Asian Studies* 33, no. 1 (1973): 51–65.

Rokuhara, Hiroko. "Local Officials and the Meiji Conscription Campaign." *Monumenta Nipponica* 60, no. 1 (2005): 81–110.

Sagamiharashi. *Sagamihara shishi dai-3-kan*. Vol. 3, *Sagamihara shishi*. Sagamihara: Sagamiharashi, 1968.

——. *Sagamihara shishi dai-4-kan*. Vol. 4, *Sagamihara shishi*. Sagamihara: Sagamiharashi, 1971.

——. *Sagamihara shishi dai-6-kan*. Vol. 6, *Sagamihara shishi*. Sagamihara: Sagamiharashi, 1968.

Sasaki, Junnosuke. *Yonaoshi*. Vol. 5, *Minshū Nihon no rekishi*. Tokyo: Sanseidō, 1974.

Sawada, Janine Tasca. *Practical Pursuits: Religion, Politics, and Personal Cultivation in Nineteenth-Century Japan*. Honolulu: University of Hawai'i Press, 2004.

Shibusawa, Eiichi. *The Autobiography of Shibusawa Eiichi: From Peasant to Entrepreneur*. Tokyo: University of Tokyo Press, 1994.

Shibusawa, Keizo. *Japanese Life and Culture in the Meiji Era*. Tokyo: Ōbunsha, 1958.

Sippel, Patricia. "Popular Protest in Early Modern Japan: The Bushu Outburst." *Harvard Journal of Asiatic Studies* 37, no. 2 (1977): 273–322.

Smethurst, Richard J. *Agricultural Development and Tenancy Disputes in Japan, 1870–1940*. Princeton: Princeton University Press, 1996.

———. "The Creation of the Imperial Military Reserve Association in Japan." *Journal of Asian Studies* 30, no. 4 (1971): 815–28.

Smiles, Samuel. *Self-Help.* London: John Murray, 1858.

Smith, Thomas. *The Agrarian Origins of Modern Japan.* Palo Alto, CA: Stanford University Press, 1959.

Steele, M. William. *Alternative Narratives in Modern Japanese History.* London: RoutledgeCurzon, 2003.

Suzuki Masayuki. *Kokumin kokka to tennosei.* Tokyo: Azekura Shobō, 2000.

Szijarto, Istvan. "Four Arguments for Microhistory." *Rethinking History* 6, no. 2 (2002): 209–15.

Takeda Kiyoko. *Tennōsei shisō to kyōiku.* Tokyo: Meiji Tosho Shuppan, 1964.

Takemitsu Makoto. *Myōji to Nihonjin: Senzo kara no messeji.* Tokyo: Bunshun Shinso, 1998.

Tsuchiya Takao, and Ono Michio, eds. *Meiji shonen nōmin sōjōroku.* Tokyo: Nanboku shoin, 1931.

Tsutsui, Masao. "The Impact of the Local Improvement Movement on Farmers and Rural Communities." In *Farmers and Village Life in Twentieth-Century Japan,* edited by Ann Waswo and Yoshiaki Nishida, 61–78. London: RoutledgeCurzon, 2003.

Vlastos, Stephen. "Opposition Movements in Early Meiji, 1868–1885." In *The Cambridge History of Japan,* edited by Marius Jansen, 367–431. Cambridge: Cambridge University Press, 1989.

———. "Yonaoshi in Aizu." In *Conflict in Modern Japanese History: The Neglected Tradition,* edited by Tetsuo Najita and J. Victor Koschmann, 164–76. Princeton: Princeton University Press, 1982.

Waswo, Ann. "The Transformation of Rural Society, 1920–1950." In *The Twentieth Century,* edited by Peter Duus, 541–605. Cambridge: Cambridge University Press, 1988.

Watson, W. Petrie. *The Future of Japan.* London: Duckworth, 1907.

Weber, Eugen. *Peasants into Frenchmen: The Modernization of Rural France, 1870–1914.* Stanford, CA: Stanford University Press, 1976.

White, James. *Ikki: Social Conflict and Political Protest in Early Modern Japan.* Ithaca, NY: Cornell University Press, 1993.

Wilson, George. *Patriots and Redeemers: Motives in the Meiji Restoration.* Chicago: Chicago University Press, 1992.

Yamaguchi Sōkichi. *Gaisei no igyō: Doitsu saishō Bisumaruku Kō jitsuden.* Translated by Yamaguchi Sōkichi. Tokyo: Shunyōdō, 1887.

Yoshizō Kubo. *Tennōsei kokka no kyōiku seisaku.* Tokyo: Emuti Shuppan, 1995.

Index

Adachihara Eiko (wife of Shigeharu), 150

administrative village system: conscription and, 34; Meiji reforms and, 63–65; Meiji tax system and, 26–27, 98–99; natural village and, 64–65, 191–92; status of hamlets in, 96; village and state relationship and, 190–92. *See also* Aizawa Kikutarō, as mayor

Afuri Shrine on Mount Ōyama, 78–81

Agricultural Association: in Aihara, 101, 118, 147, 172, 177; government initiatives and, 126, 127

agricultural equipment, 54, 55, 90–91

Agricultural Industries Bank Law (1886), 93

Agricultural Journal (Nōgyō zasshi), 56

agricultural journals, 54, 56, 59

agriculture: annual cycle of, 43–46; in Kantō region, 12–13; loss of tenant farmers and, 157–58; post-war economics and, 152–55; uncertainty and, 87–90, 153–55. *See also* rice; silk production; wheat

Agriculture and Sericulture School, 156, 159, 171

Aihara village: Agricultural Association in, 101; amalgamation into, 64–65, 96; bureaucratic influences in, 125–28; earthquake damage in, 170–71; elementary school in, 130, 138–39; Hashimoto railway station and, 114–15; health concerns in, 101–3; identity

of Hashimoto and, 191–92; mayors of, 117, 177; memorial stone in, 129; school system in, 100–101; shrine mergers and, 122–24; tax system in, 98–99; telephone service in, 162–63. *See also* Aizawa Kikutarō, as mayor

airplanes, 159–60

Aizawa family: Aizawa diary and, 4; community of Hashimoto and, 191–92; conscription and, 130–31; contributions to community by, 156; earthquake and, 164–65; family businesses of, 47–51; hereditary position of, 10–11; landholdings of, 51–52; modernization and, 155–64; printed media and, 59; silk production and, 43–44; spiritual allegiances of, 76–81; wealth of, 10, 11–12, 18–19, 47. *See also entries for specific family members*

Aizawa Asako (daughter of Aizawa), 88, 130, 141; death of mother and, 149, 150; marriage of, 175–76

Aizawa Chōichi (nephew of Aizawa), 170, 172, 175

Aizawa Hanako (daughter of Aizawa), 118, 176; death of mother and, 149, 150; earthquake and, 164–65

Aizawa Jungorō (cousin of Aizawa), 50–51, 150, 174

Aizawa Kikutarō: agricultural cycle and, 42–46; business investments and, 90–93, 110–11, 114–15, 153; deaths of friends and, 174–75; earthquake and, 165; education of, 30–31, 56–57;

Text: 10/13 Sabon
Display: Sabon
Compositor: BookMatters, Berkeley
Indexer: Marcia Carlson
Cartographer/Illustrator: Bill Nelson
Printer and binder: Maple-Vail Book Manufacturing Group